CREATING *the* OPPORTUNITY TO LEARN

ASCD MEMBER BOOK

Many ASCD members received this book as a
member benefit upon its initial release.

Learn more at: **www.ascd.org/memberbooks**

CREATING *the* OPPORTUNITY TO LEARN

MOVING FROM RESEARCH TO PRACTICE
TO CLOSE THE ACHIEVEMENT GAP

A. Wade Boykin
Pedro Noguera

Alexandria, Virginia USA

1703 N. Beauregard St. • Alexandria, VA 22311-1714 USA
Phone: 800-933-2723 or 703-578-9600 • Fax: 703-575-5400
Website: www.ascd.org • E-mail: member@ascd.org
Author guidelines: www.ascd.org/write

Gene R. Carter, *Executive Director;* Judy Zimny, *Chief Program Development Officer;* Gayle Owens, *Managing Director, Content Acquisitions and Development;* Scott Willis, *Director, Book Acquisitions & Development;* Julie Houtz, *Director, Book Editing & Production;* Jamie Greene, *Editor;* Ines Hilde, *Senior Graphic Designer;* Mike Kalyan, *Production Manager;* Valerie Younkin, *Desktop Publishing Specialist*

Portions of Chapters 2, 8, and 9 are adapted from the article "Creating schools where race does not matter: The role and significance of race in the racial achievement gap" by Pedro Noguera, which was published in the September 2, 2008, issue of *In Motion* magazine. Adapted with permission.

Printed in the United States of America. Cover art © 2011 ASCD. ASCD publications present a variety of viewpoints. The views expressed or implied in this book should not be interpreted as official positions of the Association.

All web links in this book are correct as of the publication date below but may have become inactive or otherwise modified since that time. If you notice a deactivated or changed link, please e-mail books@ascd.org with the words "Link Update" in the subject line. In your message, please specify the web link, the book title, and the page number on which the link appears.

ASCD Member Book, No. FY12-1 (Sept. 2011, PSI+). ASCD Member Books mail to Premium (P), Select (S), and Institutional Plus (I+) members on this schedule: Jan., PSI+; Feb., P; Apr., PSI+; May, P; July, PSI+; Aug., P; Sept., PSI+; Nov., PSI+; Dec., P. Select membership was formerly known as Comprehensive membership.

PAPERBACK ISBN: 978-1-4166-1306-0   ASCD product #107016

Also available as an e-book (see Books in Print for the ISBNs).

Quantity discounts for the paperback edition only: 10–49 copies, 10%; 50+ copies, 15%; for 1,000 or more copies, call 800-933-2723, ext. 5634, or 703-575-5634. For desk copies: member@ascd.org.

Library of Congress Cataloging-in-Publication Data
Boykin, A. Wade, 1947-
   Creating the opportunity to learn: moving from research to practice to close the achievement gap/ A. Wade Boykin & Pedro Noguera.
     p. cm.
   Includes bibliographical references and index.
   ISBN 978-1-4166-1306-0 (pbk.)
   1. African American students. 2. Hispanic American students. 3. Educational equalization—United States.
I. Noguera, Pedro. II. Title.
   LC2717.B59 2011
   379.2'60973--dc23

2011019694

20 19 18 17 16 15 14 13 12 11   1 2 3 4 5 6 7 8 9 10 11 12

CREATING *the* OPPORTUNITY TO LEARN

Preface

It is abundantly clear that students from certain ethnic groups, most prominently African Americans and Latinos, do not fare well in U.S. schools. It is widely documented that Black and Latino students perform substantially less well than their White counterparts (Hollins, King, & Hayman, 1994; Jencks & Phillips, 1998; King, 2005). This concern cries out for immediate, sustained, and profound attention. Until our schools do a far better job of educating Black and Latino students, to the very highest levels of achievement, our society will fail to tap a vast reservoir of human talent that we will greatly desire—indeed, require—in the years and decades ahead.

As the new century began, with the growing recognition in educational, business, and political spheres that the underachievement of minority students remained a vexing problem, No Child Left Behind (NCLB) was enacted. In its wake, more federal pressure was put on schools and school systems to raise achievement levels for all children, but particularly for children in groups that perform at levels notably below their mainstream counterparts. Nevertheless, the achievement gap today remains virtually unchanged.

A large part of the problem lies in the fact that many educators do not understand what it means to engage in educational practices that promote equity. Equity involves more than simply ensuring that children have equal access to education. Equity also entails a focus on outcomes and results. In *Inequality* (Jencks et al., 1972), Christopher Jencks and his colleagues argue that Americans are generally comfortable with the principle of equal opportunity, but they tend to be divided over the question of equality in results. This is because Americans tend to see talent and ability as unevenly distributed in the population. The so-called bell curve has permeated our consciousness, so we accept the idea that high intelligence is possessed by a relatively small number of people, whereas a greater number of people hover in the average range, and a smaller but still significant number are at the lower levels of intelligence. Research on IQ (intelligence quotient) and testing support these assumptions, so it is hardly surprising that these beliefs are difficult to dislodge.

However, No Child Left Behind is to a large degree based on a different set of assumptions about human intelligence and ability. In its requirement that schools produce evidence that all children, regardless of their status or background, are learning, NCLB calls for a revision of the paradigm that has guided educational policy and practice for the last 200 years. Instead of measuring student ability and sorting students accordingly—separating the "gifted" from the "giftless"—NCLB requires schools to cultivate talent and ability in all children. The simple fact that all schools within a state are held to the same academic standards suggests that our policymakers now believe that children in Watts should be able to do as well as children in Beverly Hills, and that children in the South Bronx can compete with children in Scarsdale.

There are certain problems with these assumptions, especially because we have done very little to address the inequity in resources among schools and because many poor children have a variety of nonacademic needs that affect their ability to learn. Still, the mere idea that we would hold children to similar expectations regardless of their race, language, socioeconomic status, or nationality is a major breakthrough. We have never had such expectations before.

Clearly, our society (and the rest of the world) will have an ongoing need for individuals capable of advanced intellectual performance. Likewise, schools will continue to play a major role in identifying students with talent and making sure they receive the support needed to reach their potential. However, we must acknowledge that the process used for identifying those with talent or potential is not precise and often deeply flawed. In many cases, individuals who possess the capacity to achieve—and even produce greatness—are denied that opportunity simply because the educators charged with cultivating talent are unable to identify and support students whose gifts are not readily apparent.

We know this because there are many individuals who have displayed intellectual brilliance and accomplished great things not because of the schools they attended but in spite of them. For example, Netscape founder Jack Clark performed so poorly in school that he failed the test to enter the U.S. Navy. Required to enroll in a remedial math course before retaking the exam, Clark was fortunate: His teacher recognized that he possessed an extraordinary (though undeveloped) talent in math. The teacher encouraged Clark to pursue his education, and after enrolling in a local community college, Clark soon demonstrated so much ability that he was able to transfer to Stanford University, where he studied computer science and received a full scholarship. The rest of Clark's story is better known because he went on to establish one of the leading technology companies in the world.

There are, of course, many others: Dean Kamen was placed in special education classes due to a learning disability, but through hard work and support from his parents, he was able to excel in school and went on to found one of the nation's leading biotechnology firms. Ben Carson, one of the nation's most prominent heart surgeons, nearly dropped out of school after his teachers confused his Black southern dialect with a speech impediment and placed him in remedial classes.

We cite these individuals as examples because they were denied educational opportunities but still went on to achieve greatness. None of them exhibited the traits typically associated with talent and ability. Either they struggled in school or they were denied opportunities because of circumstances beyond their control—the schools they attended; the parents to whom they were born; or simply the fact that they were poor, non-White, or both. They are noteworthy individuals because they managed to succeed in life despite their failures in school. Their stories should do more than give us a reason to celebrate their perseverance and resilience; they should also serve as a pointed reminder that these people are the lucky ones. The question that should keep us, as educators, awake at night is this: How many others have slipped through the cracks simply because they weren't as lucky?

For the longest time, the strongest predictor of academic success in school has been family income combined with parents' level of education (Jencks et al., 1972). In many respects, this is hardly surprising. After all, affluent children generally attend the best schools, and their parents often use their education and wealth to ensure that they receive the support and nurturing needed to excel. Likewise, highly educated parents tend to pass on the benefits of their education to their children. They consciously devise strategies to provide their children with certain kinds of intellectual stimulation (e.g., taking them to museums and other cultural centers, providing music lessons and a literacy-rich home environment), and they tend to be careful and discriminating about the schools their children attend. Such actions are understandable, and parents who play an active and thoughtful role in supporting the education of their children should be commended.

However, what about those children from certain minority groups, who are not born affluent, or whose parents are not well educated? Unless we believe that those who have more are inherently superior to those who have less, we should be troubled by the fact that patterns of achievement are often fairly predictable, particularly with respect to children's race and class background. We should be troubled because there are undoubtedly other children with potential similar to that possessed by Jack Clark, Dean Kamen, and Ben Carson. We should be particularly disturbed if our schools fail to enable the children of the poor to escape poverty and instead do little more than reproduce existing patterns of inequality in U.S. society.

Sadly, there is considerable evidence that this is exactly how many public schools in the United States work. In most U.S. schools, race and class are strong predictors of achievement, and it is rare to find poor or ethnic minority children from less educated families achieving at high levels. In fact, these patterns are so consistent that when we see schools ranked by their test scores, we are not surprised to find that wherever poverty is concentrated and schools are segregated, achievement tends to be lowest.

Fortunately, this isn't always the case. A small but significant number of high-performing, high-poverty schools do exist. A report entitled *Dispelling the Myth Revisited* (Education Trust, 2002) identifies more than 3,000 such schools across the United States. The existence of such schools is all the proof we need that, under the right conditions, poor and minority-group children can achieve at high levels. The question is this: How do we make it possible for more schools to produce similar results? In this book, we will explore this vital question.

This book is divided into three distinct but overlapping sections. In Part I, we discuss the salient components of the achievement gap. We provide documentation of its existence and complexities. We situate the gap in terms of historical, sociopolitical, and societal contexts. We also take on the thorny issue of how matters of race and academic achievement have been and should be linked. In Part II, we provide a fine-grained presentation of research that supports certain promising approaches and practices that need to occur in our nation's schools. By examining the research findings presented in Part II, we hope that researchers, practitioners, and policymakers will come to appreciate how rigorous empirical research informs what can work in teaching and learning contexts to help eliminate or reduce the achievement gap. Part III examines practical applications on a broader scale. We focus on what certain schools and districts are doing to successfully address the achievement gap as they create greater opportunities to learn for all students. We also move from research to practice by posing policy directions that should be pursued to better ensure that effective programs, approaches, and practices are successfully implemented.

—A. Wade Boykin and Pedro Noguera

Acknowledgments

This book project was a labor of love, so we want to thank the ones we love and who have supported us throughout the writing and research that went into the production of this book.

I, Wade Boykin, would like to thank my sons Wade III and Curtis, who continuously provide me with unconditional positive regard as I strive to do the same for them. I want to acknowledge with loving memory my aunt Eleanor Boykin Jones, a consummate educator, without whom I would never have succeeded. Of course, I wish to thank CME for being there.

I, Pedro Noguera, would like to thank my loving wife Allyson Pimentel who provided me with support, encouragement, and inspiration throughout this process. She came into my life at a moment when I was down and in desperate need of support. She provided that and much more, and she has given me a renewed sense of hope and happiness.

Finally and most importantly, we dedicate this book to the children of America who urgently need an education that nurtures their imagination, cultivates their creativity, and provides them with the courage, skills, and knowledge they will need to deal with the many challenges they will confront in the years ahead. We are counting on them to create a more just, peaceful, hopeful, and equitable world, and we are confident that they can. We also dedicate this book to the educators who will teach those students, and we hope that, in these pages, they may find encouragement, guidance, and even a renewed sense of possibility that through education we truly can make a difference.

PART I

Understanding the Achievement Gap

Before undertaking efforts to eliminate the disparities in academic outcomes that, in most districts, correspond to the race and class backgrounds of students (what we now refer to euphemistically as "closing the achievement gap"), it is essential that educators understand the nature of the gap and why it exists. Absent a clear understanding of the causes of the gap, it is easy for schools to adopt strategies that either do not work or, in some cases, even exacerbate the problem. We have a long history in this country of pursuing "quick-fix" reforms—phonics-based reading programs, smart boards and computer-based learning programs, scripted curricula, "teacher-proof" curricula—that promise a great deal but often seem to deliver little.

In many schools, it is also common for educators to fall into the trap of blaming others for the underperformance of their students. Uninvolved parents are a frequent target of blame, as are students typically accused of being unmotivated and not working hard enough. Misplaced priorities of district administrators and politicians are also commonly cited as reasons why more progress in raising student achievement has not been made. Although these issues may not be irrelevant to the persistence of the achievement gap, it would be a mistake for them to be treated as the cause. In the following chapters, we show that the achievement gap is actually a multidimensional phenomenon—one that must be confronted with an awareness of how the dimensions interact. Unless such an approach is taken, it is highly unlikely that efforts to counter the achievement gap will succeed. Importantly, to the degree that a school or district is mired in debate over who is to blame for the existence of the gap, and there is a reluctance to accept responsibility for finding solutions, there is little chance that the achievement gap will be closed or even reduced.

What Are the Dimensions of the Gap?

01

In the United States, there are striking, persistent achievement gaps between Black and Latino students (both boys and girls) and their White counterparts.[1] These gaps show up even before students start formal schooling—in their knowledge of vocabulary, for example (Jencks & Phillips, 1998). Gaps in math and reading achievement have been documented at the beginning of kindergarten, and these gaps tend to widen over the course of the kindergarten year (Barbarin, 2002; Chatterji, 2006).

Gaps grow even wider within the same cohort of children by the 3rd grade, and the disparities are more pronounced in higher-order skill domains such as deriving meaning from text, drawing inferences beyond the literal text, and understanding rate and measurement in mathematics (Early Childhood Longitudinal Study, 2004; Murname, Willett, Bub, & McCartney, 2006). Black–White achievement gaps have been captured over time in results from the "nation's report card," the product of the periodic National Assessment of Educational Progress (NAEP). Over the last 30 years, test score disparities have shown up in successive cohorts of 9-, 13-, and 17-year-olds in reading, mathematics, and science (NAEP, 2005).

It is widely documented that the gap is multidimensional. Achievement and attainment gaps are revealed through a host of schooling indexes, including grade point averages; performance on district, state, and national achievement tests; rates of enrollment in rigorous courses; and differential placements in special education and gifted-and-talented programs, as well as across behavioral indicators such as school dropout, suspension, and referral rates.

These achievement and attainment gaps show up across the spectrum from preschool to college and across the full range of academic skills and content areas (Ryan & Ryan, 2005). It is instructive, for example, to examine math-performance differences inside high schools that serve White, Black, and Latino students together. James Byrnes (2003) has done so by examining NAEP math proficiency scores. Results gleaned from this national data set show that, overall, these mixed-race schools enrolled 79 percent, 13 percent, and 8 percent White, Black, and Latino students, respectively. Yet among the students who scored at or above the 80th percentile in math proficiency, 94 percent were White, whereas only 3 percent were Black and 3 percent were Latino. Representing these numbers somewhat differently, 26 percent of all the White students enrolled in these schools performed at or above the 80th percentile, but this was the case for only 7 percent of the Black and Latino students. White students were almost four times more likely than Black and Latino students to reach this performance level.

Moreover, when U.S. students are compared with students from other nations, especially in Europe and Asia, and with those students' tests of achievement in reading, mathematics, and science, they fall in the middle of the pack, suggesting that there is room for improvement for U.S. students in general. For example, data from the Trends in International Mathematics and Science Study (TIMSS) show that 4th and 8th grade students in the United States fall significantly behind the math performance levels of students from nations such as Singapore, South Korea, Japan, Belgium, the Netherlands, Hungary, Slovenia, and the Slovak Republic (Mullis, Martin, Gonzalez, & Chrostowski, 2004; TIMSS, 2003).

Closing these achievement and attainment gaps is a laudable goal for us as a society. However, whatever methods we use should not aim merely to catch up Black and Latino students to the levels of their White counterparts. We must also raise achievement for all students so we can close the gaps between the performance of U.S. students and their counterparts from around the world—*but also simultaneously raise levels at a steeper rate for certain students of color.* This should be our goal (Hilliard, 2003). Even successful schools and school districts cannot afford to rest on their laurels. If they are not proactively closing achievement gaps, raising achievement for all students, and preparing their students for the demands of the 21st century, they will soon fall short of what our society and communities require of them.

This examination of schooling calls for a two-tiered scheme to capture academic performance outcomes. We refer to these two levels as first-order and higher-order learning outcomes. First-order outcomes are those that have historically been used as the measuring sticks for student performance. They include what we would call basic knowledge and skill accumulation. In language arts, this would encompass such factors as mastering the alphabetic code, word reading fluency, comprehension, vocabulary, and language conventions (grammar, syntax, etc.); in math, it would include basic facts, algorithm fluency, calculation proficiency, basic problem solving, measurement, estimation, and so on. This category also includes long-term retention of information, as well as information retrieval when it is called for. Of course, performance on standardized tests and grade point averages also generally fall within this category. These outcomes are well justified, and although their relative importance has been disputed over the years, their successful attainment has generally served U.S. schooling well.

To achieve success in the 21st century, however, students must also achieve higher-order learning outcomes. In closing achievement gaps while raising achievement for all students, we must increasingly use these outcomes as essential academic barometers. These outcomes include knowledge-transfer skills—that is, being able to use knowledge to understand or solve similar problems, or to extrapolate from present understandings to a novel body of information or concepts. This category also requires students to do more than consume knowledge. They must become adept at generating knowledge and applying their knowledge and skills to solve real-world problems. Students should become adept at reflecting on what they have learned, to understand it more deeply and to process its implications and nuances. Rather than just accept what they have learned at face value, or assume that what is on the printed page or comes from the teacher's mouth is immune to challenge, students must judge what they have learned and be constructively critical of it—and of their own knowledge as well. Certainly, in this Information Age, when information itself is becoming a commodity, skills at knowledge communication will serve students well.

In all, there are three "achievement gaps" that must be confronted simultaneously: the one between White students and their Black and Latino counterparts; the one between U.S. students and students in other parts of the world; and the one between what it took to be prepared for the 20th century and what will be required for adequate preparation in the 21st century.

The Impact of NCLB

Finding ways to close (or at least reduce) the achievement gap—the disparities in test scores and academic outcomes that follow well-established patterns typically corresponding to the race and class of children—has been a national priority for nearly a decade. Since the enactment of No Child Left Behind (NCLB) in 2001 and the implementation of its requirement that schools and students be held accountable for achievement through annual standardized tests, a sense of urgency has developed over the need to improve the educational outcomes of underperforming students. The priority given to closing the achievement gap has not diminished under the Obama administration, even though it remains unclear what the administration will do about NCLB. (At the time of this book's publication, the reauthorization of ESEA [Elementary and Secondary Education Act], which was adopted in 1965 and modified by President George W. Bush to include the provisions of No Child Left Behind, was the subject of intense debate in Congress.) It is clear from statements made by President Obama during the 2007 presidential campaign that the effort to close the achievement gap and improve the performance of U.S. schools will remain a national priority for years to come (see Dillon, 2010a).

NCLB compelled schools to focus on improving the academic achievement of children who have traditionally not done well in school. This resulted in greater attention to the educational needs of poor and disadvantaged children; students with learning disabilities; recent immigrants and English language learners; and, in many communities, African Americans, Latinos, Native Americans, and other students of color (Miller, 1995). Such children often come from families that wield little or no influence over decision making within school districts. Not surprisingly, in the small number of districts where the greatest gains have been made in closing the gap during the last several years, it has generally been due to the willingness of educational leaders to prioritize the learning needs of their most vulnerable students, even when such efforts have not been popular (Dessauer, 2011).

With this history as context, the emergence of a federal education policy that made the goal of eliminating racial gaps in achievement a national priority is nothing short of remarkable. Despite its flaws, NCLB constituted a radical break from the idea that the relationship between race and intelligence was immutable. Although policymakers never pointed out that NCLB represented a repudiation of our country's historical views on race, a close examination of history reveals that this was indeed the case. Of course, attitudes and beliefs that were shaped by ideological assumptions concerning the nature of racial inequality cannot be erased merely by the adoption of a new law. In fact, many educators and parents who have been part of the effort to address achievement gaps have encountered resistance related to attitudes and beliefs about the ability of underperforming children to achieve at higher levels. The prevalence of such opposition in school districts across the country suggests that beliefs about the relationship between race and intelligence have not disappeared. Such beliefs, even when they are masked as a desire to erect "race neutral" policies, invariably become major obstacles to the effort to eliminate racial disparities in academic outcomes. If we are not willing to acknowledge and confront the numerous barriers to the opportunity to learn that many poor and minority children experience, greater progress in reducing racial disparities will be difficult to bring about.

Certainly, it will require more than lofty pronouncements about education as the civil rights issue of the 21st century.[2]

In many schools throughout the United States, race continues to be implicated in patterns of student achievement in predictable and disturbing ways. Nine years after the adoption of NCLB, the persistence of these patterns compels us to ask why? If closing the achievement gap and elevating the achievement of poor and minority students is a national priority, what is preventing the nation and its schools from making greater progress? Unless we believe that educators across the country are racist, incompetent, or lazy,[3] the relative lack of progress in closing the gap compels us to ask whether we have been approaching this task in the wrong way. Such reconsideration is only reasonable, given that efforts to alter the long-standing relationship between race and achievement have largely been unsuccessful.

This book offers a critical examination of what is wrong with popular approaches to closing the achievement gap, and it presents a framework and set of strategies for a direction that we believe could be far more promising. In Part I, we begin by exploring the social and cultural factors that influence the role of race in educational performance. We confront race directly because, although it is increasingly less likely for educators or public officials to explain the persistence of disparities in academic outcomes on the basis of innate racial differences, certain social and cultural factors have been espoused as a cause in recent years, and these explanations end up having a similar effect. In the following sections, we show why it is a mistake for schools to use poverty, family background, or some vague notion of "culture" to explain and rationalize the persistence of the achievement gap. Though such factors may indeed have an impact on student learning and development, there is evidence that they can be successfully addressed—and they should not be obstacles that prevent schools from being more successful in closing the gap.

Recent Research on the Achievement Gap

Perhaps the best-known and most reliable measure of academic performance is the National Assessment of Educational Progress (NAEP), a congressionally mandated measure of student achievement that has been administered by the National Center for Educational Statistics since 1969. Also known as the "nation's report card," NAEP scores have gained importance as a means of determining whether increases in test scores reported by several states are due to lowered standards or genuine improvements in student learning outcomes.

The NAEP long-term trend assessment scores in reading show that achievement of Black and Latino students has risen, with statistically significant—though still relatively modest—reductions in the percentage of students scoring at the lowest performance levels and with increases in the percentage of students scoring at the highest performance levels.[4] In 1975, just under half of 9-year-old Black and Latino students scored at the lowest performance level, whereas only 2 percent of 9-year-old Black students and 3 percent of 9-year-old Latino students scored at the highest performance level.[5] In 2008, by contrast, less than one-third of 9-year-old Black and Latino students were at the lowest performance level, and approximately 10 percent of Black and Latino students scored at the highest performance level.

A similar trend of improvements in reading achievement is evident among 13-year-old Black and Latino students—though slightly less dramatic. In 1975, approximately half of all 13-year-old Black and Latino students scored at the lowest performance level, whereas approximately 2 percent of Black and Latino students scored at the highest performance level.[6] In 2008, however, approximately 43 percent of 13-year-old Black and Latino students scored at the lowest performance level, with 6 percent of 13-year-old Black students and 5 percent of 13-year-old Latino students scoring at the highest performance level.

Compared to reading achievement, Black and Latino students have made even larger gains in mathematics. The NAEP long-term trend assessment scores in mathematics reveal that the achievement of Black and Latino students has risen alongside significant reductions in the percentage of students scoring at the lowest performance levels and increases in the percentage of students scoring at the highest performance levels.[7] In 1978, approximately 46 percent of 9-year-old Black students and 39 percent of 9-year-old Latino students scored at the lowest performance level, whereas only 4 percent of

9-year-old Black students and 9 percent of 9-year-old Latino students scored at the highest performance level. In 2008, by contrast, approximately 21 percent of 9-year-old Black students and 14 percent of 9-year-old Latino students scored at the lowest performance level, and 25 percent of 9-year-old Black students and 34 percent of 9-year-old Latino students scored at the highest performance level.

The same trend of improvements in math achievement is evident among 13-year-old Black and Latino students. In 1978, approximately half of all 13-year-old Black and Latino students scored at the lowest performance level, whereas less than 5 percent of Black and Latino students scored at the highest performance level. In 2008, however, the percent of 13-year-old Black and Latino students that scored at the lowest performance level was cut nearly in half, and 10 percent of 13-year-old Black students and 14 percent of 13-year-old Latino students scored at the highest performance level.

As significant as these gains in achievement are, they do not necessarily translate into reductions in the achievement gap. This is because achievement levels of White and Asian students also improved over the last 40 years. Despite the fact that NAEP long-term trend data demonstrate marked improvements in the achievement levels of Black and Latino students, the extent to which these improvements have translated into a reduction in the achievement gap is inconsistent. More important, reductions in the achievement gap are difficult to produce because disparities in achievement, at their root, are often predicated on broader issues of deeply entrenched social inequality. This is an important point that many policymakers fail to acknowledge or address.

Between 1970 and 1990, changes in the achievement gap were defined by two unique patterns (Lee, 2002). From the 1970s through the late 1980s, Black student achievement in both reading and math increased at a faster rate than that of their White peers, leading to a reduction in the Black–White achievement gap. During the 1990s, however, these trends reversed, and the gap began to widen (Ferguson, 2007). Latino student achievement underwent a similar pattern, with achievement rising from 1970 through the late 1980s and then holding steady in the 1990s. This led to a reduction in the

Latino–White achievement gap during the 1970s and 1980s and then to an increase in the gap in the 1990s.

The most recent data on the achievement gap reveal a disturbing pattern of relative stagnation. Between 1998 and 2007, the reading achievement gaps have appeared to fluctuate—growing during the early and mid-2000s and then shrinking back to pre-2000 levels by the end of the decade. Based on national data from the NAEP, the 2007 4th and 8th grade Black–White and Latino–White reading achievement gaps were statistically the same as they were in 1998 (Figures 1.1 and 1.2).[8]

FIGURE 1.1 ⟶ 4TH GRADE READING ACHIEVEMENT (MAIN NAEP)

	AVERAGE SCALE SCORE			ACHIEVEMENT GAP	
Year	White	Black	Latino	Black–White	Latino–White
2007	230	203	204	–27	–26
2005	228	199	201	**–29**	–26
2003	227	197	199	**–30**	**–28**
2002	227	198	199	**–29**	–28
2000	223	189	188	**–34**	**–35**
1998	223	192	192	–31	–31

Source: U.S. Department of Education, Institute of Educational Sciences, National Center for Educational Statistics, National Assessment of Educational Progress (NAEP), 1998–2007 Reading Assessments. Bold numbers indicate gaps that are statistically different from the 2007 gaps as calculated by the U.S. Department of Education's NAEP Data Explorer.

The 2007 4th grade Black–White math achievement gap has improved only slightly since 1996, whereas the 4th grade Latino–White math achievement gap has remained relatively unchanged (Figure 1.3). Similarly, the 2007 8th grade Latino–White math achievement gap was statistically the same as it was in 1996. The 2007 8th grade Black–White math achievement gap, however, was the smallest it has been in the past 10 years (Figure 1.4). Still, this was the only area in which either the Black–White or Latino–White achievement gaps made any significant and sustained improvement.

FIGURE 1.2 ⟶ 8TH GRADE READING ACHIEVEMENT (MAIN NAEP)

Year	AVERAGE SCALE SCORE			ACHIEVEMENT GAP	
	White	Black	Latino	Black–White	Latino–White
2007	270	244	246	−26	−25
2005	269	242	245	−27	−24
2003	270	244	244	−27	**−27**
2002	271	244	245	−27	−26
1998	268	242	241	−26	−27

Source: U.S. Department of Education, Institute of Educational Sciences, National Center for Educational Statistics, National Assessment of Educational Progress (NAEP), 1998–2007 Reading Assessments. Bold numbers indicate gaps that are statistically different from the 2007 gaps as calculated by the U.S. Department of Education's NAEP Data Explorer.

Overall, trends in the Main NAEP show that efforts to close the achievement gap have been characterized by stagnation. This is significant because this period coincides with the advent of the No Child Left Behind law and the focus it placed upon increasing standards and accountability through high-stakes assessments and other measures. Coupled with the bifurcated achievement gap patterns of the 1970s through the 1990s, this period of stagnation indicates that, as a nation, we are no closer to closing the achievement gap today than we were two decades ago.

FIGURE 1.3 ⟶ 4TH GRADE MATH ACHIEVEMENT (MAIN NAEP)

Year	AVERAGE SCALE SCORE			ACHIEVEMENT GAP	
	White	Black	Latino	Black–White	Latino–White
2007	248	222	227	−26	−21
2005	246	220	225	−26	−21
2003	243	216	221	−27	−21
2000	233	203	207	**−30**	**−26**
1996	231	198	207	**−33**	−24

Source: U.S. Department of Education, Institute of Educational Sciences, National Center for Educational Statistics, National Assessment of Educational Progress (NAEP), 1996–2007 Mathematics Assessments. Bold numbers indicate gaps that are statistically different from the 2007 gaps as calculated by the U.S. Department of Education's NAEP Data Explorer.

FIGURE 1.4 ⟶ 8TH GRADE MATH ACHIEVEMENT (MAIN NAEP)

	AVERAGE SCALE SCORE			ACHIEVEMENT GAP	
Year	White	Black	Latino	Black–White	Latino–White
2007	290	259	264	–31	–26
2005	288	254	261	**–33**	–26
2003	287	252	258	**–35**	**–28**
2000	283	243	252	**–40**	**–31**
1996	279	239	249	**–40**	–30

Source: U.S. Department of Education, Institute of Educational Sciences, National Center for Educational Statistics, National Assessment of Educational Progress (NAEP), 1996–2007 Mathematics Assessments. Bold numbers indicate gaps that are statistically different from the 2007 gaps as calculated by the U.S. Department of Education's NAEP Data Explorer.

The NAEP long-term trend assessment reading scores show that the performance gaps between Black and White students and Latino and White students are only slightly better than two decades ago. In 2008, the Black–White achievement gap in reading for 9-year-old students and 13-year-old students were statistically the same as they were in 1988 (Figures 1.5 and 1.6). Similarly, in 2008, the Latino–White achievement gap in reading for 9-year-old students was virtually the same as it was in 1988, and the gap for 13-year-old students was virtually the same as it was in 1975.

The NAEP long-term trend in mathematics shows that the performance gap between Black and White students and Latino and White students has remained relatively unchanged. In 2008, the Black–White achievement gap in mathematics for 9-year-old students was virtually the same as it was in 1982. For 13-year-old students, the Black–White gap was virtually the same as it was in 1986 (Figures 1.7 and 1.8). Similarly, in 2008, the Latino–White achievement gap in mathematics for 9-year-old students was virtually the same as it was in 1978 (increasing in the 1990s), and the gap for 13-year-old students was virtually the same as it was in 1982.

Thus, despite gains in reading and math achievement among Black and Latino students, the national achievement gap today is strikingly similar to what is was 20 (and in some cases nearly 30) years ago. The relatively fixed nature and magnitude of the achievement gap paints a bleak picture

FIGURE 1.5   ⟶   NINE-YEAR-OLD READING ACHIEVEMENT
(NAEP LONG-TERM TREND)

	AVERAGE SCALE SCORE			ACHIEVEMENT GAP	
Year	White	Black	Latino	Black–White	Latino–White
2008	228	204	207	−24	−21
2004	224	197	199	−27	−25
2004*	226	200	205	−26	−21
1999	221	186	193	−35	−28
1996	220	191	195	−29	−25
1994	218	185	186	**−33**	**−32**
1992	218	185	192	**−33**	−26
1990	217	182	189	**−35**	**−28**
1988	218	189	194	−29	−24
1984	218	186	187	**−32**	**−31**
1980	221	189	190	**−32**	**−31**
1975	217	181	183	**−35**	**−34**

*Two NAEP long-term trend assessments were given in 2004 to re-norm the exam.

Source: U.S. Department of Education, Institute of Educational Sciences, National Center for Educational Statistics, National Assessment of Educational Progress (NAEP), 1975–2008 Reading Assessments. Bold numbers indicate gaps that are statistically different from the 2008 gaps as calculated by the U.S. Department of Education's NAEP Data Explorer.

and poses some critical questions. Why hasn't it been possible to narrow the achievement gap over the last nine years? Is there something wrong with— or missing from—the strategies that we have been using?

One crucial question is whether the achievement gap can be narrowed substantially without simultaneously addressing the inequities in health, housing, and income that have a bearing on child welfare and development. From a purely practical perspective, what makes reducing the achievement gap so difficult is that it requires Black and Latino students to play catch-up with their typically more affluent White peers.[9] Catching up is difficult, particularly when one considers that middle-class White students often have access to substantially superior resources, both within school and at home, that affect learning outcomes. Unless a deliberate effort is made to provide those who are behind with additional learning time, better instruction, and more resources (especially funding), it appears highly unlikely that the gap will close. From a policy perspective, if we were serious about closing the gap, then federal, state, and local policies would need to promote greater equity in learning conditions and greater external support to Black and Latino students to mitigate the effects of disadvantage.

Although a small number of school districts—such as Montgomery County, Maryland; Aldine Independent School District, Texas; and Abington,

FIGURE 1.6 ⋯→ THIRTEEN-YEAR-OLD READING ACHIEVEMENT (NAEP LONG-TERM TREND)

	AVERAGE SCALE SCORE			ACHIEVEMENT GAP	
Year	White	Black	Latino	Black–White	Latino–White
2008	268	247	242	–21	–26
2004	265	239	241	–25	–24
2004*	266	244	242	–22	–24
1999	267	238	244	**–29**	–23
1996	266	234	238	**–32**	–28
1994	265	234	235	**–31**	–30
1992	266	238	239	**–29**	–27
1990	262	241	238	–21	–24
1988	261	243	240	–18	–21
1984	263	236	240	**–26**	–23
1980	264	233	237	**–32**	–27
1975	262	226	232	**–36**	–30

*Two NAEP long-term trend assessments were given in 2004 to re-norm the exam.

Source: U.S. Department of Education, Institute of Educational Sciences, National Center for Educational Statistics, National Assessment of Educational Progress (NAEP), 1975–2008 Reading Assessments. Bold numbers indicate gaps that are statistically different from the 2008 gaps as calculated by the U.S. Department of Education's NAEP Data Explorer.

FIGURE 1.7 → NINE-YEAR-OLD MATH ACHIEVEMENT (NAEP LONG-TERM TREND)

	AVERAGE SCALE SCORE			ACHIEVEMENT GAP	
Year	White	Black	Latino	Black–White	Latino–White
2008	250	224	234	−26	−16
2004	245	221	229	−24	−16
2004*	247	224	230	−23	−18
1999	239	211	213	−28	**−26**
1996	237	212	215	−25	**−22**
1994	237	212	210	−25	**−27**
1992	235	208	212	−27	**−23**
1990	235	208	214	−27	−21
1986	227	202	205	−25	−21
1982	224	195	204	−29	−20
1978	224	192	203	**−32**	−21

*Two NAEP long-term trend assessments were given in 2004 to re-norm the exam.

Source: U.S. Department of Education, Institute of Educational Sciences, National Center for Educational Statistics, National Assessment of Educational Progress (NAEP), 1978–2008 Mathematics Assessments. Bold numbers indicate gaps that are statistically different from the 2008 gaps as calculated by the U.S. Department of Education's NAEP Data Explorer.

Pennsylvania—have chosen to take this path, the vast majority of states and school districts have not (Ferguson, 2010). The districts mentioned above have produced significant gains in achievement for Black and Latino students, and their success serves as evidence that greater progress can be made. Why other districts are not pursuing similar strategies, and why such strategies do not have a greater bearing on state and federal educational policies, is an issue that must be addressed if we hope to see greater progress.

At the federal level, there is very little evidence to suggest that NCLB has been effective at reducing the achievement gap (Lee, 2006). Individual states, however, have fared better in their efforts to reduce achievement gaps between Black and White students and Latino and White students. In comparing 2007 state NAEP scores to those from 1998, the Education Trust (2009) identified five states that have significantly reduced the Black–White achievement gap—Arizona, Arkansas, Connecticut, Georgia, and Louisiana—yet no state has demonstrated a significant reduction in the Latino–White achievement gap. Although the gains achieved by some states are encouraging, it is hardly surprising that so little progress has been evident in other states. Several studies have shown that top-down policies enacted by state governments are blunt tools for reducing the achievement gap, and they are only moderately effective (e.g., Braun, Wang, Jenkins, & Weinbaum, 2006). Most existing research on the achievement gap suggests that even though a small but statistically significant number of individual schools and districts have made real progress, the impact of large-scale reforms has been far less promising.

FIGURE 1.8 ⟶ THIRTEEN-YEAR-OLD MATH ACHIEVEMENT (NAEP LONG-TERM TREND)

	AVERAGE SCALE SCORE			ACHIEVEMENT GAP	
Year	White	Black	Latino	Black–White	Latino–White
2008	290	262	268	−28	−23
2004	287	257	264	−30	−23
2004*	288	262	265	−27	−23
1999	283	251	259	−32	−24
1996	281	252	256	−29	−25
1994	281	252	256	−29	−25
1992	279	250	259	−29	−20
1990	276	249	255	−27	−22
1986	274	249	254	−24	−19
1982	274	240	252	**−34**	−22
1978	272	230	238	**−42**	**−34**

*Two NAEP long-term trend assessments were given in 2004 to re-norm the exam.

Source: U.S. Department of Education, Institute of Educational Sciences, National Center for Educational Statistics, National Assessment of Educational Progress (NAEP), 1978–2008 Mathematics Assessments. Bold numbers indicate gaps that are statistically different from the 2008 gaps as calculated by the U.S. Department of Education's NAEP Data Explorer.

What's Race Got to Do with It?

02

For much of our nation's history, Americans have been both preoccupied with and confused about race. The confusion is understandable; throughout U.S. history, racial categories have changed over time and varied from state to state (Omi & Winant, 1986). There was a time when certain groups of people, such as Jews, Armenians, and even the Irish, were not afforded the same legal privileges as other people considered to be White (Ignatiev, 1991). Moreover, as recently as 1982, states across the country used different definitions to determine who would be regarded as an African American (Takaki, 1989). Latinos and Asian Americans pose an even greater quandary to the nation's ever-evolving racial classification system, because there is so much diversity among the groups lumped together within these categories. Furthermore, the categories and racial definitions we use in the United States are not universal and do not necessarily correspond to racial categories used by other countries (Bonilla-Silva, 2002).

Despite the confusion that surrounds the ways Americans think about it, race continues to have a profound effect upon life experiences in our society. Despite the ambiguity within racial categories, race is implicated in undeniable ways in a number of important quality-of-life indicators. From life expectancy to infant mortality, from dropout rates to incarceration rates, race remains a highly significant variable within the U.S. population. Ignoring these patterns under the guise of pursuing color-blind social policies does not cause them to disappear, though it does typically make them harder to detect and address.[1]

Confusion about the role and significance of race is particularly evident with respect to the ways in which Americans think about the relationships among race, education, and achievement. As we pointed out earlier, much of this confusion can be explained by history. The view of intelligence that prevailed throughout most of the 19th and 20th centuries held that non-Whites, particularly Blacks, Native Americans, Latinos, and even some Eastern Europeans, were genetically inferior and possessed lower levels of intellectual capacity than Whites, particularly those who originated in north-western Europe (Gould, 1981). Such views about the relationships between and among race, ethnicity, and intelligence had considerable influence on social science research, psychology, and theories of education (Lehman, 1996).

Racial Reasoning in America's History

Early in the 20th century, advocates of eugenics—the so-called science of genetic engineering—propagated the notion that groups with superior intellects and physical abilities should be encouraged to procreate in order to strengthen the national gene pool, but inferior groups should be discouraged and even prevented from reproducing (Duster, 2003). Some eugenicists were leaders in the effort to devise tests for measuring intelligence (Lehman, 1996). These individuals sought to ensure that intelligence tests and later exams such as the Scholastic Aptitude Test (SAT) would be used to provide an "objective" measure of talent and ability. There were, of course, other noneugenicists who saw testing as a meritocratic approach to ensuring that talent—rather than privilege—would be used to determine who should be recruited for high-ranking positions in the military, for professional occupations, and for enrollment at elite universities (Fischer et al., 1996).

This history of the relationship between race and intelligence in the United States is highly relevant to current efforts aimed at closing the academic achievement gap. Though it is no longer acceptable to attribute differences in achievement to genetic differences among racial groups, this point was made as recently as 1994 (Herrnstein & Murray, 1994). *The Bell Curve* received a mix of condemnation and acclaim at the time of its release (see Fischer et al., 1996). Even though such views have never been supported by research on genetics, or advanced by scientists who research the links between human biology and intelligence, they continue to find adherents throughout U.S. society. Neither of the authors of *The Bell Curve* studied genetics (Richard Herrnstein was a psychologist, and Charles Murray is a political scientist), but their lack of knowledge about genetics did not stop them from supporting the genetic basis of intellectual ability or the inferiority of racial minorities.

Not long ago, former Harvard University president Lawrence Summers suggested that one of the reasons why women were not well represented in math- and science-related fields was due to innate differences in intellectual ability (Bombardieri, 2005). If the president of Harvard University, an econo-mist by training, felt comfortable making remarks about the relationships among genetics, gender, and intelligence (at least in science and math), it would not be a stretch to conclude that similar views about the relationships between innate ability and categories such as race and gender may be widely held throughout U.S. society.

In place of arguments about the genetic inferiority of minority groups, it is becoming increasingly common for a variety of spokespersons to attri-bute differences in achievement to broad and undefined notions of "culture" (McWhorter, 2000; Ogbu, 1987), parental influences (Epstein, 1994), and even rap music (Williams, 2006). Though these arguments vary in substance, such perspectives on the influence of culture are not unlike earlier views that regarded racial differences in academic performance as the result of genetic differences. Like the eugenicists and their intellectual offspring, many of those who attribute achievement differences to culture explain racial dispari-ties as a by-product of pathologies that are inherent to norms, attitudes, and behaviors embraced by underperforming groups.

The confusion and misguided logic associated with such views about cul-ture become apparent as soon as one looks closely at the arguments that are made. Most demographers recognize that there is a high degree of diversity within racial and ethnic groups that is related to income, education, speech and linguistic patterns, and outlook on a variety of social and political subjects. Moreover, researchers who have studied academic performance over the years note that a broad array of factors—individual motivation, family income, parental education, school quality, and so on—have a powerful bearing on student achievement. Despite the prevalence that more is in play than merely some broad notion of culture, arguments about the influence of culture as a factor that undermines student achievement continue to be made. They are also not easily refuted when they are made by highly respected figures such as Bill Cosby and noted African American psychiatrist Alvin Poussaint. In their book *Come on, People* (Cosby & Poussaint, 2007), the two authors make statements such as the following:

> As if poor black kids didn't have trouble enough, they often turn to those rappers, even the gangsters, as role models. Some middle-income males do the same. All these misguided souls, poor or not, saunter through school imitating the rappers and ignoring Standard English because it is "white." Unfortunately for them, gangsta rappers don't design standardized tests or do the hiring for jobs. And no translator at the UN can tell you what "fo' shizzle, ma nizzle" means. Hanging on to such styles in school can spell doom for these kids. (p. 119)

Though there is no doubt that some children exhibit oppositional behavior that may contribute to academic failure, without citing any evidence to support their arguments, Cosby and Poussaint never explain where these attitudes come from, how widely they are held, or why it is that some children who gravitate toward rap music still manage to do extremely well in school. More important, they fail to consider that if culture, as conceptualized here, is responsible for low achievement, why have some schools managed to create environments where high levels of achievement among Black and Latino children are the norm? A close examination of schools such as Thurgood Marshall High School in Harlem or Elmont High School on Long

Island reveals that such schools manage to create a culture where learning is valued and students don't perceive a need to choose between their racial/ethnic identities and their desire to be successful (Chenoweth, 2009). Given the existence of such schools, it seems reasonable to conclude that perhaps there is more going on than a pervasive culture of anti-intellectualism (McWhorter, 2000).

Unlike biology, culture has been embraced by some scholars as a less politically distasteful explanation of the achievement gap, because it is assumed that cultures are not immutable and can be changed over time. Among those advocating this perspective are scholars, such as anthropologist John Ogbu (1987; Ogbu & Davis, 2003), who have argued that involuntary minorities—groups that were incorporated into the United States through conquest, slavery, or force (i.e., Native Americans, African Americans, Puerto Ricans, and Mexican Americans)—consistently do less well in school because they adopt an oppositional culture in relation to schooling. According to Ogbu, to the degree that involuntary minorities regard schooling as a form of forced assimilation, they are less likely to embrace the behaviors that contribute to school success (obeying school rules, studying for exams, speaking Standard English, etc.). Ogbu's views have been embraced by many scholars as an effective way to explain why many voluntary immigrant minorities (especially Asians) outperform the involuntary minority groups mentioned above.

Similarly, linguist John McWhorter (2000) has attributed the lower achievement of many Black students to a "culture of anti-intellectualism," whereas former English professor Shelby Steele (1996) has attributed it to what he calls "victimology"—the tendency on the part of Blacks to blame "the White man" for their problems. McWhorter contends that "victimology stems from a lethal combination of this inherited inferiority complex with the privilege of dressing down the former oppressor," and he adds that it "condones weakness and failure" (2000, p. 28). Others, such as sociologist Orlando Patterson and journalist Juan Williams, have cited the culture of gangsta rap—with its emphasis on bling (flashy jewelry), violence, and disdain for hard work—as producing a "culture of failure" (Patterson, 2009; Williams, 2006) Finally, a number of others (e.g., Ruby Payne, whose work has been embraced by a number of school districts) have cited a "culture of poverty" as the reason why poor children of all races often fail to perform well in school (Payne, 1996). Even if unacknowledged, such theories draw on the work of anthropologist Oscar Lewis, who argued that intergenerational poverty among Puerto Ricans was reproduced because the poor embraced norms that perpetuate a culture of poverty (Lewis, 1966).

Cultural explanations of the achievement gap, including those articulated by Ogbu, Steele, and McWhorter, have been widely embraced by researchers, policymakers, and educators (Noguera, 2003). Even though such explanations of academic performance fail to account for individuals who deviate from established patterns but have cultural similarities with others who conform to these patterns—for example, poor Black students who excel and middle-class White and Asian students who struggle—these theories continue to be embraced. A recent article in the *New York Times Magazine* put the cultural argument this way: "Kids from poor families might be nicer, they might be happier, they might be more polite—but in countless ways, the manner in which they are raised puts them at a disadvantage in the measures that count in contemporary American society" (Tough, 2006, p. 31). Recognizing how difficult it will be to achieve the goals of NCLB if cultural differences are at the root of the achievement gap, the article goes on to ask, "Can the culture of child-rearing be changed in poor neighborhoods, and if so, is that a project that government or community organizations have the ability, or the right, to take on?" (p. 36).

When asked whether low achievement among Black students might be explained by a fear they have of being accused of "acting White," or if Asian students are culturally oriented to excel in mathematics, it is important to point out that such arguments are based upon gross generalizations of culture and overlook the powerful role that schools can play in promoting or hindering academic achievement. For example, such cultural arguments cannot explain the large number of Asian students at schools such as Galileo High School in San Francisco or Richmond High School in Richmond, California, who drop out of school. Conversely, such theories are useless in explaining the large number of low-income Black students who excel at schools such as New York City's Frederick Douglass Academy or Middle College High School at Medgar Evers. Such examples serve as powerful reminders that the success or failure of students cannot simply be attributed to the amount of culture they do or do not possess. Rather, a close examination of achievement patterns at these schools reveals that conditions there play a major role in shaping students' academic outcomes.

Ironically, broad generalizations about culture are so deeply embedded in popular thinking about race and school performance that they manage to survive even when empirical evidence undermines their validity. For example, Julian Ledesma, an undergraduate student at the University of California, Berkeley, tested the strength of the Asian "model minority" stereotype in a paper he wrote (1995). At a high school in Oakland, California, he surveyed students and teachers about which ethnic group they believed was most academically talented. The vast majority of those he surveyed identified Asian students as the highest performers. This was even true for the Asian students he interviewed who were not performing well themselves. Most interviewees justified their answers by pointing out that Asian students were overrepresented in the school's honors and advanced placement courses and that several of the school's valedictorians had been Asian. However, in his analysis of student performance data, Ledesma showed that even though many of the school's academic stars happened to be Asian, such students were by no means representative of Asian students as a whole. In fact, the grade point average for Asian students at the school was 1.9 on a scale of 1.0 to 4.0. Because Asian students were perceived as academically successful, little effort had been expended to provide them with the kind of academic support or special services that had been made available to other students.

Examples such as this do not prove that cultural influences are irrelevant to student achievement. At an aggregate level, Asian students outperform other groups in mathematics, White students achieve at higher levels than Black and Latino students on most standardized tests, and middle-class children generally outperform poor children (Farkas, 2004). Individual exceptions exist, of course, but the patterns cited are fairly consistent (Ferguson, 2007). To some degree, these patterns may be attributed, at least in part, to characteristics that are loosely associated with culture. However, to find ways to reduce disparities in achievement, the specific aspects of culture that seem to have the greatest bearing on achievement must be identified (see also Chapter 6). For example, certain childrearing practices, such as parents reading to children during infancy or posing questions rather than issuing demands when speaking to children, are associated with the development of intellectual traits that contribute to school success (Rothstein, 2004b). Similarly, parental expectations about grades, homework, and the use of recreational time have been shown to influence adolescent behavior and academic performance (Ferguson, 2007).

In his research at the University of California, Uri Treisman found that many Asian students studied in groups when they completed homework or prepared for exams. He found that this practice helped individuals excel in math while reinforcing norms that contribute to the importance of academic success among Asian students. By contrast, the Black students he studied were more likely to socialize together but study alone (Treisman, 1993). Whether such behaviors can be attributed to culture can be debated, but clearly identifying specific behaviors that seem to boost academic achievement—parents reading to children, studying in groups, teaching study habits and organizational skills—is more helpful than making broad generalizations about "oppositional" behavior and "anti-intellectual" attitudes. When studies of cultural norms and practices are specific and focused, we can use the information gleaned to teach others (even teachers) how to emulate behaviors that lead to success. For example, we need more research that explores the influence of popular culture—videogames, rap music, television—on student achievement and attitudes toward school. Broad generalizations about the presumed negative influences of such aspects of popular culture won't suffice. We need to know how they influence students, and if we find an adverse impact on some individuals, we need to investigate how this harm can be countered.

It is hard to imagine how we might go about changing the culture of individuals who seem to embrace attitudes and norms that undermine possibilities for academic success. For that reason, although we should not ignore those influences that are broadly termed "cultural," we should also recognize that it is more practical to focus on factors that influence learning (and that we can actually do something about). There is much that our nation can do to reduce the concentration of poor children of color in struggling schools, to equalize funding between schools that serve middle-class and poor children, to lower class size, to extend learning opportunities after school and during the summer, and to ensure that we are hiring teachers who are qualified, are competent, and receive high-quality, appropriate professional development. These are all factors that research has shown can have a positive effect on student achievement (Darling-Hammond, 2004, 2007; Miller, 1995), and none of them involves trying to figure out how to change a person's culture.

Understanding Race and Its Influence on Academic Achievement

As a result of the high degree of mixing among so-called racial groups, and because of the amorphous nature of racial categories themselves, a growing number of scholars have rejected the notions that race should be regarded as a biological concept or that differences among racial groups should be attributed to essential genetic differences. Instead, scholars in recent years have advanced the idea that race should be considered largely as a socially constructed political category (Lipsitz, 2006).

We take the position that if racial categories are indeed social and not primarily biological in nature,[2] then it should be possible to fundamentally alter the predictability of racial patterns related to academic ability and per-formance *if we can eliminate the ways in which those patterns are entrenched within the structure and culture of a school.* This does not mean that the racial patterns manifest in most academic outcome data can be dismissed as a fig-ment of our collective imagination. Rather, it suggests that we must address the institutional practices and social conditions that produce, perpetuate, and give meaning to these disparities. In order for schools to produce aca-demic outcomes that demonstrate that race is irrelevant to achievement, they must address the many ways in which racial identity and stereotypes are reinforced and even reproduced within academic settings (Steele, 2010). The notion that Black, Latino, and Native American children are not as smart or capable as White students is not only deeply rooted in U.S. history but also propagated in the media and popular culture. Because schools generally reflect the larger values and beliefs of society, stereotypes about the relationship between race and intelligence are often reinforced within the structure and culture of schools. If unchallenged, we should not be surprised to see Black male students gravitating toward basketball and football while avoiding math and science. Stereotypes are powerful; unless educators make a deliberate and concerted effort to challenge them, they can have the same impact on student achievement as older views about the relationship between race and intellectual ability.

Unfortunately, the number of schools where race is not a strong predictor of academic performance and no longer "matters" with respect to its ability to predict academic outcomes is relatively small (Ferguson, 2007). Although there are a few schools where it is common to find Black or Latino students among the highest achievers (Jencks & Phillips, 1998), and there are also a number of high-performing high-poverty schools (Education Trust, 2002), most schools in the United States continue to exhibit the racial achievement gap, despite many exhortations to eliminate it.

Changing the Discourse on the Relationship Between Race and Achievement

In an unusual break from past practice, NCLB significantly expanded the role of the federal government in the operation of the nation's public schools. With its requirement that states adopt clear academic standards and accountability measures for schools and students, the federal government ended the practice of local control by extending its influence over public education in ways that significantly altered the tradition of state and local control (Katznelson & Weir, 1985). Few have disputed the need to improve public education, and the requirement that schools produce evidence that all students are learning is generally seen as laudable. However, even though the law remains controversial, especially among educators who object to the excessive emphasis on testing, many features of the law remain popular within the federal government.

Undoubtedly, at least part of the reason NCLB generated such strong opinions is that, for the first time in U.S. history, schools were required to produce evidence that *all* students were learning. Many schools and districts found themselves struggling under the new law simply because they were unprepared to demonstrate their ability to educate all children, and they had difficulty fulfilling the basic requirements of the law. This was and is true in large urban school districts where the majority of students are poor, Black, and Latino and where achievement has historically been low. Likewise, this was and is also true in many affluent suburban communities where the underperformance of a relatively small number of poor and/or non-White children was previously overlooked or ignored. NCLB's requirement that schools disaggregate test scores by race and other designated subgroups exposed the fact that, even in schools and districts with ample resources and a track record of academic success, poor and racial minority students typically have not been well served. Not surprisingly, much of the opposition to NCLB emerged first in these communities, in response to the law's heavy emphasis on standardized testing and to resentment and embarrassment at having some of their schools labeled as "failing" because of the performance of students of color.

Understanding the Relationships Among Race, Culture, and Teaching

Although a variety of factors contribute to the disparities in academic performance that correspond to the race and class background of children (e.g., parental support, peer influences, health, nutrition, media), the need to provide teachers with the requisite skills to teach effectively, regardless of race, class, and culture, is now widely recognized as essential. Clear and consistent evidence has emerged over the years that when teachers lack such skills, students are less likely to achieve and classrooms are more likely to be disruptive and disorderly (Irvine, 2003; Lipman, 1995; Sleeter, 2000). The reason for these problems is also clear—students learn through relationships. When educators experience difficulty establishing respectful, caring, and mutually beneficial relationships with the students they teach, it is often difficult to create an atmosphere that is supportive of teaching and learning (Bryk & Schneider, 2003).

Race, class, and linguistic and cultural differences between students and teachers certainly do not cause the achievement gap; however, they do contribute to its persistence and often complicate efforts to reduce or eliminate disparities in student learning outcomes. In the United States, it has taken some time for educators and school districts to recognize the importance of what is now widely referred to as "cultural competence." For the longest time, there were two prevailing views on race and class differences and teaching. The first and most traditional view held that teachers were, in effect, emissaries of the dominant culture; as such, their job was to deliberately facilitate the assimilation of students from culturally different backgrounds (Cremin, 1988; Fass, 1989; Katznelson & Weir, 1985). Under this educational paradigm, schools were expected to impart the values, norms, and language of the dominant culture to the immigrant, poor, and minority students they taught (Jiobu, 1988). This was seen as an essential part of preparing disadvantaged and culturally diverse students for citizenship and integration into mainstream U.S. society. No apologies were offered for such an approach, nor was it common to hear complaints from those who were expected to carry it out. Eliminating cultural differences was typically equated with providing the social skills students would need to enter the U.S. workforce and assume adult roles in society (Glazer & Moynihan, 1963). "Americanization" was regarded as the price certain students had to pay for mobility (Fass, 1989).

Though never fully repudiated (it is, in fact, still widely practiced in many schools throughout the United States today), this approach to education has been gradually replaced in some schools by what is best described as the "color-blind" approach. Unlike its predecessor, the color-blind approach grew out of the idea that the best way to educate all children was to ignore differences related to race, class, and culture and to treat all children equally regardless of their backgrounds (Fine, Weis, Powell, & Mun Wong, 1997; Sleeter, 2000). By ignoring differences, it was assumed that teachers could minimize the possibility that prejudice and bias would influence their perceptions of students and interfere with their ability to teach. Advocates of the color-blind approach envisioned it as a way to ensure that teachers' expectations would not be determined by students' backgrounds, and they saw it as epistemologically linked to the civil rights goal of creating a society in which race no longer determines a person's status or social standing (Delpit, 1995; Kirp, 1982).

Before explaining why both approaches have come under attack and gradually been replaced, it is important to at least acknowledge their merits. The assimilationist approach is based on a certain degree of realism—students who do not learn English, who do not become conversant in Standard English, and who fail to adopt mainstream social norms are less likely to be successful in higher education and the U.S. workforce. As Lareau (1989) has shown through her research on the ways in which class differences affect the ways in which children and parents are treated by schools, education is not a neutral process; it occurs in social settings that are necessarily influenced by the hierarchical arrangements that exist in society. Those who do not acquire the cultural capital of the dominant classes are invariably regarded as less suitable for inclusion in mainstream roles in society (García, Wilkinson, & Ortiz, 1995; Olsen, 2000). Though critics may regard it as unfair that the onus for change and acculturation is on subordinate groups, it is nonetheless the reality. In a controversial and seminal article entitled "The Silenced Dialogue: Power and Pedagogy in Educating Other People's Children," noted educator Lisa Delpit (1988) argues that students who do not acquire what she refers to as the "tools of power" tend to be less successful in school and often find their future options for employment adversely affected. Although Delpit does not endorse the eradication of cultural differences, she does recognize, as do a number of language educators and linguists, that the ability to code switch (knowing when the use of Standard English is expected) is an essential requisite for educational success (e.g., Fordham, 1988; Ogbu, 1988). According to Delpit, teachers who fail to impart such skills to their students, and who do not provide them with a critical understanding of how and when they are to be used, end up short changing them.

Similarly, advocates of the color-blind approach to teaching frequently point out that there is a slippery slope between acknowledging differences related to race, class, and culture and lowering expectations to accommodate these differences. Though it may be true that adopting a color-blind stance is nearly impossible in a society where racism, ethnocentrism, and class snobbery are rooted in historical and contemporary social relations (Fredrickson, 1981), acknowledging differences does not guarantee that teachers won't be influenced by biases that continue to be pervasive in U.S. society (Hacker, 1992). According to this view, when teachers strive to adopt a stance of neutrality on matters related to race, class, and culture, they may be more likely to strive for fairness in the way they treat students and to avoid practices that give certain groups of students unfair advantages. Of course, critics of the color-blind approach frequently point out that such striving rarely occurs; even if teachers refuse to acknowledge the ways in which their biases influence their teaching, they are invariably influenced nonetheless (Sleeter, 2000). According to the critics, when teachers recognize that student differences influence their academic needs and acknowledge the likelihood that personal biases influence teacher–student interactions, they will be more likely to take measures that address these issues.

Beginning in the 1980s, a new approach to preparing teachers to teach in ethnically and socioeconomically diverse classrooms began gaining credibility and adherents. Advocates of multicultural education argued that the only way to effectively prepare teachers to teach across these differences was to expose them to a curriculum that focused on the history of race and class oppression in the United States and that forced them to recognize and unlearn their biases. According to Enid Lee, one of the leading proponents of multicultural education, such an approach is essential because "it provides teachers, students and parents with the tools needed to combat racism and ethnic discrimination, and to find ways to build a society that includes all people on equal footing" (1995, p. 8).

For the most part, critics of both approaches to teacher education and advocates of multicultural education have won. In most teacher-education programs based in universities throughout the United States, courses on multiculturalism and courses that attempt to prepare teachers to teach effectively across race, class, and cultural differences are common (Davidman & Davidman, 1994; Gay, 2000). There are, of course, colleges that have not embraced this change, but it is now widely accepted that teachers must receive special training to enter classrooms filled with students from ethnically diverse backgrounds. This is especially true in programs designed to prepare teachers for urban public schools, but as the demographic changes caused by immigration and suburbanization have transformed the composition of suburban and rural schools, teacher-education programs throughout the country have adopted similar courses (Banks, 1981).

Unfortunately, winning the struggle over how to prepare teachers has not guaranteed that teachers, even those who graduate from programs that embrace multiculturalism, are fully prepared for, much less effective at, teaching students from diverse backgrounds. Though numerous studies of such programs have been conducted, there is not yet clear evidence that mere exposure to multicultural approaches to teaching actually result in more preparation for or effectiveness in classrooms comprised of children of color and from low-income backgrounds. Courses in multiculturalism do not inoculate those who take them from the influence of bias, nor do they provide them with the social and emotional skills required to relate and establish rapport with students from diverse backgrounds. The same is true of the various cultural sensitivity programs that some schools and school districts have implemented. Like the preservice courses offered at colleges and universities, training seminars offered by noted diversity experts such as Ruby Payne (*A Framework for Understanding Poverty,* 1996) do not seem to impact student outcomes directly, even when they do show some degree of success in raising awareness.

Moving Beyond Rationalizations of the Gap

As we mentioned previously, certain cultural explanations of the achievement gap that overemphasize the importance of race are often associated with a tendency to blame students, their parents, and communities for failure and underachievement. In schools where race and class are strong predictors of achievement, where few Black or Latino students are enrolled in gifted or honors courses but are overrepresented in special education and remedial courses, and where the link between race and achievement has been firmly established in the minds of educators, a sense of inevitability often leads to complacency about the effort to raise student achievement. In such communities, the failure of students of color can become normalized as educators and others rationalize and accept low performance as the by-product of factors they cannot control.

Too often, attitudes and beliefs that contribute to the normalization of failure are unchallenged, and when failure is normalized, educators often grow comfortable seeing minority students underperform and fail in large numbers. In such schools, students of color may also grow accustomed to receiving failing grades, and they may actively avoid academic pursuits or challenging courses. In educational settings such as these, race and gender stereotypes flourish, can have a powerful effect on attitudes and behavior, and can undermine efforts to raise achievement. Likewise, parents and the broader community can become so conditioned by pervasive and persistent failure among certain groups of students that, over time, low test scores, discipline problems, and high dropout rates generate little outrage or concern.

When failure is normalized and educators are no longer disturbed by low student achievement, it can be extremely difficult for student outcomes or schools to change. Reforms may be implemented—new textbooks and new curricula may be adopted, schools may be reorganized and restructured, principals may be replaced—but unless there is a strategy for countering the normalization of failure, it is unlikely that disparities in achievement will be reduced or that schools will ever change. Like certain cultural explanations of underachievement, the normalization of failure can reinforce beliefs about the link between race and intelligence, and unless these beliefs are countered, it is less likely that patterns of achievement will be altered.

The factors that contribute to normalization are often quite real and should not be dismissed as merely a form of whining. Student motivation and the attitudes that students display toward learning profoundly affect patterns of achievement. We address many of these factors in the following chapters. Schools that do not have an effective strategy for convincing students to become invested in their education—to work hard, study, arrive at school on time and prepared, and generally care about learning—are unlikely to reduce disparities in academic outcomes and raise student achievement. Similarly, parents who are negligent about reinforcing the value of education, who fail to encourage their children to apply themselves, or who do not regard education as an effective means to improve the lives of their children may engage in behaviors that contribute to the failure of their children.

All of these factors can contribute to the normalization of failure and complacency related to racial patterns in achievement. This is why the normalization of failure must be addressed if progress is to be made. Educators who are serious about closing the achievement gap and raising achievement for *all* students must be willing to confront these obstacles, rather than merely dismiss them as excuses. What is needed is a strategy that makes it possible to change the discourse about the relationship between race and achievement from one that is focused on who's to blame to one in which all of the key stakeholders—teachers, parents, students, and administrators—accept responsibility for their roles in raising achievement (Perry, Steele, & Hilliard, 2003).

President George W. Bush called for the nation to "end the soft bigotry of low expectations," as his way of describing what we call the normalization of failure (Noe, 2004). We have not found slogans such as these useful in helping educators figure out how to approach the challenge of raising achievement for all students. However, the president was also making an important point: It is clear that how we feel about the persistence of the racial achievement gap has a strong bearing on what we do about it. If we feel some students won't achieve because they are intellectually deficient, because they come from a dysfunctional culture, or simply because such students have never done well before, chances are that no reform measure will change academic outcomes. Whenever educators blame low student achievement on some factor they cannot control, there is a strong tendency for them to reject responsibility for those factors they can and do control. For this reason, countering the normalization of failure must be seen as the first step in any effort to close (or at the very least reduce) the achievement gap.

Closing the racial achievement gap and pursuing greater equity in schools will undoubtedly be a long-term, uphill struggle that is fraught with difficulty because of our history of racial inequality and because our nation remains so profoundly unequal and racially segregated. Sociologist Orlando Patterson has argued convincingly that the persistence of racial segregation (and our policymakers' retreat from doing anything about it) contributes to the perpetuation of the racial achievement gap because it denies many children of color access to the opportunities they need to succeed (2009). We must recognize that the sources of inequity typically lie outside schools—in income and wealth disparities and in unequal access to health care, well-paying jobs, and vital social services. We may be approaching a time when the political interest and will to close these vital gaps in quality of life will increase. Certainly, reforms to social policy that promote greater equality and justice would help efforts to close gaps in academic achievement (Anyon, 2005).

However, until the time for promoting equity on a larger scale comes, we will have to take advantage of our nation's proclaimed commitment to closing the academic achievement gap, even if it may only be lip service. Even if many of those who have embraced this call do not truly believe that it can be done, the mere fact that the call has been made provides an opportunity to create a broader agenda for equity in schooling. The effort to promote educational equity and close the achievement gap is consistent with the basic promise of public education in the United States: Schools should function as the equalizers of opportunity (Jencks et al.,1972; Sizer, 1984). No matter how difficult and elusive such an effort might be, closing the achievement gap remains a key feature of educational policy. It is also a goal that schools must pursue if they are to retain the trust of the families they serve and remain viable as public institutions. For those of us who can see how it is connected to other forms of equality, closing the achievement gap is also a goal we must press for our entire society to embrace—to avoid greater racial polarization and conflict and to realize the enormous potential that our diversity has bestowed upon us.

In Part II of this book, we will explore what research tells us about some of the most promising approaches for closing the achievement gap. By grounding our efforts in credible research, we can increase the likelihood that our work to close the gap will be rewarded with success—both our own and our students'.

PART II

Analyzing
the Research

We face a daunting number of challenges as we work to eliminate academic achievement gaps. Our task becomes more feasible, however, when we embrace an evidence-based framework (Slavin & Fashola, 1998). Too much educational practice is based on hearsay, on what sounds good, on how things have always been done, or even on who knows whom. Instead, we must build our practices on sound, rigorous research and systematic evidence—evidence of what works but also on *how* and *why* things work, *where* things work, and *for whom* they work (Slavin, 2002).

What does an evidence-based framework entail? First, we must glean the research literature to identify the best evidence that can help shape and direct the practices to be implemented. What qualifies as best evidence? To determine this, ask three questions. Did the obtained findings actually result from the practices that were implemented, or are there plausible alternative explanations for the outcome(s)? Are there indications that the results have been repeated and are not just one-time occurrences? Have the results been obtained at other sites beyond the place of origin? (In other words, is there evidence for similar findings occurring more generally and not just under a special circumstance or in a unique situation?) These three questions (and the framework they imply) are familiar to research methodologists and have been correspondingly labeled as matters of internal validity, reliability, and external validity (or generalizability).

Having stated these standards, we believe some cautions are in order. The literature that focuses on learning and performance among Black and Latino students has not produced a sizable number of studies that yield definitive results born out of methodologies that meet the highest standards of research evidence. Such a barometer would make use of rigorous experimental research designs in which treatment groups/conditions are contrasted with control groups/conditions or in which there are varying treatment conditions, and assignment to condition is done on a strictly random basis. Deploying such techniques is the best way to ensure that outcomes meet the highest test of internal validity, whereby competing or alternative explanations for results can be substantially ruled out.

Although several studies included in our review did deploy experimental designs, much of the work we present deployed correlational designs. Nonetheless, these designs incorporated sophisticated multivariate analyses, so predictor variables for relevant outcomes have been discerned, and insights can be attained on causal pathways among potentially operative factors. In this way, factors that have direct impact or indirect influence (or no impact at all) on relevant outcomes can be systematically ascertained.

Many studies have drawn on national secondary data sets, rather than on primary data. This approach has its advantages in that it yields findings that are generalizable across the United States, rather than applicable only to a particular locale. However, it requisitely relies more on self-report data and instruments that are of the investigators' own choosing. Thus, constructs are formulated in a post-hoc fashion and may not be as precisely captured as they could be. Beyond this, many studies have not asked specific and direct questions to discern which actual learning processes are at play, whether there are racial or ethnic divergences, or whether certain factors or conditions would lead to gap-closing performance outcomes.

The Pursuit of Promising Conceptions and Processes

In spite of these limitations, certain conceptions and processes have emerged in recent research studies that promise to account for ethnic-group performance differences; provide insights into the *whys* behind performance deficits; explain or predict academic proficiency levels for certain minority students; and suggest avenues to improve minority student achievement outcomes, close majority–minority achievement gaps, raise the achievement of U.S. students relative to international standards, and better prepare all of our students for the 21st century.

The logic behind what evidence should be used to judge whether processes or practices are gap closing deserves further discussion. We look especially for findings where the achievement gap closes or narrows under a certain condition or intervention, which contrasts with conditions in which the gap does not narrow. We also look for cases where students in general seem to benefit from a particular practice or intervention or where the presence of a given attribute is associated with or correlates with a desired outcome. This is particularly helpful if the cases are coupled with empirical data that show the attribute is markedly lower in its expression—or, if maladaptive, markedly higher in its expression—among Black and Latino students. Finally, we look for cases where lower-performing or less skilled students seem to benefit comparatively more from a given practice, intervention, or strategy than do skilled or high-performing students.

A fourth decision rule that is deployed in the absence of other, more convincing evidence is when a given practice seems to elevate performance. This is the least compelling option; if the intervention lifts all students to the same degree, then it is not gap closing, but it cannot be ruled out in the absence of countervailing evidence. Of course, having low-achieving students achieve at a proficient level of functioning has merit in its own right, even if it does not close gaps. Having a greater number of students function at or above an acceptable level of performance has greater societal good than if this were not the case. In fact, the effective schools movement of the 1980s had this as its objective (Edmonds, 1986). Cutting off the proverbial tail of academic failure was the benefit that such practices were supposed to produce—not closing achievement gaps per se.

When we examine the extant literature, a picture emerges of what makes certain processes particularly effective in raising achievement and closing performance gaps. The chapters that comprise Part II are devoted to identifying, explaining, and providing the research support for these attendant factors and how they seem to interrelate. In examining the extant research that meets the standards outlined in this introduction, a set of interconnected factors emerge and form into a reasonably coherent scheme of what should occur inside classrooms on a daily basis in the transactions that transpire between teachers and students and among students themselves.

It will be argued and documented that if more of these factors are manifested in the ongoing teaching and learning activities that occur inside classrooms, then we can make significant progress in raising achievement for all students while closing achievement gaps between minority and majority group students across the K–12 spectrum. This proposed scheme is presented in the graph on the next page. As depicted, the most proximal factor to achievement outcomes is student engagement in academic tasks. Engagement is the bellwether for enhanced student achievement. It is the precursor to gap-closing academic outcomes. It is the beacon of greater opportunities to learn for all students.

Engagement is impacted by what we term guiding functions, or adaptive learning postures. We label these as such because they represent beliefs about or ways of orienting toward academic tasks and demands that will likely promote positive academic outcomes when they are embraced by students. It is further argued here that suitable engagement levels and appropriate guiding functions are more likely to occur when they are functionally connected to or impacted by asset-focused strategies. These are practices, techniques, or approaches that are explicitly designed to optimize learning opportunities for all students.

RESEARCH-BASED SCHEME FOR PROMOTING ENHANCED
CLASSROOM TEACHING AND LEARNING

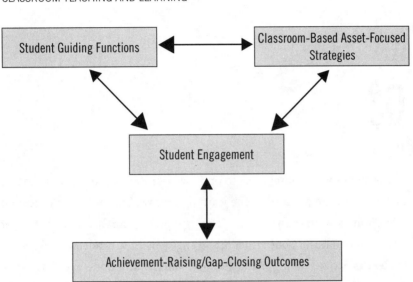

Note: Although arrows between boxes are bidirectional, the larger arrowheads indicate the more typical direction of influence.

Engagement

03

At the most fundamental level, to optimize learning, a teacher must ensure that students are engaged in the learning process. The kind of engagement that optimizes task performance is not simply measurable time on task or attending to a lesson, but rather active engagement in academic tasks—the student is actively doing math, reading material at a non-superficial level, and making strides toward task accomplishment (Greenwood et al., 1987). A growing amount of research points to such engagement as particularly linked to favorable learning outcomes for minority students who have been placed at risk for academic failure (Borman & Overman, 2004; Tucker et al., 2002; Wenglinsky, 2004).

Classroom-based engagement can be of three types: behavioral, cognitive, and affective (Fredericks, Blumenfeld, & Paris, 2004). These three types are distinct yet interrelated. Behavioral engagement conveys the presence of general "on-task behavior." This entails effort and persistence along with paying attention, asking pointed questions, seeking help that enables one to accomplish the task at hand (rather than being given the answer), and participating in class discussions. Cognitive engagement connotes investment aimed at comprehending complex concepts and issues and acquiring difficult skills. It conveys deep (rather than surface-level) processing of information whereby students gain critical or higher-order understanding of the subject matter and solve challenging problems. Affective engagement connotes emotional reactions linked to task investment. The greater the student's interest level, positive affect, positive attitude, positive value held, curiosity, and task absorption (and the less the anxiety, sadness, stress, and boredom), the greater the affective engagement. Based on current research and understanding, we don't know how the three types of engagement interact, and we are not certain which antecedents are linked to which types (Ladd & Dinella, 2009).

Other terms used in the literature convey the opposite meaning: lack of engagement. The term *disengagement* obviously is one case in point, but we also see synonyms for disengagement in the form of self-handicapping behaviors or inclinations such as task avoidance and procrastination. These notions have been studied in their own right (e.g., Turner et al., 2002). As expected, these factors have uniformly negative relationships with achievement outcomes.

Research on Mathematics

In reviewing research specific to math learning and the performance of Black and Latino students, the evidence strongly suggests that greater engagement leads to greater success for these populations. Indeed, findings in support of this claim have been well documented, from kindergarten through 12th grade.

A study by Borman and Overman (2004) is a case in point. These researchers set out to discern the factors that differentiate between academically successful and unsuccessful Black, Latino, and White students from low-income backgrounds. Their goal was to examine the trajectory of performance levels by a cohort of students from 3rd to 6th grade. For their outcome measure, they used the Comprehensive Test of Basic Skills, Fourth Edition (CTBS/4) math performance scores from the *Prospects* national data set. They focused on a cohort of students who performed comparably during 3rd grade but whose scores diverged substantially during 6th grade. Those students whose scores increased substantially were labeled *resilient,* and those students whose scores decreased by 6th grade were termed *nonresilient*. The percentile rank for both groups was at 39 in the 3rd grade. In the 6th grade, the percentile ranks were 59 and 11, respectively, for the resilient and nonresilient groups. The predictor variables were measured as the average annual scores for each factor, for each participant, across a four-year period.

One factor that distinguished resilient from nonresilient children was having a positive attitude toward school. Another factor, student engagement, also significantly differentiated between successful and unsuccessful students. In this investigation, student engagement was not measured by self-report, but it was instead indexed by the extent to which teachers agreed that a student's attitudes and behaviors indicated an interest in schoolwork and a desire to learn.

In a study by Balfanz and Byrnes (2006), self-reported effort emerged as a significant predictor (for Black and Latino middle school students from an "urban background") of whether students' gains in math performance exceeded what would have been expected by average yearly grade equivalent increments. According to the authors, this outcome (by implication) suggests a prediction of gap-closing math performance.

DiPerna, Lei, and Reid (2007) examined growth in math performance from kindergarten through 3rd grade. The authors set out to discern the classroom behavioral indicators of such growth. They used the Early Childhood Longitudinal Study (ECLS) data set, which included a national sample of ethnically diverse children. The grade-appropriate math competencies of interest included number sense, properties, operations, measurement, geometry, probability, and data analysis.

The behavioral indicators of interest were obtained through teacher ratings taken at four data points: the beginning of kindergarten, the end of kindergarten, 1st grade, and 3rd grade. Among the indicators examined were externalizing behaviors (aggression, hyperactivity, behavioral regulation), internalizing behaviors (anxiety, worry, distress, withdrawal), and approaches to learning (task persistence, attentiveness, eagerness to learn). Math skills were indexed through an individually administered math standardized test. It was found that the major contributor to math growth (beyond general knowledge and age) was the approach to learning, which is akin to engagement.

Furthermore, it is crucial to distinguish engagement from instructional time. This point is brought home by Bodovski and Farkas (2007), who sought to determine the pattern of math-achievement growth (and what factors account for it) in the early elementary grades. For example, do initially high-achieving students continue to gain at a faster rate, or do those who begin with low levels of achievement close the gap over time? If the rates of progress differ, why? How does time spent in instruction affect these trajectories? What role does engagement (as perceived by teachers) play?

These researchers deployed the ECLS data set to address such questions. Their design was longitudinal; they followed the same cohort of children from kindergarten through 3rd grade. They divided a "nationally representative" sample of children into quartiles based on math achievement scores at the beginning of kindergarten. They then obtained measures of the amount of instructional time these children received in kindergarten, 1st grade, and 3rd grade, along with teacher ratings of students' engagement in classroom tasks at the same points in time. Engagement was gauged in terms of students' levels of persistence, eagerness to learn, and attentiveness.

Results revealed that basic number knowledge at the beginning of kindergarten (i.e., quantity discrimination and magnitude comparison) made a great difference in subsequent achievement gains. It was found that the lowest-achieving group (those students who performed in the lowest quartile at the beginning of kindergarten) showed the least math growth by the end of 3rd grade, whereas the two highest groups essentially gained the most. Moreover, the students with the lowest initial scores had the greatest amount of instructional time but the lowest level of engagement.

In other words, engagement had a far greater effect on math gains than did instructional time. Engagement also had a far greater effect on math gains (at all measured points) for the lowest-achieving group. By implication, these lowest-achieving students gain the least when they are more disengaged. To be sure, instructional time did make a difference, but it paled in comparison to the engagement variable. Changing the amount of instructional time is easier to do than changing students' engagement levels, but the data indicate that such a change yields a relatively small return on investment. What's more, instructional time did not differentially affect the four groups.

Research on Reading

Engagement has also been found to predict or account for reading outcomes. The work of Lutz, Guthrie, and Davis (2006) is a case in point. They reviewed several studies indicating that behavioral, cognitive, and affective engagement levels are clear precursors to reading outcomes, in terms of both grades in school and performance on standardized tests of reading achievement. Structural factors such as teacher–student ratio or number of years teaching were not strongly related to reading outcomes at the elementary level. Similar findings are illuminated in the work of others (e.g., Guthrie et al., 2004; Skinner & Belmont, 1993; Stipek, 2002; Taylor, Pearson, Peterson, & Rodriguez, 2003). Many of the studies cited here highlight the special importance of cognitive engagement in the reading process—when students grapple with understanding the deeper meanings inherent in their texts. Many of these studies contain sizable proportions of ethnic minority students. Moreover, the benefits of increased engagement in reading were relatively stronger for struggling readers. The implication here is that enhancing engagement appears to be particularly important in closing the reading achievement gap.

In a recent study by Wigfield and colleagues (2008), three different approaches to reading comprehension instruction were directly compared to discern their impacts on comprehension outcomes in a racially heterogeneous sample of 4th grade students. In addition, level of reading engagement was directly measured for each approach. It was found that the approach that produced the highest level of student engagement (deploying practices such as those depicted in Chapters 5–7) led to the highest levels of reading proficiency across several different components of reading comprehension. When the researchers statistically controlled for student engagement levels across the three instructional approaches, the ensuing comprehension levels were virtually the same across the three modes of instruction. This led the researchers to conclude that the effect of instruction on comprehension level was substantially mediated by student engagement.

Elsewhere, an experimental investigation conducted by McElvain (2010) compared Transactional Literacy Circles (a reading instruction strategy), which was explicitly designed to promote more active engagement in the reading process, to a "standard instruction" condition. Not only did the Transactional Literacy Circles intervention lead to greater levels of student engagement, but it subsequently led to greater reading comprehension in a sample of 4th–6th grade English language learners (ELLs). Similarly, Taylor and colleagues (2003) found that growth in reading comprehension across time was greater in "high-poverty classrooms" when practices were implemented that explicitly promoted cognitive engagement in literacy activities.

Research by Kelly (2007, 2008; Kelly & Turner, 2009) has also shown that in classrooms characterized by literacy instruction that promotes rote recitation and memorization, high-achieving students are discernibly more engaged than their lower-achieving counterparts. This disparity in engagement levels disappears when more engaging practices are implemented. (These practices will be elaborated on in Chapters 5–7.)

Research on Avoidance Strategies

As mentioned earlier, certain factors that are the antithesis of engagement have also been examined in the literature. Prominent among these are student avoidance strategies (Turner et al., 2002). Avoidance strategies include self-handicapping in the form of procrastinating, purposely not trying hard, looking for excuses not to study, avoiding help, guessing at answers rather than asking for help, not asking questions in class, and choosing to work only on familiar problems. Turner and colleagues focused on the behaviors of 6th grade Black and White students in 65 classrooms. Data were in the form of surveys and classroom observations. Not surprisingly, it was found that these avoidance behaviors were all negative predictors of math outcomes. Of particular relevance is the finding that Black students engaged in self-handicapping techniques and avoided help more often than White students. Controlling for other factors, race clearly predicts avoidance behaviors.

Intriguingly, in a recent study by Guthrie, Coddington, and Wigfield (2009), different profiles were obtained for Black and White 4th grade students regarding the relationship between engagement (or disengagement/avoidance) and reading comprehension. For Black students, negative correlations were found between the use of avoidance strategies during reading lessons and reading comprehension levels. That is, the more these students exhibited avoidance tendencies, the lower their level of measured reading comprehension. However, the trend among White students indicated positive correlations between their levels of engagement and reading comprehension. Avoidance was the prominent factor for Black students, and engagement loomed larger for White students.

Having documented the important role that engagement plays in learning outcomes, it seems crucial to elaborate on the issue. Engagement should not be construed as the simple reaction of a student to a teacher-initiated action; the concept is much more complex than that. Sutherland and Oswald (2005) have addressed this matter in their work. They note that linear conceptual models, which examine teacher impact on the child or vice versa, need to be reconsidered in light of the need for bidirectional influences on teacher–student interactions. Teachers and students mutually influence one another in a cyclical, recursive way. This dynamic becomes problematic when, for example, low-achieving students receive fewer (and lower-quality) interactions with the teacher—often because such interactions are less rewarding to the teacher than those with high-achieving students.

Students who are more engaged in classroom activities receive more positive teacher attention in return, whereas unengaged students receive less positive attention and more "coercion" from teachers, and there is less consistency in their interactions. Therefore, more classroom engagement ensues for those students who are already engaged, whereas less develops for those who are disengaged. Over time, the initial effect gets increasingly amplified and even ritualized or regularized. As Greenwood (1996) observes, classroom interactions in inner cities—marked as they are by an absence of positive reinforcement and infrequent opportunities to respond—lead to lower levels of academic responding. Academic growth and achievement are stunted in comparison to what happens in more affluent or suburban settings.

Skinner and Belmont (1993) provide us with a concrete empirical example. They explored reciprocal teacher–student effects that are related to student engagement over the course of an academic year. They posit that student engagement is mediated by student perception of teacher behaviors. Moreover, teacher behavior is mediated by teacher perception of students' levels of motivation and engagement. They suggest that one of two possible options may occur in the face of a teacher's perception of a student's initially low level of engagement. The teacher may compensate by attempting to raise the student's level of engagement, or he or she might magnify the low engagement—that is, accentuate the low level—through exhibiting less involvement and directing fewer encouraging actions toward the student.

Skinner and Belmont pitted these possible options against each other in classrooms serving 3rd through 5th grade children in a rural/suburban school district with 94 percent White enrollment. Teacher involvement was discerned through self-reports of their liking, appreciation of, enjoyment of, understanding of, and availability to each child in their classrooms. Student engagement was indexed jointly through student self-report and teacher report. Engagement in this study tapped into behavioral and affective dimensions. The most critical finding supports the magnification stance—positive student engagement leads to positive teacher behaviors. Teachers are more positively responsive to students who initially show high levels of engagement, and they are more neglectful of those students who initially show low levels of behavioral engagement. Consequently, teachers are likely to enhance subsequent engagement for high-engagement students and to diminish engagement for low-engagement students. Clearly, such actions can snowball over time.

There is some evidence in this study that compensation by teachers does occur for students who are initially negative in their emotional engagement. However, those students who seem to lack behavioral engagement are perceived as passive and are coded as lacking internal motivation by their teachers. Thereafter, they suffer the magnified consequences—they are perceived as students who do not want to learn.

Chapter Summary

Engagement is three-dimensional, and the evidence reviewed in this chapter indicates that it is a precursor to achievement and even growth in achievement levels over the years. Engagement is not the same as the amount of teacher instructional time. What seems crucial is not how much time is devoted to a subject but, rather, how much time students are actively and progressively involved in the learning process. This seems particularly important for students who are low achieving (at least initially) or an ethnic minority. The benefits of engagement seem to be especially apparent when the learning and performance demands are more challenging. The flipside of engagement is avoidance, which may be a more informative indicator of performance outcomes than engagement is for ethnic minority students. Evidence also suggests that engagement level and instructional quality may be reciprocally related—that is, teachers tend to respond more positively to students who are already engaged and less positively to students who are not engaged. In turn, this leads to more divergent displays of engagement between these two groups of students.

Guiding Functions

04

A central cluster of factors have repeatedly demonstrated significant impact on closing achievement gaps *and* raising achievement for all students while also enhancing both basic and 21st century competencies. We refer to this class of factors as guiding functions because they can steer, shape, govern, and intensify fundamental engagement processes. The factors themselves are interrelated, and it is highly plausible that they feed on one another. They are, in short, adaptive learning orientations. When several are present at once, their impact on engagement is even more substantial. Of course, to the extent that these functions are absent or negatively manifest, they will dampen engagement. These functions include self-efficacy, self-regulated learning, and incremental ability beliefs. As with engagement, there is evidence that these factors are less evident among Black and Latino populations.

Research on Self-Efficacy

The notion of self-efficacy has a long history in social and motivational psychology. When Bandura (1977) first postulated the concept, he stated that "An efficacy expectation is the conviction that one can successfully execute the behavior required to produce the (desired) outcomes" (p. 193). Bandura later elaborated on his original definition by capturing self-efficacy as "people's judgments of their capabilities to organize and execute [the] course of action required to attain designated types of performances" (1986, p. 391). In essence, as the learner approaches a given task, he or she implicitly or explicitly is involved in a self-questioning process: "Can I do this task in this situation?" The pattern of his or her actions will be different, depending on the answer.

Self-efficacy should not be confused with self-concept. With self-concept, one conducts a generalized self-appraisal such as "I am good at math" or "I am a good speller." Self-efficacy is more a matter of confidence that one can accomplish the task at hand in the present situation. Therefore, self-efficacy tends to be situationally specific. A representative line of thinking might be "I can do two-digit multiplication word problems in this setting" or, in a different realm, "I can make these free throws at this point in this game." Self-efficacy is also domain specific—it is about confidence in math, as opposed to confidence in general academic achievement. Moreover, it is about differences in efficacy *within* academic domains, such that one could have high self-efficacy for comprehending narrative text but not for expository text; for multiplying and dividing fractions, but not for decimals (Pajares, 2003).

Generally, self-efficacy has to do with the confidence that one can accomplish a desired outcome in a given context if the requisite application of skill is put forth. There is convincing evidence that self-efficacy has more predictive potency in terms of academic outcomes than, for example, self-concept does (Pajares & Miller, 1994).

In the academic domain, Bandura (1986) has argued that "educational practices should be gauged not only by the skills and knowledge they impart for present use but also by what they do to children's beliefs about their capabilities, which affects how they approach the future. Students who develop a strong sense of self-efficacy are well equipped to educate themselves when they have to rely on their own initiative" (p. 417). Thus, enhancing self-efficacy may be no less important in academic settings than enhancing achievement. Indeed, the evidence consistently shows that self-efficacy exerts a powerful influence on academic performance, both directly and through student engagement (Schunk, 2003).

Self-Efficacy and Academic Performance Outcomes

That self-efficacy has functional value with respect to academic outcomes has been well documented (Fast et al., 2010; Williams & Williams, 2010). A case in point is the work of Borman and Overman (2004), who find that self-efficacy differentiates between resilient and nonresilient students (see Chapter 3). Elsewhere, Schultz (1993) reports that self-efficacy is a significant correlate with mathematics performance for 4th to 6th grade Black and Latino students. Similar findings on the significant predictive value of math self-efficacy are reported by Stevens, Olivarez, and Hamman (2006) for both Latino and White students from 4th through 10th grade. A similar pattern was obtained in other studies with math, reading, and science outcomes (e.g., Byrnes, 2003, for White, Black, and Latino 12th grade students; Long, Monoi, Harper, Knoblauch, & Murphy, 2007, for low-income, Black 8th and 9th graders; Navarro, Flores, & Worthington, 2007, for low-income, Latino middle school students; Stevens, Olivarez, Lan, & Tallent-Runnels, 2004, for White and Latino 9th and 10th graders).

Self-efficacy has also been positively linked to key literacy skills. For example, it has a positive influence on reading comprehension at the elementary level (e.g., Guthrie, Wigfield, Metsala, & Cox, 1999; Schunk, 2003). Other work shows that self-efficacy in writing clearly affects the quality of compositional writing outcomes. This finding has been demonstrated among students from elementary to college level (Pajares, 2003).

There is also evidence that self-efficacy levels can have long-term academic ramifications. A study by Byrnes and Miller (2007) is a case in point. Using the National Education Longitudinal Study of 1988 national data set, Byrnes and Miller endeavor to predict 10th and 12th grade math and science performance outcomes based on a host of prior operative factors from 8th and 9th grade. They find that even when controlling for factors such as middle school course grades and socioeconomic status (SES), self-efficacy for graduating (i.e., how sure you are that you will graduate from high school) is a significant predictor of math and science grades in 12th grade. More recent similar findings have been reported by Friedel, Cortina, Turner, and Midgeley (2010).

Self-Efficacy and Engagement

There is substantial evidence that self-efficacy operates, in large measure, through its direct impact on student classroom engagement. The work of Guthrie and colleagues (Guthrie et al., 2007; Guthrie, McRae, & Klauda, 2007) demonstrates, for elementary and secondary students, that self-efficacy leads to more time spent reading and to deeper levels of reading involvement, both of which in turn predict higher-quality reading outcomes. Elsewhere, Mucherah and Yoder (2008) show that middle school students with high levels of self-efficacy are more likely to read challenging texts, which in turn leads to higher performance on a standardized test of reading achievement. Similar findings, with respect to reading comprehension and quality of compositional writing, have been reported by Schunk (2003).

Dynamics of Self-Efficacy

Discussions of the relationships among self-efficacy, engagement, and academic outcomes are of special interest to us because of their implications for the racial achievement gap. Several of the studies cited here reveal lower levels of self-efficacy, on average, for Black and Latino students in math, reading, and writing (e.g., Borman & Overman, 2004; Mucherah & Yoder, 2008; Stevens et al., 2004). Interestingly, this is true even when these students report high levels of self-concept (Pajares, 2003). Given that self-efficacy seems to be firmly and positively related to engagement and academic outcomes, efforts to enhance it for Black and Latino students is a worthy pursuit toward closing the achievement gap.

Schunk (2003) suggests that self-efficacy is not a fixed attribute of the learner; rather, it is one that can be raised through targeted interventions that lead to enhanced levels of reading engagement and elevated levels of reading comprehension. Bandura (1994) proposes four dynamics linked to key information sources that impact self-efficacy. Students derive their self-efficacy level from encounters with these key information sources. One such source is past performance and experience, which has also been called enactive mastery (Margolis & McCabe, 2006). It certainly stands to reason that performing a task well begets high self-efficacy; in turn, high self-efficacy begets a higher task accomplishment level. A second source-linked dynamic is observational learning—observing others perform a task with competence, which can influence one's own self-efficacy. Seeing other people experience success or reap rewards for their efforts encourages observers to try the activity in an effort to experience similar success. A third dynamic is verbal persuasion or social influence. Other people (e.g., teachers or peers) can encourage a student to believe that his or her own efforts can be successful. The final dynamic is physiological reaction or state (before, during, and after a task activity). Feelings of anxiety or stress do not bode well for attaining a desired outcome. However, feelings of relaxation, confidence, and happiness are good signs that things are on course for a successful outcome. This physiological reaction or emotion state then feeds into subsequent self-efficacy beliefs. For example, feelings of anxiety would likely lessen self-efficacy, whereas feelings of happiness would likely increase self-efficacy.

These four factors—prior performance and experience, observational learning, social persuasion, and physiological state—foreshadow some of the considerations we will address more fully in the following chapters on asset-focused factors.

Research on Self-Regulated Learning

According to Schunk and Zimmerman, self-regulated learning or self-regulation is defined as "self-generated thoughts, feelings and actions that are systematically designed to affect one's knowledge and skills" (2007, p. 8). Pintrich extends this notion by stating that this is "an active, constructive process whereby learners set goals for their learning and then attempt to monitor, regulate, and control their cognition, motivation, and behavior, guided and constrained by their goals and the contextual features in the environment" (2000, p. 453). Zimmerman (2002) adds that self-regulated learning also involves self-evaluation of how well one is doing and reactions to the obtained outcomes relative to the goals that one has set.

Self-regulated learning is emphasized here, in large measure, because it leads to enhanced engagement and academic performance, but it also can be especially beneficial to struggling learners, beginning learners, learners diagnosed with learning disabilities, and other students who might otherwise be placed at risk for academic failure (Horner & O'Connor, 2007). Therefore, its currency with respect to the achievement gap is well justified.

Elaboration on Basic Operations

According to Horner and O'Connor (2007), learners who effectively self-regulate tend to set realistic goals for themselves, select adaptive strategies, monitor their progress, develop understanding, and evaluate how well they have accomplished their goals. As Boekaerts and Cascallar contend, "the most salient feature [of self-regulated learning] is that the learner actually has control over his own learning, steering and directing cognitive and motivational processes to achieve the learning goal" (2006, pp. 199–200). Schunk and Zimmerman (2007) conceptualize self-regulated learning as consisting of three phases: forethought, performance control, and self-reflection.

The forethought phase entails processes and beliefs that occur before attempts to learn begin. These processes provide a platform for ensuing actions. It is during this phase that learners set the goal(s) for the activity and plan what they need to do to accomplish the goal(s). The performance control phase refers to processes that transpire while learning takes place, such as the use of learning strategies, attentional focus, and task execution. Finally, self-reflection refers to perceptions and appraisals that take place after each attempt at learning. Here, learners respond by judging how well the intended goal was accomplished and by making adjustments in subsequent actions attendant to the present (or a future) task.

Domain Specificity

As with self-efficacy, self-regulated learning is domain specific. For example, a learner may deploy self-regulation tactics in math but not reading, or he or she may use them when it comes to comprehension but not vocabulary learning. Self-regulated learning can also be situational; for example, it could be used in high-interest tasks but not in low-interest tasks or in one classroom but not another (Boekaerts & Cascallar, 2006).

Schunk and Zimmerman (2007) emphasize that one's self-regulatory competence can vary from one domain or situation to the next. Indeed, self-regulated learning does not emerge all at once—full-blown and with expert proficiency. Instead, it emerges across time, and learners can be at different steps of the process at different points in time or even at different competency levels at the same time for different domains or settings (Horner & O'Connor, 2007).

Self-Regulated Learning

Schunk and Zimmerman (1997, 2007) depict four distinct steps along the path to self-regulatory competence: observation, emulation, self-control, and self-regulation. Although the distinction is not entirely perfect, the first two levels (observation, emulation) draw on social learning factors, whereas the latter two (self-control, self-regulation) depend more on self-focused factors. At the first level (observation), learners become acquainted with appropriate thoughts and actions by observing models that demonstrate the desired behaviors and thought processes. At the next step (emulation), learners attempt to carry out the appropriate behaviors and thought processes of the model. At the self-control level, learners have internalized the requisite thoughts and actions, and they can conduct the sequence of processes in a more fully independent fashion—although still tied directly to the representations of the original modeled source. In the final stage (self-regulation), learners are guided by self-produced representations, and they are able to modify thought-and-action sequences to fit the demands of the task at hand.

Ties to Persistence and Engagement

Recent research has documented that many of the educational advantages of self-regulated learning work through the three domains of engagement: behavioral, cognitive, and affective. For example, Zito, Adkins, Gavins, Harris, and Graham (2007) present findings from reviews of more than 30 empirical studies that focus on reading and writing performance among elementary school students. A general conclusion is that self-regulated learners display increased initiation, persistence, attention, and effort with respect to academic tasks. On the other hand, those learners who self-regulate to a lesser degree are likely to be less persistent and focused, have more negative reactions to their involvement, be more self-critical of their work, and engage in self-handicapping behaviors. In several of these studies, participants are described as struggling learners or defined as having learning disabilities. Other reviews have reached the same conclusions (e.g., Horner & O'Connor, 2007; Boekaerts & Cascallar, 2006).

Valiente, Lemery-Chalfant, Swanson, and Reiser (2008) examine factors that predict increases in academic performance across an academic year for a sample of 7- to 12-year-old students. Most of these children are ethnic minorities from working-class backgrounds. It is found that the more students display "effortful control" (greatly akin to self-regulated learning), the more they are involved in classroom participation, which is directly linked to and a result of behavioral engagement. Similar findings are also obtained by Soric and Palekcic (2009).

Ties to Academic Performance

Horner and O'Connor (2007) make the case that self-regulated learning is linked to increased reading and writing outcomes, especially for struggling students and novice learners. De La Paz (2007) has reviewed research particularly in the realm of writing outcomes. Her literature review indicates that self-regulated learning leads to enhanced writing performance outcomes; what's more, this enhanced outcome is not only immediate but also maintained several weeks out, and the beneficial effects generalize to performance on writing tasks different from those that were the initial focus. Elsewhere, Patrick, Ryan, and Kaplan (2007) find significant correlations between self-regulated learning and math grades for 5th grade White, middle-class children. Valiente and colleagues (2008) find that effortful control leads to increased behavioral engagement, and it also predicts changes in composite math and reading grades across an academic year for predominantly ethnic-minority students in 2nd through 6th grade.

According to Schunk (2005), research demonstrates that students' self-regulatory processes can be enhanced through targeted interventions—

expressly, in this review, by increasing students' focus on goals and self-monitoring and self-evaluation skills—and that this enhanced self-regulation results in higher academic performance (Boekaerts, Pintrich, & Zeidner, 2000; Schunk & Zimmerman, 1998; Tracy, Reid, & Graham, 2009).

Zito and colleagues (2007) report similar results in their review of the literature. They determine that raising self-regulated learning levels affects reading and writing outcomes with learning-disabled students, struggling readers and writers, and "normally achieving students" alike. In terms of writing outcomes, for example, they find improved quality of ideas, better grammar, more appropriate use of literary elements (e.g., character, plot, setting, and information details), and longer compositional lengths. They also reveal that this enhancement encompasses greater long-term maintenance of the effects and greater generalizability across genres. Even though these effects are obtained among all three student categories mentioned above, the positive impact is more pronounced for learning-disabled students and struggling writers. Zito and colleagues also report that research indicates that the benefits for learning-challenged students are manifest only when the quality of self-regulated learning has been advanced to the latter two steps—that is, the self-control and self-regulation levels. Merely observing and modeling self-regulated learning is insufficient to produce beneficial outcomes.

Mason (2004) focused on affecting reading outcomes, and her work is relevant to this discussion. The participants in her investigation were 5th graders who had low (10th to 40th percentile) reading achievement levels. Over 90 percent of the students were Black children from low-income backgrounds. These students engaged in explicit training to enhance their self-regulated learning skills, particularly in terms of goal setting, self-monitoring, and self-reinforcement (for making progress). Training consisted of 11 to 15 sessions that each lasted for 20 minutes. Reading outcomes were enhanced to a greater degree for those students who received the self-regulation intervention, when compared to students who received generic strategy instruction. The benefits were measured in terms of performance immediately after training and three weeks later. In the math domain, Montague (2007) examined training for self-regulated learning and finds that such preparation leads to higher math outcomes for students with learning disabilities in that subject.

Another crucial question still needs to be addressed. What are the conditions or prerequisites that most likely lead to the emergence of self-regulated learning? Paris and Newman (1990) underscore the importance of modeling. Particularly during the observation and emulation phases of self-regulated learning, effective modeling is crucial and demands correct use of the self-regulation procedure. Models such as talk-alouds articulate the challenges addressed in the learning task and ways to address these challenges. Models also make transparent students' fears, misconceptions, and beliefs as they work toward solutions. They encourage active participation by students, and they provide guidance, feedback, and social reinforcement for students (Schunk, 2005). As students progress to the self-control phase, it is crucial to continue to emphasize the value of actualizing the strategy. As students make progress in their use and control of the strategy, it is also critical to continually provide them with feedback and encourage them to attempt self-reinforcement for their own performance.

Schunk and Rice (1993) emphasize the effectiveness of fading for the promotion of self-regulated learning. This procedure builds on the work of Vygotsky (1962), with respect to the internalization of learning processes. It is first verbalized by the teacher or model; students are then encouraged to say out loud the various facets of self-regulated practices as they perform them and then whisper the requisite procedures to themselves. Finally, students should go through the practices silently via "inner speech" only. In their research, Schunk and Rice find that this fading procedure is particularly effective in moving students to the self-regulation phase and in maintaining use of the associated skills over the long term.

Reciprocity

Self-efficacy and self-regulated learning are distinct constructs that have arisen out of different lines of scholarship. Nevertheless, it is clear that they have reciprocal influences on each other, and the presence of one enhances the manifestation of the other. For example, according to Horner and O'Connor (2007), self-regulated learners have higher levels of self-efficacy. Moreover, the final step in self-regulated learning—referred to as self-regulation—to some degree requires self-efficacy for its maintenance over time (Schunk & Zimmerman, 2007). Self-efficacy can be a product of self-reflection, and it can therefore guide subsequent forethought, planning, and goal setting as the self-regulated learning cycle is perpetuated over time (Zimmerman, 2002).

The empirical links between self-efficacy and self-regulated learning have been well established. Camahalan (2006), for example, uses an introduction to self-efficacy as a precursor to her self-regulated learning training program. Research has also shown that self-efficacy directly affects the level of expressed self-regulated learning in young adolescent learners (Patrick et al., 2007). Elsewhere, self-regulation has been shown to directly affect the expression levels of self-efficacy (Schunk & Zimmerman, 2007). Both self-efficacy and self-regulated learning serve as antecedents to adaptive belief change among students. It is to this third category that we now turn.

Research on Incremental Ability Beliefs

For nearly 40 years, attribution theory has been an influential framework for understanding how motivation affects achievement. The major contributor to this scheme has been Bernard Weiner (1986, 1994, 2000). Attribution theory primarily addresses the belief that people seek explanations for events (and their consequences) in which they have participated. In the academic domain, this translates to reasons that students attribute to their own success or failure.

According to Weiner, there are three factors that cause students to make these attributions. These factors are whether the outcome is attributed to a controllable or uncontrollable cause, to a stable or variable cause, and to an internal or external source. The first factor has to do with whether students believe they controlled their ability to arrive at the outcome or whether they feel it was due to factors beyond their control. The second factor has to do with whether the outcome occurs constantly or fluctuates over time. The final factor has to do with whether the outcome is attributed to something within the students or from somewhere else—that is, from someone or something in the surrounding environment.

Two attributions that have received considerable attention in recent years, and that can help us understand achievement differences and raise performance outcomes in gap-closing ways, are the notions of ability and effort. Ability lies at the intersection of relatively uncontrollable, stable, and internal causes, whereas effort lies at the intersection of controllable, variable, and external causes. It is noted that these attributions, over time, convert into enduring beliefs that students hold about their prospects for success and failure in school (Weiner, 2000). Beliefs that performance is tied to fixed ability have been associated with reduced motivation over time in achievement settings, especially when students are faced with challenging tasks that may initially result in failure. By contrast, effort attributions are more strongly linked to adaptive achievement outcomes. In recent years, much attention has been given to documenting these divergent outcomes as a function of students' beliefs and on devising ways to alter those beliefs so they emphasize effort, not ability.

For example, in this domain, Dweck and her colleagues differentiate ability and effort beliefs in terms of divergent implicit theories that students hold about the nature of intelligence (Blackwell, Trzesniewski, & Dweck, 2007; Dweck & Leggett, 1988; Molden & Dweck, 2006). These beliefs are referred to as implicit, because they are not necessarily held at the level of conscious awareness. The terms *entity* (fixed) and *incremental* (malleable) have been used to capture two distinct ways in which people understand personal attributes. An entity, or fixed, view presumes that personal attributes—such as personality, competence, and intelligence—are essentially fixed and unchanging. Either you are nice or not nice, smart or not smart, a good reader or not so. Thus, these attributes are not truly under your control. An incremental, or malleable, view, on the other hand, holds that such attributes are open to change—they are malleable and dynamic, and they can improve or expand one's competence or intelligence. Thus, self-improvement is substantially under your control, and it is linked to the application of effort, persistence, and learning across time.

This dichotomy—whether intelligence is a fixed and absolute quality of an individual or whether it is changeable as a function of environmental circumstances and experiences—is one of the most widely debated issues in all of psychology. As Aronson, Fried, and Good state, "irrespective of the truth—or what psychometricians believe to be the truth—there is very compelling evidence that what a *student* thinks about intelligence can have a powerful effect on his or her achievement" (2002, p. 115).

Consequences of a Fixed Versus Malleable Belief of Intelligence

Whether a student holds a fixed or malleable view of intelligence is particularly related to the behaviors that result from failure or challenge. For example, a student with a fixed view tends to be more preoccupied with preserving self-respect than with trying to improve performance at a particular task. As such, this student is less likely to persist in the face of failure or have subsequent involvement with similar tasks. When given a choice, this student is inclined to lower his or her sights and pursue less challenging tasks.

On the other hand, students who subscribe to a malleable view are more likely to see failure as an opportunity to get better at a skill. These students seek to profit from their mistakes and redouble, rather than dampen, their efforts. They are more task-persistent, have a more positive attitude toward task involvement, and are less anxious about new learning experiences. Interestingly, these differences are evident even when students with opposing beliefs about intelligence have equivalent levels of intellectual ability (Blackwell et al., 2007).

Furthermore, Nussbaum and Dweck (2008) find that, in the face of failure, entity-focused students are more inclined to compare themselves with lower-achieving students. By doing this, they seek to verify that they themselves truly are capable. By contrast, incremental-focused students try to determine which strategies are used by higher-achieving classmates. By doing this, they hope to improve their own performance.

Predicting Performance from Belief Type

Students who adopt a malleable view of intelligence generally demonstrate high levels of achievement. Likewise, students who adopt a fixed view generally demonstrate lower levels of achievement. Stipek and her colleagues were among the first to pursue this relationship. In one study (Stipek & Kowalski, 1989), primarily of White, middle-class 5th and 6th grade students (roughly 25 percent of participants were ethnic minority students), those students who indicated a malleable view continued to use effective learning strategies in the face of failure, whereas those who embraced a fixed view abandoned such adaptive strategies.

Elsewhere, Stipek and Gralinski (1996) examined similar concerns with a sample of "ethnically diverse" 3rd to 6th grade children from poor and working-class backgrounds. Approximately 85 percent of the participants identified with an ethnic minority (45 percent Latino, 15 percent Black, 9 percent Asian, 16 percent "other" minorities, 15 percent White). Achievement tests scores in language arts, math, and social studies during the fall term predicted comparable test scores at the end of the spring term. Most striking was the finding that the more students held to a fixed belief about intelligence (as measured in the fall term), the lower were their achievement test scores and course grades in the spring.

Looking specifically at mathematics achievement, Blackwell and colleagues (2007) show that students who view their intelligence as a fixed trait fare more poorly during the transition from elementary (6th grade) to junior high (7th grade) than do their peers who believe that their intelligence is malleable and can be developed. (This study exclusively included Black and Latino participants from low-income communities.) Although both belief groups began 7th grade with equivalent math achievement, their math grades diverged by the end of the first semester and continued to move apart during the following two years. The superior performance by students who believe that intelligence is malleable was facilitated by a greater emphasis on learning, a greater belief in the importance of effort, and more improvement-oriented reactions to setbacks.

Feedback Can Alter Belief Orientation and Affect Achievement

Given the divergence in outcomes for those students who embrace fixed versus malleable views of intelligence, the question surely arises as to whether such beliefs are open to change. One important line of work suggests that they are, perhaps particularly at relatively young ages (Mueller & Dweck, 1998). These beliefs can be influenced merely by the type of feedback or praise that students receive in reaction to their performance.

A telling study in this regard was conducted by Mueller and Dweck (1998). Their study involved 5th grade students from various backgrounds—both White, middle-class children and Black and Latino children from low-income backgrounds. Mueller and Dweck argue that it is indisputable that children suffer from performance feedback that is overly critical. However, the consequence of providing praise is more complicated than what might be assumed. Praise for effort and ability have different consequences for students who have experienced challenge or failure with an academic task. For example, praise such as "You must be smart at these kinds of problems" engenders fixed-ability attributions (i.e., students are more likely to conclude they did well because of their fixed ability), and praise such as "You must have worked hard at these problems" provokes malleable effort attributions (i.e., students are more likely to conclude they did well because they exerted the sufficient level of effort). In their study, Mueller and Dweck focused on items from Raven's Progressive Matrices, which is designed to be a nonverbal measure of reasoning ability. The matrices focus on presenting students with sets of patterns that follow a logical progression; students need to identify the next step in each series.

Those students who receive "ability praise" (as opposed to "effort praise") on a set of relatively easy matrix problems have less desire to persist with more difficult problems, express less task enjoyment, and perform more poorly after experiencing a period of failure. These results are equally evident for White, Black, and Latino students. (It is worth noting that some studies have found ethnic minority students more likely to deploy fixed-ability attributions or reasons for their success; e.g., Kurtz-Costes, Ehrlich, McCall,

& Loridant, 1995) Moreover, students who receive ability praise are more likely to attribute their low performance to a lack of ability, whereas students who receive effort praise are much more likely to attribute low performance to low effort on their part.

Dweck offers the following specific examples of what effort praise sounds like in an actual classroom setting:

> "You really studied for your English test, and your improvement shows it. You read the material over several times, outlined it, and tested yourself on it. That really worked!"

> "I like the way you tried all kinds of strategies on the math problem until you finally got it."

> "It was a long, hard assignment, but you stuck to it and got it done. You stayed at your desk, kept up your concentration, and kept working. That's great!" (2007, p. 37)

Targeted Interventions to Change Beliefs

Interventions designed to foster belief changes among students susceptible to poor academic performance have been the subject of much recent research. Good, Aronson, and Inzlicht (2003) attempted to enhance performance through a systematic intervention for predominantly low-income 7th graders (67 percent Latino, 20 percent White, 13 percent Black). For an entire academic year, students in an "experimental group" were mentored by college students who provided them with school adjustment and study strategies and also encouraged them to regard intelligence as malleable (rather than fixed) and to attribute academic difficulties to the uniqueness of the setting (i.e., that middle school is tough but things will improve with time). A "control group" of students was provided with similar study and adjustment strategies by their mentors, but they also received information linked to an antidrug campaign, rather than information regarding intelligence and reasons for academic difficulties. Performance on a statewide standardized test of mathematics and reading achievement was analyzed as the outcome measure. Mathematics results revealed that girls in the experimental group performed substantially better than their peers in the control group. Boys in both groups had essentially the same math performance levels, although students in the experimental group demonstrated a slightly better performance than those in the control group. For reading, there was an overall main effect (across gender) for condition, such that students in the experimental group performed better than students in the control group.

Blackwell and colleagues (2007) also conducted an intervention with a group of Black and Latino 7th graders from low-income backgrounds who had declining math grades. Both the experimental and control groups attended a workshop composed of eight 25-minute sessions that taught useful study skills. However, students in the experimental group also received instruction in a malleable theory of intelligence. They were taught that learning leads to new neural connections in the brain and that intelligence can increase with new learning experiences. (These sessions began with a document they created, called "You Can Grow Your Intelligence," which likened the brain to a muscle.) Whereas students in the control group continued their downward trajectory, the experimental group showed a significant rebound in mathematics grades. Teachers (who were unaware of which group students had been assigned) spontaneously reported that more students in the experimental group showed increased engagement with and interest in classroom lessons.

Reciprocity with Other Guiding Functions

There is good reason to believe that a malleable view of intelligence facilitates self-regulated learning and self-efficacy. Therefore, the more self-efficacious a student is, the more likely he or she will pursue adaptive self-regulatory learning strategies and believe that effort matters. The more self-regulated a student is, the more confident he or she will be about the possibility of success and believe that efforts will make him or her "smarter." Likewise, the more a student believes that ability is malleable, the more likely he or she will be to seek out adaptive learning strategies. The literature is replete with examples of conceptual and empirical links between a malleable view of intelligence, self-efficacy, and self-regulation (e.g., Aronson et al., 2002;

Bandura, 1993; Chan & Moore, 2006; Dweck, 1999; Linnenbrink & Pintrich, 2003; Lynch, 2008; Molden & Dweck, 2006; Seifert, 2004; Shell & Husman, 2008).

In light of the research reviewed in this chapter, it behooves us to consider interventions that simultaneously and directly raise the levels of these three guiding functions—a malleable view of intelligence, self-efficacy, and self-regulated learning—to see if such an approach would produce synergistic results and thus enhance students' outcomes even more substantially. Further research should be done, particularly for ethnic minority students who are likely to be placed at risk for academic failure.

Chapter Summary

Three guiding functions (or adaptive learning postures) were identified in this chapter, and research evidence linked them to increased engagement levels and academic performance, especially for certain ethnic minority students. These functions are self-efficacy, self-regulated learning, and incremental beliefs about ability. These three factors also appear to be mutually reinforcing of one another; that is, the expression of one can promote the expression of the others. Moreover, research shows that these functions can distinguish between students whose achievement levels improve and decline over the years. Self-efficacy, self-regulated learning, and incremental ability beliefs are positively correlated with math and literacy achievement for Black and Latino students at the elementary, middle, and high school levels. These factors are also positively related to academic performance for low-achieving students in general. Evidence indicates that the impact these three guiding functions have on achievement operates through level of student engagement. It also seems evident that the typical expressions of these guiding functions are lower for Black and Latino students than they are for White students. However, these guiding functions are not fixed or hardwired attributes. Their expressions can be enhanced by providing students with certain targeted experiences. It seems to follow, then, that providing these experiences helps promote gap-closing outcomes.

Asset-Focused Factors:
Interpersonal Relationships

05

The third focal point we will discuss—along with engagement and guiding functions—are asset-focused factors, which deal with the contextual conditions in which teaching, learning, engagement, and guiding functions are manifest. We refer to these factors as asset focused for several reasons— primarily because they involve learning exchanges that build on the assets students bring into the classroom and because they provide conditions that allow these assets to flourish. In addition, when key assets are not readily apparent for students, these factors provide the conditions that directly teach or provide those assets, rather than penalize learners for not knowing the material or having the requisite intellectual tools. This discussion raises the issue of how we define *assets*. They can be personal, social, experiential, cultural, and intellectual. Simply put, they are existing or emerging interests and preferences, motivational inclinations, passions and commitments, attitudes, beliefs, opinions, self-perceptions, personal or collective identities, and prior experiences, knowledge, understandings, skills, and competencies. When asset-focused factors are present in the classroom, they are likely to lead to gap-closing outcomes. We have divided these factors into three distinct but interrelated groups: interpersonal relationships, intersubjectivity, and information-processing quality.

Interpersonal relationships involve social exchanges (and their consequences) that occur between teachers and students and among students and their peers. This covers teacher–student relationship quality, teacher expectations, learning goals, and learning collaborations.

Intersubjectivity deals with the extent of compatibility in the interests, values, perceptions, and learning objectives of teachers and students, as well as how these various objectives mesh with the curriculum. Intersubjectivity also refers to the extent to which teachers and students are on the same educational page or how closely their respective goals are aligned. This covers cultural factors (e.g., core values, popular culture, and family traditions) and meaningful learning in the form of personal relevance, prior knowledge, personal experiences, and interests.

Information-processing quality concerns configuring subject matter content, as well as interacting with content, in ways that promote deep understanding, higher-order thinking, effective and efficient information processing, and long-term retention. Information-processing quality encompasses notions such as cognitive load reduction, opportunities for practice, multiple representations of knowledge, strategic learning, and critical and higher-order thinking tied to the elaboration and expansion of one's existing knowledge.

Research on Teacher–Student Relationship Quality

Of all the asset-focused factors, teacher–student relationship quality (TSRQ) has gathered the most evidence to support its gap-closing importance. Several interpersonal features involved in classroom dynamics are encompassed in TSRQ. These include the degree to which teachers display empathy, support, encouragement, and optimism and to which they are perceived to be fair, genuine, and nonpatronizing in their praise and feedback. High TSRQ embodies socially proactive communication with students (i.e., interacting with students socially to anticipate communication problems and address them before they even happen), along with establishing constructive rapport and a positive classroom tone (Baker, 1999; Byrnes & Miller, 2007; Hamre & Pianta, 2005; Hughes & Kwok, 2007; Murray, 2009).

TSRQ Predicts Academic Achievement

Hamre and Pianta (2001) conducted a study to discern the impact of TSRQ on academic performance during the kindergarten year. In this project, the same cohort of children was followed from kindergarten through 8th grade. The quality of teacher–student relationships was measured in kindergarten by teacher ratings. Students who received negative ratings in kindergarten eventually performed worse, as far out as the 8th grade. Academic performance was measured by both classroom grades and standardized achievement. Although the impact on children was present in 8th grade, the relationship between rating and performance was, not unexpectedly, strongest in the early primary grades. Hamre and Pianta's sample was 60 percent White and 40 percent Black. A more recent study, whose sample was exclusively Black, produced similar findings (Iruka, Burchinal, & Cai, 2010).

Stevens, Olivarez, and Hamman (2006), in a study of 4th through 10th grade Latino and White students, report that "emotional feedback" is among the two strongest predictors (along with self-efficacy) of math achievement. According to those authors, emotional feedback refers to teachers' praise and positive feedback to students, as well as their attempts to reduce student anxiety. Other studies demonstrate the connection between TSRQ and academic performance. For example, Borman and Overman (2004) find that positive teacher–student interactions in the classroom help differentiate resilient and nonresilient elementary students through test performance.

A qualitative study by Brand, Glasson, and Green (2006) deserves mention. They conducted in-depth interviews with five Black students (four high school seniors and one college freshman) who were participating in a highly selective teacher-training program and were, thus, considered high-achieving students. One central theme (about academic success) present in all of the students' responses dealt with high-quality interactions with their teachers. This was taken to mean positive experiences with teachers who validate their students' capabilities, who are accessible and approachable, who are supportive, and who hold high expectations for their students.

Research by Stewart further documents the role of TSRQ in achievement outcomes. One study of 8th and 12th grade Black students shows that a positive perception of the school environment—more specifically, the perception that students get along well with teachers, have caring teachers, and receive praise for good efforts—is a significant predictor of math standardized achievement scores (Stewart, 2006). Another study uses a national data set to demonstrate that, for a sample of 10th grade Black students, students who agree with items such as "My teachers are interested in students," "Most of my teachers care about me," "My teachers praise my effort," and "Discipline is fair" tend to perform better in math, English, history, and science classes (Stewart, 2008).

TSRQ Helps Close the Gap

Hamre and Pianta (2005) look at whether emotional support can boost achievement outcomes for 1st grade students who have been placed at risk for educational failure. They consider high-quality classrooms to be ones where such support is abundantly provided to students during daily instruction, and students are understood to be at high risk if they demonstrated problematic classroom behaviors, such as sustained inattentiveness, low academic skills, and low social competence, during kindergarten. Emotional support (present in the 1st grade classroom) is represented by factors such as teacher sensitivity to students' needs and a positive classroom climate. Woodcock–Johnson composite scores for math and reading were used as outcome measures. Hamre and Pianta find that emotional support helps close the gap between high- and low-risk students. (Low-risk students do not display the attributes listed above.) They also find that putting high-risk students in classrooms with low levels of emotional support fans the fire and increases the risk these students face during the academic year. These students display less engagement, more conflicts, and lower levels of achievement.

Exposing elementary students to caring adults, helping students feel comfortable with sharing their ideas in class, listening to students' personal and academic concerns, and providing supportive and nonjudgmental (but rigorous) feedback are all associated with smaller achievement gaps in reading, writing, and math between minority (Black and Latino) and nonminority students (Griffith, 2002). Balfanz and Byrnes (2006) also report that when middle school Black and Latino students participate in "supportive classrooms," gap-closing math performance becomes evident. Finally, Liew, Chen, and Hughes (2010) show the ability of TSRQ to close achievement gaps in reading and math among 1st grade Black and Latino children who were judged to be at risk for academic failure.

TSRQ Affects Student Engagement

There is compelling evidence that the level of TSRQ directly affects the level of classroom engagement for students. Moreover, evidence has mounted that the association between relationship quality and student engagement is ultimately a reciprocal one. The research of Ladd, Birch, and Buhs (1999) demonstrates that the connection between TSRQ and engagement shows up as early as kindergarten. They find that teacher–student relationship quality—indicated by factors such as the presence of close, warm, and nurturing interactions with positive verbal exchanges and the absence of oppositional interactions that are marked by argumentation and negative exchanges and gestures—directly affects kindergarteners' levels of classroom participation, which is measured by students' ability to cooperate, follow classroom directives, and display independent, self-directed behaviors. Not surprisingly, these displays of engagement strongly relate to school achievement, as measured by a standardized test administered during the spring term.

Hughes and Kwok (2007) examined the interplay of TSRQ, student engagement, and academic outcomes among students in the earliest primary grades, and they discern certain clear and striking trends. They examined the quality of teacher–student relationships as it relates to academic performance across two school years for students deemed vulnerable to school failure because of low-level literacy skills. Furthermore, they examined how TSRQ measured in one year relates to achievement outcomes in the subsequent year. Participating students were Black, White, and Latino in relatively equal numbers. Results reveal that the perceived quality of teacher–student relationships positively relates to student engagement, which in turn predicts reading test scores in the first year. Moreover, student engagement levels from the first year predict both math and reading achievement scores in the second year.

Sutherland and Oswald (2005) offer a convincing formulation that illuminates the interwoven, reciprocal relationships among academic performance, student engagement, and TSRQ. In short, academically proficient or appropriate responses lead to increased teacher praise and positive inclinations toward children, which in turn lead to more and higher-quality opportunities to learn. On the other hand, student inattention leads to teacher reprimands, which lead to noncompliant behaviors by students, which lead to avoidance, punishment, or coercion by teachers, which ultimately leads to student failure—an escalating cycle of negativity.

This line of reasoning has been further supported in several high-quality research investigations. For example, consider the work of Hughes, Luo, Kwok, and Loyd (2008).

They set out to examine the interplay of engagement and achievement across a three-year span for early elementary school children. One particular focus was on what they called effortful engagement. This factor refers to "volitional or effortful involvement akin to trying hard and not giving up in the face of failure, and directing of one's attention to instructional activities" (p. 3). They specifically examined how TSRQ affects changes in children's levels of effortful classroom engagement and ultimately affects academic achievement. They postulate that they should see reciprocal effects—that is, children's engagement levels should both influence and be influenced by TSRQ and academic competence—and they deem it quite plausible that teachers find it easier to display support and affection for students who try hard and pay attention in class. They discuss these dynamics in terms of a "lag effect," which refers to the idea that children's early relationships with teachers are carried forth as "enduring mental representations" that affect subsequent relationships with teachers and help account for long-term prediction of achievement.

The sample for this study was composed of children from diverse ethnic backgrounds. Approximately 35 percent of participants were White, 37 percent were Latino, 23 percent were Black, and 5 percent were Asian. In addition, roughly 60 percent of the children were eligible for the free or reduced-price school lunch program; thus, participants were substantially from low-income backgrounds. During the first year of the study, children were in 1st grade, and the study followed these children through 3rd grade. In order to be eligible for the study, children must have scored below the median (for their district) on the most recent state math and reading achievement tests (individually administered Woodcock–Johnson). Effortful engagement was measured by a teacher report questionnaire that focused on level of effort, attention, persistence, and cooperative participation in learning. Teachers were the rating source for TSRQ. Pertinent items included "I enjoy being with this child," "This child gives me opportunities to praise him/her," and "This child talks to me about things he/she doesn't want others to know." Measures of engagement and TSRQ were obtained for each child, for each of the three years.

The results show that TSRQ in 1st grade affects reading and math achievement for the following two years. Moreover, TSRQ in earlier years predicts effortful engagement in later years, and effortful engagement in earlier years predicts achievement in math and reading in later years. The results also show cyclical relationships where prior achievement predicts later engagement, and prior effortful engagement predicts later TSRQ.

Consequently, TSRQ during 1st grade shapes children's patterns of engagement in learning, which leads to more supportive relationships with teachers and higher levels of achievement. Nevertheless, if a child experiences high levels of positive TSRQ during 2nd grade, but not 1st grade, the positive effects for that child will still show up in 3rd grade. Likewise, a child who is highly engaged in 2nd grade, but not 1st grade, will still show elevated TSRQ in 3rd grade.

TSRQ Is Critical for Black and Latino Students

Findings from several recent investigations lead to reasonable confidence that the quality of teacher–student relationships is crucial for the engagement and academic outcomes of Black and Latino students. The work of Burchinal, Peisner-Feinberg, Pianta, and Howes (2002) is a case in point.

They examined factors that predict the development of academic skills for children from preschool through 2nd grade, and they found that a close relationship with the teacher is uniquely and positively related to language skills (and reading scores) among Black children.

Elsewhere, Mooney and Thornton (1999) polled Black and White 7th graders, from a range of socioeconomic backgrounds, about their attributions for success in school. They found that White students, more so than their Black counterparts, attribute success to their own abilities. On the other hand, Black students—to a much greater extent than White students—attribute success to rapport with their teachers.

A study by Casteel (1997) is also worth noting here. In a survey of more than 1,600 Black and White middle school respondents from diverse socioeconomic backgrounds, students were asked "Whom do you most want to please with your class work?" Seventy-two percent of Black students answered that they want to please "their teacher." This was only the case for 30 percent of White respondents. Among these students, the most common response was "their parents." This pattern suggests that many Black students don't just learn from their teachers, they also learn for their teachers.

Tucker and colleagues (2002) conducted a multivariate path analytic study that examined Black students from low-income backgrounds in 1st through 12th grades. They found a direct relationship between classroom engagement and students' recognition that their teachers care about and are interested in their academic performance and show a personal interest in them as people. Recent investigations by Woolley, Kol, and Bowen (2009) and Mireles-Rios and Romo (2010) have documented the distinctive potency of TSRQ in enhancing engagement and academic achievement for adolescent Latino students.

Work by Irvine (1990) and Ware (2006), among others, claim that a teaching approach known as "warm-demander pedagogy" may be particularly effective with Black students. This method entails sternness (to the point of reprimanding students who don't live up to expectations) in a way that conveys compassion, unyielding support, and nurturance. Ferguson (2003) presents direct empirical support for the special responsiveness of Black and Latino students to warm-demander pedagogy. A nationwide sample of high school students from various ethnic groups was asked "When you work really hard in school, what of the following reasons are most important to you?" Among Black and Latino students, 47 and 41 percent, respectively, agreed with the statement "My teacher encourages me to work hard." However, only 31 percent of both White and Asian students agreed with this statement. Only 15 and 19 percent of Black and Latino students, respectively, agreed with the response option "The teacher demands it," whereas 29 percent of White students and 20 percent of Asian students agreed with it. When the teacher is seen only as demanding, positive responsiveness is not indicated by Black and Latino students. Favorable reactions, however, are indicated when the demands are tied to the "warmth" of encouragement.

Despite all of the benefits already discussed, evidence clearly points to the probability that TSRQ is problematic for many Black and Latino children. Saft and Pianta (2001) report findings from a national data set on teachers' perceptions of their relationships with preschool and kindergarten students. Black students are rated by teachers as more problematic than White students, in terms of teacher–student relationships, school adjustment matters, and academic competence, and they are perceived to have poorer educational prognoses.

In their investigation, Ladd and colleagues (1999) found that TSRQ among kindergarten students varies as a function of racial background. Teacher–student interactions were observed across an entire academic year. It was found that White and affluent children formed closer, more positive emotional relationships and fewer conflict-ridden relationships with their teachers, and they were more accepted by their classroom peers (as rated by teachers) than were their poor, Black, and Latino peers.

In the Hughes and Kwok (2007) study cited above, the quality of teacher–student relationships is measurably lower for Black students than it is for their White and Latino counterparts. These poor-quality relationships account, in part, for the lower achievement trajectories among Black students and contribute to the widening of the Black–White achievement gap.

In a telling study by Noguera (2003), graduating seniors in a mixed-race high school were asked questions concerning matters of school climate.

Approximately 75 percent of Black students disagreed with the statement "My teachers support me and care about my success in their class." By contrast, this was the case for only 37 percent of White students and 32 percent of Asian students. What makes these results all the more intriguing is that the school was a selective-admittance magnet school for high-achieving students.

Research on Teacher Expectations

Ever since the publication of Rosenthal and Jacobson's classic text *Pygmalion in the Classroom* (1968), teachers' low expectations have been blamed as the root of poor academic performance among minority students. Teacher expectations, then, is another interpersonal factor that deserves our attention. Although the original works on this subject were more anecdotal, the past 25 years have seen systematic empirical data support many of the original claims and document the fact that low expectations have adverse academic effects for many Black and Latino children (e.g., Hinnant, O'Brien, & Ghazarian, 2009; Mistry, White, Benner, & Huynh, 2009).

How do teachers demonstrate lower expectations for some students? To the casual observer, the method by which differential expectations are conveyed may be elusive. However, the work of Good (1987) and Ferguson (1998) has shown that very specific and concrete behavior differences can convey differences in expectations. For example, these authors document that teachers

→ Call on low-expectation (LE) students less often than on high-expectation (HE) students.

→ Are likely to give LE students less praise and more criticism for failure.

→ Show less acceptance of ideas put forth by LE students.

→ Provide briefer and less informative feedback to questions raised by LE students.

→ Give LE students less benefit of the doubt.

→ Allow LE students less time to answer questions.

→ Are more likely to provide LE students with correct answers, whereas they are more likely to provide clues or rephrase a question for HE students.

Ferguson's (2003) research reveals that different teacher expectations fall along racial lines. Teacher expectations of future performance for Black students are regularly more negative than they are for White students. Further, teacher perceptions and future expectations may affect Black students' future mathematics performance, both positively and negatively, to a greater degree than they affect White students' performance. On the basis of data furnished by Ferguson (Jussim, Eccles, & Madon, 1996), it is found that teachers' relative influence is nearly three times larger for Black students in elementary school than it is for White students.

A recent meta-analysis by Tenenbaum and Ruck (2007) provides further evidence concerning teacher expectations. Their review covers research performed between 1968 and 2003. The majority of the studies they review focus exclusively on elementary students (approximately 60 percent), and the remainder include students at the secondary or university level or students across school levels. Results indicate that teachers have more positive expectations for White students than they do for Black or Latino students. Moreover, teachers direct more positive speech (in the form of praise, affirmations, and positive feedback) toward White students. White students also receive more product- and process-based questions, which require them to generate a product or explain a process; therefore, Black and Latino students have fewer opportunities to respond academically in their classrooms.

McKown and Weinstein (2002) provide us with further documentation of differential expectations and the resulting academic impact. They studied approximately 1,900 elementary (3rd and 5th grade) students from more than 80 classrooms and tried to discern whether teacher expectations could be differentiated by students' racial backgrounds. They find that in race-heterogeneous classrooms, teacher expectations for Black and Latino students are substantially more negative than they are for White and Asian students, even though all student groups have comparable histories of achievement. Furthermore, these expectation differences are tied to student perceptions that teachers treat high- and low-achieving students differently. Even more, the lower expectations for Black and Latino students are functionally linked to lower levels of reading achievement at the end of the school year. Similar findings were obtained by Hinnant, O'Brien, and Ghazarian (2009).

Research on Learning Goals

Classroom learning goals deal with how teachers and students discern, understand, or approach their purposes for teaching and learning the material at hand. The study of goals is a topic that has received considerable attention, specifically in terms of its potential to address achievement gaps among groups of students. Evidence has mounted that learners' goals (or the goals structured for learners by teachers) can significantly affect academic functioning—particularly for Black and Latino students—in ways that can address the achievement gap.

Several different taxonomies have been suggested to classify goal types. Nicholls, Cheung, Lauer, and Patashnick (1989) offer task versus ego goals; Dweck and Leggett (1988) present learning versus performance goals; and Ames (1990) discusses mastery versus performance goals. These goal orientations can be understood as an individual's dispositional qualities (or enduring characteristics) or as situational perceptions tied to the motivational fabric of the learning setting.

The most prevalent classifications, perhaps, are mastery and performance goals. These goals speak to the reasons why students seek to achieve in a given setting. Mastery goals focus on gaining comprehension or competence and on effort and personal improvement as standards for achievement. They focus on gaining skills, making progress, and acquiring a deep understanding as end results. The more academically conventional performance goals, however, focus on competence in comparison to others and on being the best. Motivation is thus tied to the personal gratification that stems from recognition that one is, for example, smartest among peers. These two goal types are cast as ways in which students construe and respond to achievement experiences, and they are associated with distinctly different patterns of cognition, affect, and behavior (e.g., Dweck & Leggett, 1988; Kaplan & Maehr, 1999; Nichols et al., 1989; Pintrich, 2000).

Graham and Golan (1991) show that instructions that prompt a mastery-focused approach (as opposed to ones that prompt a performance-focused approach) lead to higher academic outcomes for college students, particularly when the task calls for depth in processing, which is when more than a shallow mental effort is needed for successful performance. One other advantage to mastery-focused strategies is that, in the face of great challenge or failure, students are likely to attribute the result to insufficient effort on their part, rather than to a lack of ability where others are simply smarter or more capable.

A focus on performance goals is more likely to link to ability attributions and, thus, more likely to induce lower levels of effort as students could likely conclude that they don't have the requisite competence to perform well. When students pursue performance goals, they typically focus on outperforming their peers, and they seek out tasks in which they are already competent (i.e., "easy tasks"). They are also more prone to seek quick solutions than to think and worry about making mistakes (Kaplan & Maehr, 1999). A focus on mastery goals likely yields an increased effort toward ultimate task accomplishment (Ames, 1992). A mastery goal orientation should not be confused with Bloom's notion of mastery learning (1971, 1981). This latter notion refers to an instructional approach whereby teachers lead students through a discrete set of learning units, with progression predicated on established criteria for proficiency at each step.

In recent years, performance goal orientation has been bifurcated into performance approach and performance avoidance inclinations (Elliot & Harackiewicz, 1996; Middleton & Midgley, 1997). Performance approach links to the desire to surpass the performance of others, whereas performance avoidance links to the desire to avoid appearing stupid or incompetent. This distinction has led to the assertion that approach goals are as adaptive as mastery goals in achievement settings, leading to greater achievement and performance (Harackiewicz, Barron, Pintrich, Elliot, & Thrash, 2002);

avoidance goals, on the other hand, have been identified with maladaptive motivational patterns and task performance (Harackiewicz, Barron, & Elliot, 1998). Work that documents the utility of this distinction has principally been conducted with college-level students, so this distinction has yet to be proven useful with K–12 students (e.g., Kaplan, Gheen, & Midgley, 2002).

With respect to math outcomes, Linnenbrink (2005) finds that among 5th and 6th grade students (roughly equal numbers of Black and White children from "working-class" backgrounds) studying statistics and graphing, those who demonstrate a high level of mastery goal orientation report greater self-efficacy, more personal interest in math, less test anxiety, more adaptive help seeking, and more success on the unit exam than those students who demonstrate a high level of performance goal orientation. Elsewhere, Wolters (2004) shows that among middle school students (in a sample composed of 70 percent White and 18 percent Black and Latino suburban students), a mastery orientation is positively related to cognitive engagement in adaptive learning strategies and math grades, but no systematic relationships occur for a performance goal orientation.

Another notable investigation was conducted by Kaplan and Maehr (1999). The participants in this study were all 6th graders in the first year of their transition to middle school. The sample's demographic profile was 54 percent White, 39 percent Black, and 11 percent "other minorities." Students are described as coming from working-class backgrounds, with roughly half of the sample eligible for the school's free and reduced-price lunch program. Students filled out a 90-item survey that targeted their perceptions and opinions concerning school-related affect, perceived academic efficacy, and personal and perceived emphasis on mastery versus performance goals in school. Data were also collected for disruptive behaviors, peer relationships at school, and the emotional tone of the classroom.

Generally speaking, the pattern of results is comparable for Black and White students and for personal and perceived classroom goal emphases. Generally, the more students embrace mastery goals (or perceive their emphasis in the classroom), the more favorable are students' ratings of classroom emotional tone, peer relationships, perceived academic efficacy, and grade point averages. With respect to performance goals, the more students embrace them (or perceive they are emphasized in classroom activities), the more they exhibit disruptive behavior and positively rate emotional tone, peer relationships, efficacy, and grade point averages. Further analyses reveal one important distinction between Black and White students: The perceived presence of performance goals in classrooms has a more detrimental effect on Black students' academic self-efficacy.

Gutman (2006) shows a link not only between mastery goals and academic performance but also between mastery and the key guiding function of self-efficacy. For a sample of Black high school students, she finds that exposure to mastery goals in the classroom leads to increased self-efficacy and higher grades in math classes. Similarly, students who actively espouse mastery goals have higher self-efficacy and course grades in math. Other investigations confirm the fact that an emphasis on mastery goals is associated with higher levels of student engagement, self-efficacy, and standardized achievement among ethnically diverse K–12 students (Fast et al., 2010; Friedel et al., 2010; Walker & Greene, 2009).

Mueller and Dweck (1998) also give empirical support to the connection between mastery goals and another guiding function. They find that, for Black and White 5th grade students, receiving effort praise leads directly to the adoption of mastery goals, whereas the use of ability praise leads directly to the adoption of performance goals. Hence, it can be inferred that mastery goals are more readily linked to malleable beliefs about competence and smartness, and performance goals are linked to conceptions of fixed ability.

The preponderance of work that examines the academic virtue of mastery goals has focused on the proactive consequences of engagement and performance. Turner and colleagues (2002) examine connections between the classroom context and students' reports of avoidance and other self-handicapping strategies. They focus on mathematics, a domain in which anxiety and avoidance are frequently reported, and they set out to discern what factors might militate against such expressions. They find that classrooms with high levels of avoidance are low in mastery goal structures. In these settings, the emphasis is more on errorless performance, a premium placed on goals for completion, and on acknowledging perfection and high scores linked to social comparisons among students.

In this study, data were collected from Black and White 6th grade students across 65 classrooms. The data show that perceived classroom mastery goal structures significantly predict lower levels of self-handicapping behaviors, which manifest in several ways. Students procrastinate, purposely do not try hard, look for excuses not to study, avoid help, guess when they don't understand, and refrain from asking questions in class even when they don't understand. Moreover, in the face of hard problems, students simply do not do the work. Students are also more likely to choose to work on problems they already know how to do. Of special interest here is that more Black students utilize self-handicapping strategies and avoid asking for help than do their White peers.

Research on Autonomy Motivation

Another approach to learning goals grows out of a conception known as self-determination theory (Ryan & Deci, 2000). This conception is itself an outgrowth of White's (1959) seminal work on the notion of competence. The claim is that accomplishing a challenging task and causing a desired effect to occur are inherently enjoyable. The logic follows that the more self-determined the act, the more a sense of competence ensues. Being guided by self-determination, while engaged in an activity, results in optimal motivation levels. It is further postulated that people are more self-determined when they feel a sense of autonomy in their pursuits, rather than when they feel their pursuits are controlled through coercion, external rewards, or guilt/shame avoidance. Autonomy is conceived as distinct from notions such as individualism and independence. Ryan and Deci (2006) refer to it succinctly as "self-governance," which is distinct from "other governance." Elsewhere, Chirkov and colleagues state that a person is autonomous in his or her functioning "when his or her behavior is experienced as willingly enacted and when he or she fully endorses the action in which he or she is engaged"

(Chirkov, Ryan, Kim, & Kaplan, 2003, p. 98). The litmus test, they argue, is whether the person is acting consistent with his or her own "authentic" interests, values, and desires.

Learning climate is also crucial. This conceptual scheme distinguishes between autonomy-supporting and autonomy-suppressing learning contexts. The weight of evidence indicates that autonomy support leads to greater student engagement and a deeper processing of information, whereas settings that suppress autonomy (or convey control) lead to less positive affect and reasonably adaptive performance on superficial, relatively simplistic learning tasks but not on more challenging tasks that require deep information processing.

The interactional elements that foster autonomy support include empathy for the student's perspective/point of view, a compelling rationale for involvement, independent thinking and criticism, and choice within the limits of the situation (Vansteenkiste, Lens, & Deci, 2006; Vansteenkiste & Sheldon, 2006). Factors that control or suppress autonomy include a lack of criticism and independent thinking, the imposition of authority as the rationale for involvement, and the use of rewards, punishments, and social coercion as bases for student involvement in inherently uninteresting tasks.

Research over the years has shown the positive values of intrinsic over extrinsic goals (i.e., goals beyond the task at hand) in motivation, of autonomous over controlled motives, and of performance in the face of autonomy support rather than control. These concepts have also been applied with similar success in other life domains, such as mental health, physical health, and the adaptive pursuit of increased physical activity (Ryan & Deci, 2000, 2006).

Other studies provide further support to the claims of self-determination theory. For example, Assor, Kaplan, and Roth (2002) examined several autonomy-supporting and -suppressing teacher behaviors to ascertain their impact on student outcomes. Participants in their study were 3rd–8th grade Israeli children who were described as coming from middle- to lower-class backgrounds. Salient among the autonomy-supporting behaviors targeted in this study were

→ Fostering relevance (clarifying how learning tasks contribute to students' personal goals and paying attention to students' feelings and thoughts regarding learning tasks).

→ Providing a choice of tasks to pursue (that are consistent with a student's interests and goals).

→ Allowing critical feedback.

→ Encouraging independent thinking.

Among the autonomy-suppressing behaviors were

→ Stifling student criticism and independent opinions.

→ Intruding on students' "natural" learning rhythms.

→ Compelling students to engage in personally meaningless and uninteresting activities.

Data were gathered in the form of student questionnaires. For example, a question concerning relevance asked whether the teacher explains why it is important to study certain subjects in school, a question about choice asked whether the teacher allows students to choose how to do class work, and a question about criticism asked whether the teacher allows students to talk about things they find unacceptable in school. With respect to autonomy-suppressing behaviors, the questionnaire asked whether the teacher is unwilling to admit his or her mistakes (for stifling student criticism), forces students to prepare uninteresting homework (for compelling students to engage in meaningless and uninteresting activities), or interrupts when a student is in the middle of interesting activities (for intruding on natural learning rhythms).

For students in grades 3–5 and in grades 6–8, the results indicate that the more students report autonomy-suppressing behavior by their teachers, the lower are their positive feelings and levels of engagement in the classroom. On the other hand, the more they report teachers using autonomy-supporting behaviors, the greater are their positive feelings and engagement. Roth, Assor, Kanat-Maymon, and Kaplan (2007) further advance this line of work. They examined self-reports by 132 teachers in Israel, along with the corresponding reports provided by their 3rd–5th grade students from middle- and lower-class backgrounds. It was found that the more teachers report autonomous motives for teaching, the more their students report both autonomy-supporting teaching behaviors and autonomous motivation in themselves. Vansteenkiste, Simons, Lens, Sheldon, and Deci (2004) conducted similar work in Belgium with high school students. They found there was greater task persistence, deeper processing of content, and higher levels of test performance in the presence of autonomy-supporting teacher behaviors, compared with autonomy-suppressing behaviors.

In all, impressive outcomes have been obtained for students across several investigations. The tenets of self-determination theory seem highly plausible, and the value of the constructs and processes, in terms of addressing achievement gaps, seems highly promising. However, to date, little evidence has been directly accrued with low-income Black and Latino students. The practical merits of such an approach await more direct empirical testing. Given the impressive results in several domains and from other countries, this testing should be spiritedly pursued.

Research on Collaboration

A preponderance of evidence seems to indicate that, when properly structured, collaboration for learning can boost academic performance and may have a positive impact on the performance of minority students, particularly those from low-income backgrounds (Ginsburg-Block, Rohrbeck, Lavigne, & Fantuzzo, 2008). This finding appears to be especially robust at the elementary school level. Research on the effectiveness of collaborative learning at the middle and high school levels has been generally absent from the literature, but a recent review suggests that similar outcomes also obtain for secondary students (Slavin, Lake, & Groff, 2009).

Perhaps the best source to discern relevant effects of collaborative learning on math outcomes comes from a meta-analytic review conducted by Rohrbeck, Ginsburg-Block, Fantuzzo, and Miller (2003). They set certain stipulations for the inclusion of studies in their review: ethnic group comparisons, explicit peer assistance, interdependent reward contingencies, and independent accountability or evaluation procedures. The latter two stipulations were necessary because the extant literature on peer-assisted learning documents that these conditions are critical to produce positive outcomes. All studies reviewed were at the elementary school level. Other qualifiers were that all studies had to appear in peer-reviewed journals, and these studies had to deploy experimental or quasi-experimental designs. Moreover, the interventions had to be classroom based and occur for more than one week. Ninety studies met these criteria, and they were published between the years 1966 and 2000.

What were the findings of this meta-analytic review? Overall, peer-assisted learning contexts lead to greater math performance outcomes than do contexts that are individually or competitively structured. Larger effects on performance are found for urban over rural and suburban settings, for low-SES over mid- and high-SES levels, and for minority status (Black and Latino) over majority (White) status. Positive effects on achievement for collaborative learning occur among samples of Black and Latino children, and the difference in the effects of collaborative learning on math performance is greatest between these children and their White counterparts. A more recent empirical investigation by McMaster, Kung, Han, and Cao (2008) corroborates these findings with a sample of English language learners at the kindergarten level.

Among the most widely researched and empirically successful collaborative learning methods is classwide peer tutoring (Greenwood, Carta, Kamps, & Hall, 1988; Greenwood, Delquadri, & Carta, 1997; Greenwood, Delquadri & Hall, 1989). Classwide peer tutoring (CWPT) operates by randomly assigning students to two teams within the classroom and then randomly assigning students to pairs (within teams). These pairs work together for approximately 20 minutes, between three and five days a week. Students in each pair alternate playing the roles of tutor and tutored. Typically, the learning activities are scripted and structured by the teacher so that instructions can be easily followed, regardless of a student's skill level. As the two teams compete for recognition awards (e.g., special classroom privileges, classroom applause, tangible rewards), students accrue points for their team by answering questions correctly. CWPT is especially useful for reinforcing and practicing basic academic skills. A variant of this technique is Peer-Assisted Learning Strategies (PALS) (Mathes, Howard, Allen, & Fuchs, 1998; Mathes, Torgeson, & Allor, 2001). PALS is designed to adapt CWPT procedures for more advanced academic skills such as reading comprehension or phonemic awareness fluency embedded in connected text.

Another intriguing strategy is known as Numbered Heads Together (Kagan, 1992; Maheady, Mallette, Harper, & Sacca, 1991). This strategy is relatively simple to implement, and it is well suited to classrooms that have students with markedly different skill levels. Students are assigned to mixed-skill groups of four, in which each member is randomly assigned a number. After the teacher poses a given question, he or she provides time for group members to "put their heads together" and consider the appropriate response. The teacher then calls on group members by number to provide the appropriate response. Since they do not know who from the group will be called, group members must ensure that every member understands the material, as any one of them may be called on to represent the group's response. A recent study chronicles the effectiveness of this strategy for addressing the educational challenges of minority students (Maheady, Michielli-Pendl, Harper, & Mallette, 2006). This technique was used in a middle school chemistry class (compared to more standard whole-class instruction). Of the students, 57 percent were Latino and the rest were White. Performance was substantially better with Numbered Heads Together, in terms of active student response, daily quiz performance, and unit test performance. These results essentially replicate findings from previous studies with younger children (Maheady et al., 1991; Maheady, Michielli-Pendl, Mallette, & Harper, 2002).

Chapter Summary

This chapter introduced the notion of asset-focused strategies, which refer to activities that benefit from students' interests, experiences, and prior knowledge. These asset-focused factors are key strategies that promote student engagement and guiding functions and lead to gap-closing academic outcomes. Three categories of asset-focused factors are presented. They are interpersonal relationships, intersubjectivity, and information-processing quality.

This chapter addressed interpersonal relationships. It centered on interaction quality inside classrooms between teachers and students and among students themselves, concerning matters of student learning, learning potential, and learning aims. One factor addressed was teacher–student relationship quality (TSRQ), and it was shown that, across the K–12 continuum, students (especially Black and Latino students) are more positively responsive when teachers display genuine caring and support for them yet are still demanding and have high expectations. The importance of this factor is underscored by the finding that high TSRQ in kindergarten continues to have a positive effect on academic performance as far out as 8th grade. In addition, there is more evidence to support the benefits of TSRQ than there is to support any other factor reviewed in this book. What's more, TSRQ and engagement appear to mutually influence each other. Not only does high TSRQ lead to greater student engagement, but the presence of high student engagement in turn leads to greater TSRQ. Unfortunately, evidence also abounds that classrooms serving low-income Black and Latino students typically have low levels of TSRQ. Similarly, low teacher expectations are more likely to be directed at Black and Latino students, and these students are more susceptible to the negative influences of low teacher expectation.

This chapter also presented evidence for the potential gap-closing benefits of (1) mastery (understanding, effort, and improvement) over performance (doing better than others) goal structures, and (2) autonomy-supporting learning contexts (intrinsic or self-determined involvement in learning) over autonomy-suppressing learning contexts (involvement for extrinsic reasons). Collaborative learning was also found to boost academic performance and yield gap-closing outcomes, but this is the case only when the collaboration entails authentic intellectual exchanges that occur among student participants.

Asset-Focused Factors: Intersubjectivity

06

This chapter centers on the asset-focus factor of intersubjectivity. This factor grouping speaks to how well the values, interests, and learning priorities of the teacher are aligned with those of the students and the extent to which these aligned emphases are reflected in the curriculum. The two areas of intersubjectivity covered here are meaningful learning and cultural concerns.

Research on Meaningful Learning

Over the last two decades, as experts have tried to address the achievement gap, attention has centered on making academic material personally meaningful and relevant to students. The notion is that educators—by centering the learning process on children's actual experiences, relating what students learn to matters of personal interest, linking classroom learning to relevant events and experiences in students' lives, tying what is learned to the community or the larger society, and drawing connections across topics and subjects—can bring about better learning outcomes for students. The literature that supports such beliefs is substantial.

Newby (1991) recorded the percentage of time elementary school teachers used various motivational strategies to support student learning. The most frequently observed approach was labeled *rewards and punishments* (either verbal or tangible), and it occurred approximately 58 percent of the time. Less frequently observed was an approach labeled *emphasizing relevance*, which occurred roughly 8 percent of the time. In this latter approach, teachers tied a given lesson or presentation to previous experiences that students found familiar.

Interestingly, there was a substantial negative correlation between the use of rewards and punishments by teachers and the amount of task engagement by students ($r = -.50$). The more the teacher invoked rewards and punishments to induce learning, the less children were engaged with the learning activity. By contrast, a strong positive correlation was obtained between the use of relevance strategies and the level of student engagement ($r = .61$). That is, the more a teacher directly tied a lesson to familiar experiences, the more students were discernibly engaged in the lesson and task at hand.

A randomized field experiment by Cohen, Garcia, Apfel, and Master (2006) addressed the usefulness of linking school performance to matters of personal relevance for Black students. The participants were Black and White 7th graders from middle- to lower-middle-class backgrounds. They all attended the same school. The authors describe their experimental treatment as a "self-affirmation" intervention. Students who were randomly assigned to the experimental group selected one or more values that were important to them and then wrote brief paragraphs in which they justified why those values were chosen. The exercise was presented to the students as a normal lesson and took approximately 15 minutes to complete. Students who were randomly assigned to a contrasting group were asked to select one or more values that were least personally important and then write about why those values might be important to someone else. Teachers were not aware of which students participated in either group. Two parallel studies were conducted, separated by one year. In the first study, students completed the exercise once, and they wrote about only one value. In the second, students completed the exercise twice, and they could choose up to three values.

For both studies, course grades for Black students in the experimental group were significantly higher than those obtained by Black students in the control group. No treatment effect was obtained for White students in either study. Significant race-by-treatment interactions were found in both studies. Black students in the experimental group even performed better than their contrasting-group counterparts in other courses for which the treatment did not occur. For this investigation, the course subject in which the treatment was provided was not specified.

Research on Personalization

Do students perform better when they see themselves in their coursework? D'Ailly, Simpson, and MacKinnon (1997) found that using the word *you* in one-step math problems that called for comparisons generally improved problem-solving performance. Participants were 3rd through 5th grade students whose ethnicity was unspecified. Consider this problem (presented orally): "John has nine sticks. Peter has four sticks fewer than John. How many sticks does Peter have?" If the problem is reworded to be self-referencing, more correct answers result. For example, "You have nine sticks. Peter has four sticks fewer than you. How many sticks does Peter have?" or "John has nine sticks. You have four sticks fewer than John. How many sticks do you have?" When the question is self-referencing, students ask for it to be repeated fewer times, and they are able to solve the problem faster.

Several studies explore the idea of customizing academic material to the individual interests and personal experiences of the learners. One of the earliest deployments of such personalization was carried out by Anand and Ross (1987). This study centered on a personalized approach to math and the effects on elementary students' performance. The researchers' concern was that, beyond computational skills, many children falter in math because of an inability to understand what is asked of them in a given problem. Context, therefore, influences a student's comprehension of the problem's task demands. Increased comprehension of a problem's task demands should improve that student's ability to focus on relevant information and solve the problem. Moreover, incorporating a child's particular interests and background experiences into the problem context should result in a greater focus on relevant information, which in turn should enhance performance outcomes. Anand and Ross sought to individualize problem presentation for each student through personalizing the context in which the problem was presented. This was accomplished by encasing each problem in computer-generated information that was greatly familiar, meaningful, or of personal interest to each student. Thus, for this condition, each child's problem set was unique.

Participants in this study were primarily Black 5th and 6th graders. For this investigation, students were randomly assigned to one of three practice/learning conditions. These were labeled (1) abstract, (2) concrete, and (3) personalized. The problems that students were assigned in these conditions were germane to a math unit on division of fractions. This was a unit with which students at the school had struggled. For all conditions, the set of problems contained identical mathematics information and operations. However, across the conditions, the manner in which the problems were described differed.

In the abstract condition, problems were described in general terms, not unlike the typical presentation of math problems in a standard curriculum. In the concrete condition, problems were presented with specific but hypothetical referents. In the personalized condition, problem text incorporated personalized information about the given student. Consider these three versions of the same problem:

> **Abstract:** There are three objects. Each is cut in half. In all, how many pieces would there be?
>
> **Concrete:** Billy has three candy bars. He cuts each one of them in half. In all, how many candy bar pieces does Billy have?
>
> **Personalized:** Mrs. Williams surprises Joseph on December 15th when she presents him with three Hershey bars. Joseph cuts each of them in half so that he can share the birthday gift with his friends. In all, how many Hershey bar pieces does Joseph have for his friends?

For the personalized condition, information about each child was gleaned from a questionnaire that was administered prior to the lesson. The questionnaire asked students to provide information such as birthday; parents' names; teacher's name; friends' names; favorite foods, hobbies, magazines, TV shows; and the like. This information (via computer generation) was then incorporated into the given child's problem set. In the personalization example provided, the student's name is Joseph, his teacher is Mrs. Williams, his birthday is December 15th, and Hershey bars are his favorite candy.

Two major performance outcome measures were deployed in this study. There was an immediate posttest, which consisted of problems that had a similar structure and challenge level as the lesson problems. There was also a transfer measure, which consisted of a set of problems on the same material—division of fractions—but were structured differently, thereby creating a novel format for students.

It was generally found that students performed best under the personalized condition, and performance under the concrete condition was slightly better than the abstract context. The superiority of the personalized condition was stronger with the transfer outcome than with the posttest outcome. It was also found that students' performance patterns differed, based on participants' standardized achievement levels. Students were divided into two groups, low–medium and high levels for both language arts and math. Students who scored below the 70th percentile in achievement scores composed the low–medium level, and students who scored above this threshold composed the high level. It was found that, for both outcome measures, students in the low–medium group performed significantly better in the personalized condition, whereas those in the high group performed similarly in the personalized and concrete conditions. It seems plausible to infer, then, that the personalization condition results in stronger performance levels for comparatively lower-achieving students.

Similar findings have been obtained in a study emphasizing 2nd and 5th graders in both urban and rural schools (Davis-Dorsey, Ross, & Morrison, 1991), further confirming that infusing personalization into problem texts creates an increased opportunity for students to link the problem to well-known and (personally) interesting information, which then leads to higher performance outcomes.

Cordova and Lepper (1996) took the work on personalization even further by factoring in whether students had a choice in what personalized information would be included in the problems, as well as manipulating the descriptive quality and general interest value of the problems themselves (contextualization). A complex multistep problem-solving task was designed to help students learn the mathematical order of operations. Personalization was factored into the approach, but a new twist was added: the factor of choice. Either children had their personalized information embedded in the task by a computer-generated process or they had the freedom to choose which biographical elements to include at designated points in the problem text. For this study, participants were 4th and 5th graders, of whom 71 percent were White, 13 percent were Latino, 9 percent were Black, and 7 percent were Asian. Students' backgrounds ranged from working class to upper-middle class, and they were drawn from two private schools.

Personalization, choice, and contextualization yielded substantially more favorable outcomes than when each of these options was not present. Differences favoring these three conditions occurred with respect to engagement and motivation level, perceived competence, and problem-solving performance (measured one week after the interventions).

Research on Cultural Resources

Closely related to matters of meaningful learning are factors that concern cultural resources. Cultural matters should be closely aligned with learning and performance dynamics. To the extent that there is cultural congruency or linkages attached to the academic requirements at hand, intersubjectivity can be obtained.

To be sure, *culture* is a seductive concept fraught with explanatory pitfalls. It has defied precise definition. Indeed, efforts to define it often lead to distortion or oversimplification. People in general, and scholars in particular, use the term *culture* frequently but do not necessarily nail down its exact meaning. Most people appreciate its importance and understand that it is a real, credible, and important factor in individuals' unique experiences, but, at the same time, they fail to ascribe too much specificity to it. The explanatory potency of the concept, and its value in discerning strategies to close achievement gaps, compels us to examine its role in this section.

The Problems of Culture

Understandably, those who employ the notion of culture do so with great promise but also at some peril (as indicated in Chapter 2). There are several potential problems associated with its use. For example, cultural accounts fall prey to overgeneralization. Many educators unfortunately fall prey to the belief that race and culture are interchangeable. If a student is Black, then he or she must possess Black culture. One danger of overgeneralizing is the specter of stereotyping a population of people. This becomes particularly problematic when cultural factors are attributed to groups that have been historically marginalized by society. Those aspects of culture could be assumed to account for the marginalization and explain why the group performs inadequately or is unable to function as well as other cultural groups.

Related to this is the pitfall of assigning common cultural features to all members of a given population. When this is done, insufficient attention is given to individual variation. An oft-voiced critique is that there is more within-group variation than between-group variation. Another related concern deals with the notion of cultural determinism. The worry here is that if one student is designated as a member of a given cultural population, he or she must necessarily act, think, or feel certain ways.

Perhaps the most cogent critique raised in recent times about cultural analyses has to do with the problem of essentialism (Carlassare, 1994; Fuchs, 2005). Many who reject a cultural analysis do so because they believe that culture implies essentialism. Many who are favorable toward cultural arguments are emphatic about distancing themselves from an essentialist position. More particularly, essentialism is the stance that people have underlying, unchanging qualities that are their "essence" or their "nature." This is the way they are, the way they will always be—the innate characteristics of individuals, or the fixed, inherited, biological factors that by definition cannot be altered. Individuals of a certain group were simply born that way. The essentialist assertion is also that these unchanging attributes are located inside individuals and are characteristic of entire populations. If you are Black, then you have a "rhythmic" essence in you. If you are a woman, then you are more emotional than a man. Thus, the essentialist critique for our present purpose is launched against positing that people of a given cultural group possess certain fixed traits that an entire group of people possess. This does not allow for changes in expressions, in behaviors over time as a function of circumstances and experiences, or among members of an identified population. The counterargument for culturalists who eschew essentialism is that culture is a dynamic—not a static—phenomenon. It is a variable—not a homogenous—phenomenon. The focus should not be on how people are, but rather on what they do and how their actions depend on the exigencies of the pattern of situational demands that they individually or collectively face as a people.

An Informed Conception of Culture

Within a multiracial and multicultural society such as the United States, cultural expressions for a subpopulation or racial/ethnic group are not only dictated by the dominant culture. There can be cultural divergences among the various subpopulations or groups, but we cannot judge the cultural book by the racial cover. "Black culture," for example, is not the sum total of what Black people do. We must be mindful of overgeneralizations, of variation within a subpopulation, and of making essentialist claims. For our present purposes, culture can be conceived as the prism or lens through which people interpret life events. Cultural elements can exist independent of a given person or subpopulation as abstract concepts, values, or ways of thinking. They take the form of commonly held assumptions about what makes sense, what is appropriate, and what does or does not violate commonly held sensibilities. Even though such considerations typically exist independent of a given person or population, they can be identified with specific groups.

One qualifier for this discussion is in order: the issue of overdetermination. So much of the specification of culture is tied to the interpretation of behavior expressions, even verbal ones. Indeed, behavior is notoriously overdetermined. That is, any given behavior may occur for a variety of reasons, or the same behavior may itself have had multiple determinants for multiple reasons. Trying to decipher root causes of a given behavior becomes challenging at best; the same behaviors may have occurred for different reasons or different behaviors may have occurred for the same reason. Likewise, behaviors may have been displayed for cultural reasons in some instances or unrelated to culture considerations in other instances. This complexity urges caution in what we infer from our observations or from what we are told.

A more suitable framework for understanding the effects of culture is gained by taking a cultural patterning approach that conceivably encompasses the expressive, structural, functional, and fundamental domains of culture (Boykin & Allen, 2003). For any given cultural designation, there can be a particular constellation of what is emphasized, prioritized, valued, embraced, adhered to in terms of institutional rules, produced, practiced, done with regularity, and symbolized at particular points in time or in different historical moments. Thus, cultures differ in the patterning of their elements. This is in opposition to the belief that a relatively small set of universal cultural elements have different surface manifestations and expressions and to the relatively rigid either-or classification of cultural prototypes.

What about the connections between cultural displays and the groups that display them? This is a crucial matter. The achievement and opportunity gaps that are the subject of this book are couched in terms of differences between racial/ethnic groups. In common parlance, we speak of Black–White or Latino–White gaps in academic performance. This book discusses how to eliminate such disparities. Therefore, we must consider how this matter relates to these issues of culture.

We have already said that you cannot tell the cultural book by the racial cover. Nor can you tell the racial book by the cultural cover. Matters of race and culture are not the same, but they very likely overlap. That is, it is highly plausible that certain patterns of behavior, practices, values, priorities, salient sensibilities, and even products may be more prevalent, apparent, or observable in one racially designated group. Nevertheless, that a certain feature might be distinctive of a given racial group does not mean it is unique to that group—just that it is particularly evident. Differences in the pattern of expressions of certain cultural factors may indeed be obtained when groups are compared. When distinctive cultural features are associated with a given group, it should be taken literally to mean that it is associated with, not connected to, that group.

Cultural Transmission

Culture is transmitted in three ways: through deliberate teaching, through observational learning, and through direct participation. It is transmitted from a range of sources, including parents, siblings, other family members, peers, friends, teachers, ministers, and other authority figures. It is transmitted from role models or cultural icons in the community or from society at large. It is also transmitted through culturally produced artifacts, technologies, recreational events, and tools for conventional learning and communication (Boykin & Ellison, 1995).

The home environment provides the earliest elements of a cultural meaning system. Cultural themes are linked to the most significant people in a child's life and associated with positive affective reactions. These themes are generally primeval; they are learned and embraced securely and tacitly, and they are positively coded and valued, without ever needing justification for why they are responded to or resonated with in these ways.

Moreover, as children venture outside the home into the surrounding neighborhood and community, they very likely encounter cultural experiences that are extensions of those encountered in the home environment. This then reinforces what was appropriated in the earlier experiences. Thus, what occurs early will likely remain more meaningful or salient, but this is subject to change as cultural horizons expand through participation in a wider array of culturally structured settings and with divergent cultural agents. What is culturally acquired early on can remain most meaningful if children, as they develop and grow, choose to participate in, "allow" to be taught by, and choose to be influenced by observations that are consistent with their primary cultural schemes. In this regard, a complicating factor is context—the notion that different elements, values, and expressions may be more salient or likely to manifest in certain settings. How children understand to operate at home may differ from what is expected in school or among peers.

Educational Importance of Culture

Even though cultural phenomena have proven difficult to pin down, their presence in school settings has been convincingly argued. Schooling in our society does not take place on culturally neutral terrain (Hollins et al., 1994; Spring, 2009; Warikoo & Carter, 2010). School is a cultural context. There are structural cultural elements present. There are codified rules and regulations that govern how schools function. There are procedures for how the school day is organized; for how students are to behave; and for what is considered permissible in terms of dress codes, lengths of class periods, staff organizational culture, systems for evaluation, and promotion of school personnel and students. Contractual and legal considerations are also in play.

In addition to these structural cultural elements, there are also expressive cultural considerations. Schools at all levels have opportunities for recreational games and athletic sports participation. There are classes for art and music. There are opportunities for creative writing and other forms of creative expression. Students participate in school-based artistic and creative events such as plays, talent contests, and assemblies.

Closer to the heart of schooling purposes are adaptive cultural components. There are desired ends and goals that are viewed as essential for academic success, including grades, achievement test performance, academic recognition, certificates of various kinds, and credentials. Schools also impart skills that are deemed useful, even essential, by the broader society, and the extent to which these competencies are acquired signifies how prepared students are for participation in society (as part of a specific profession or the general labor force). These, of course, include literacy and numeracy skills, fluent use of technologies, communication skills, and, to some degree, social relational skills. Thus, many skills and competencies acquired from formal schooling are instrumental in school- and society-based, adaptive outcomes.

There are also what we would call instrumental, or functional, values such as hard work and good grades, persistence, a love for reading, and the importance of teacher recognition.

Finally, there is fundamental culture, which speaks more to the fabric of the academic experience. On what terms is schooling done? What are the foundational modes of operation? What are the overarching themes for living that are prioritized with respect to how people negotiate their lives, relate to others, and discern their place in the world? These themes, if embraced consciously or tacitly, are intrinsically valued. The written record shows, for example, that certain fundamental themes such as self-contained individualism (i.e., accomplishing things alone), interpersonal competition, and material gains are greatly privileged in our society and, as such, extend into U.S. classrooms. Moreover, learning is typically seen as a sedentary pursuit that requires very little physical activity and is best done in quiet settings with minimal distractions. However, other fundamental themes can emphasize and serve as candidates for the fabric of classroom life and learning. These include collectivism, communalism, and the linking of learning to high levels of movement expression, where music is integral to the learning and performance process. These fundamental themes have salience to children who have grown up largely outside the racial and socioeconomic mainstream U.S. experience (Boykin, 1986; Boykin & Ellison, 1995).

Culturally Relevant Pedagogy

In recent years, a sizable chorus of scholars has brought attention to the ways that students' experiences outside school—including those of ethnic minority students placed at risk for educational failure—can be a valuable resource inside classrooms (e.g., Morrison, Robbins, & Rose, 2008).

Ladson-Billings (1995, 2002) has been a prominent advocate for infusing culturally relevant pedagogy into classroom practices. The notion here is for teachers to blend Black students' home and community experiences into their instructional methods. This approach affirms students' cultural identities as they strive for high academic attainment while they exercise critical reasoning skills about academic and economic inequalities. In doing so, students' levels of achievement are tied to their pursuit of service to the community. Thus, in their instruction, teachers raise community-based issues that amplify, for example, challenges that students and their families face in their everyday lives. Still further, teachers urge students (in age-appropriate ways) to confront the realities of power and privilege in the larger society or link events that happen in their lives to the school's official curriculum.

González, Moll, and Amanti (2005) advanced another approach to developing culturally familiar adaptive practices. They advocate drawing on the funds of knowledge to be found in students' family and community experiences. The ultimate goal of this approach is to create greater experiential familiarity among teachers, students, and their families. The weight of responsibility often falls on teachers, as they strive to enhance their students' educational outcomes by gaining insights into the actual conditions under which their students live. Teachers, in effect, engage in ethnographic research in their students' communities to learn about the knowledge, skills, and assets that can be found there. For example, teachers might make home visits to better appreciate what their students' lives are actually like, or they might interact with their students' family members on their own "turf." In this way, teachers are better positioned to witness and appreciate their students' unique exchanges, skills, and knowledge. Teachers are then expected to collaborate with their colleagues and with students' family members to determine the best ways to take advantage of these knowledge funds in the course of classroom teaching and learning.

The research of González, Andrade, Civil, and Moll (2001) provides an illuminating example of the educational potential of a "funds-of-knowledge" approach.

They define funds of knowledge as "historically accumulated bodies of knowledge and skills essential for household functioning and well-being" (p. 116). In their work, they sought to discern the "mathematical potential" in regularly occurring household practices. Thus, they sought to connect everyday, real-life mathematics to school-based mathematics lessons. They also wanted to identify how students and their family members use mathematics at home—in other words, how they are already regular practitioners of mathematics.

More specifically, their approach was to extract mathematics from the everyday activities of household seamstresses, for example. This extraction is not done by asking these dressmakers to identify the mathematics principles that undergird their work. Such conceptual insights are rarely known by them. Instead, the idea is to get them to be conscious of how the measurements in which they intuitively engage can be seen as systematic and quantifiable and then to use the practice of dressmaking as an activity to build measurements around. The women in the household then helped provide insights into how this could be done by discussing the dressmaking process either directly with students or indirectly through a teacher who presents the mathematics procedures linked to that practice.

Fundamental Cultural Themes

When it comes to culture, certain general themes serve as blueprints for living. Among these themes are individualism, interpersonal competition, communalism, and movement expression. Individualism, generally speaking, has to do with a premium placed on working alone or being independent and on valuing self-reliance, self-containment, or self-sufficiency. Competition connotes an emphasis on rivaling and surpassing others, desiring to be the best, or beating opponents in some form of contest. Communalism implies a premium placed on social interdependence, mutuality, and reciprocity; on identity and duty tied to group membership; and on the primacy of social relationships. Movement expression, as used here, conveys special significance to the interwoven mosaic of movement, rhythm, music, percussiveness, and syncopation. Keeping in mind all the caveats and qualifiers about culture discussed earlier in this chapter, the latter two themes have been prominently (but not exclusively and certainly not universally) manifested in the lives of many Black children and youth from socially marginalized backgrounds (Boykin, 1983; Boykin & Allen, 2003). Over the years, Boykin has sought to discern if and how the incorporation of such themes into teaching and learning contexts might benefit Black students, especially those from low-income backgrounds, who live in primarily Black "cultural enclaves."

One study (Ellison, Boykin, Tyler, & Dillihunt, 2005) examined the learning preferences of Black and White 3rd and 4th grade children, all from low-income backgrounds who lived and attended school in the same neighborhood. The team of investigators administered a questionnaire to the students to gauge their preference for learning in an individualistic, competitive, or cooperative/communal fashion. The students responded to a set of questions that fell into three categories. An example of an "individualistic" question was "I like to work alone." An example of a "competitive" question was "I like to be the best when I learn." A "cooperative/communal" example was "I like to work in groups." Children responded to each question along a 7-point scale from *strongly disagree* to *strongly agree*. Black students showed a very strong preference for cooperative/communal learning as well as a dislike (with ratings below the midpoint) for competitive or individualistic learning. A different pattern emerged for their White counterparts, who displayed a greater preference for individualism and competition relative to cooperation.

In another study, Boykin, Tyler, and Miller (2005) drew inferences, based on several hundred hours of direct classroom observations, about the dominant cultural practices in classrooms that serve low-income Black elementary students. They found that individualism and competition (rather than communalism) were much more frequently observed. When these themes occurred, they were almost always teacher-initiated. When the far less frequent theme of communalism was manifest, it was virtually always initiated by Black students themselves, and, more often than not, it was associated with negative teacher feedback.

Other studies have systematically analyzed whether differential learning outcomes arise from different fundamental cultural conditions. One line of research has focused on the cultural theme of communalism. As mentioned, this theme implies that an intrinsic premium is placed on collaborative interdependence. Moreover, if some students prefer communalism, then the opportunity to work under such conditions should enhance academic outcomes from them. This notion has been examined in several investigations.

One such study was conducted by Hurley, Boykin, and Allen (2005). Black 5th grade children from low-income backgrounds were asked to learn strategies for solving mathematics estimation problems, and then they took a test on the relevant material. After completing a pretest on grade-appropriate multiplication problems, students were randomly placed in one of two conditions.

In the individual learning condition, children were given a 20-minute practice exercise in which they had to complete a workbook to help them become more adept at mathematics estimation, and they were directed to work on this task independently and exercise individual effort. They were also told that if they reached a certain level on the follow-up test, they would receive a reward. Other children were assigned to the communal condition. After the pretest, these children were formed into groups of three and given a prompt that emphasized the importance of working together for the good of the group and of helping one another learn. These children were not offered a reward for good performance. They were told to work together but not told *how* to work together. It was reasoned that if collaborative interdependence was a salient theme for them, they would not need external incentives to do well, nor would they require explicit instructions on how to work together. Participants in both conditions individually completed a 15-item mathematics estimation posttest. Results revealed that students in the communal condition had superior performance on the posttest, even in the absence of external incentives or explicit collaborative instructions.

In another recent study (Hurley, Allen, & Boykin, 2009), ethnic group differences were obtained across learning conditions, this time with the same math estimation task deployed in Hurley, Boykin, and Allen's (2005) investigation discussed above. Low-income Black and White 4th and 5th grade children were randomly placed in one of three different learning conditions (which lasted for 15 minutes). In turn, the conditions were interpersonal competition, group competition, and communal work. For the former two conditions, contingent rewards were offered. For the communal condition, there was no reward. Black students did significantly better than their White counterparts under the communal condition, whereas the opposite was true under the interpersonal competition condition.

A study more directly analogous to classroom performance was conducted by Boykin, Lilja, and Tyler (2004). They examined the effects of communal and individualistic contexts on students' learning during a three-week social studies unit. Participants were Black 5th grade students from a low-income community. They received a social studies/geography lesson from the school district's official curriculum (given under communal or individualistic conditions) for two weeks. After each lesson, they took a quiz. During the third week, they took a cumulative test that covered all the material taught. It was found that students performed better when the lessons were encased in a communal condition. This finding was also true for the weekly quizzes and cumulative final exam. Students working under the individualistic condition attained average scores of 45, 47, and 50 percent, whereas students in the communal condition earned average scores of 81, 88, and 87 percent. Put in different terms, students working individually would have failed the unit, and students working communally would have earned a high *B*. Nevertheless, all of these students were exposed to the same lesson information and took the same exams. They all attended the same schools and classrooms and lived in the same neighborhoods. Yet their school-relevant performance was strikingly different.

Several studies have focused on the impact of movement expression on academic performance. One of the earliest such studies was conducted by Allen and Boykin (1991). In this investigation, Black and White 1st and 2nd graders from low-income backgrounds served as participants. The task required students to recall a set of randomly generated picture pairs (of familiar objects). Two basic learning conditions were constructed, and they varied in the number of music and movement opportunities that were presented. In the low-movement-expression condition (LME), children were told to sit still while they rehearsed the picture pairs presented by the tester, and no music was played during this session. In the high-movement-expression condition (HME), children were presented with the picture pairs in a rhythmic fashion, accompanied by a rhythmic-percussive tune. Students were encouraged (but not forced) to stand, clap their hands, and move to the beat of the music as they rehearsed the pairs.

During the subsequent testing phase, students were presented with a set of picture cards that each depicted one of the items presented during rehearsal, and they were asked to put the cards into the proper pairs. All students received the rehearsal and testing sessions under both LME and HME conditions. This participation was separated by a five-day interval. The results revealed that White children performed better under the LME condition, and Black students performed better under the HME condition. Moreover, these performance levels were roughly equivalent.

This task was tapping a relatively low level of cognitive functioning, and the picture pairings were done on a random basis. The rationale for this was to tap into pure learning, since children could not draw upon prior experience with the pairings of the objects depicted. Although the performance pattern differences between the two cultural groups were quite striking, the question remains whether such data relate to more high-level cognitive tasks that are more meaningfully related to academic learning demands.

To address such concerns, Allen and Butler (1996) studied Black 2nd and 3rd grade children from low-income backgrounds and White children from middle-class backgrounds. Children were exposed to the same LME and HME conditions described above, but the target task in this case was analogical reasoning—students had to draw inferences from a story that had been read to them. It was found that Black children performed better in the HME condition, whereas the opposite was true for White children. Despite the different socioeconomic backgrounds, the performance of Black children in the HME condition and of White children in the LME condition were comparable.

In a subsequent study, Boykin and Cunningham (2001) sought to determine if movement expression imagery could benefit children if it was included in the content of text information. The participants in this study were all Black 2nd and 3rd graders from low-income backgrounds. This study generally deployed the same paradigm used in the Allen and Butler investigation, with one major modification. The content of the stories was manipulated to include movement expression themes. In the HME stories, characters were engaged in high-movement-expression activities—they ran, skipped, jumped, and danced. In the LME versions, characters walked, sat, and stood. This manipulation in no way altered the plot or substance of the story narrative. The results revealed that overall performance was better for students in the HME condition. Moreover, there was a compounding of effects when high-movement-theme content was present with high-movement-expression context. That is, when movement expression was present in both the learning context and the story content, performance was at its best.

Expressive Culture

Carol Lee (2001, 2006) has called for cultural modeling of instructional strategies in classrooms that serve primarily low-achieving Black students. These strategies build on students' popular and expressive cultural interests. The notion here is that, under culturally familiar circumstances, students often use reasoning, analysis, and problem-solving strategies that are not unlike those expected and required in academic settings (yet those same students do not typically display such cognitive—even metacognitive—skills in their classrooms with respect to academic subject matter).

Lee began to make links between the everyday and school domains in which she worked with secondary school students in Chicago, where an alarming number of Black 9th grade, inner-city students were failing English Literature. She discerned that the official curriculum required students to use orthodox literary analyses (e.g., symbolism, irony, paradox, double entendres, and character analyses) to understand the works of Shakespeare and Chaucer. As a student of Black youth culture, Lee was keenly aware that many of these elements are present in popular songs and hip hop lyrics. Many of these elements are also part and parcel of youths' discussions with one another about the songs, lyrics, and the people who perform them. They routinely use symbolism and metaphor in their own speech, and they analyze the motives of performers and the intentions and messages of song lyrics. Indeed, substantial use of satire and figurative language appears in the everyday language of many Black children and youth, and other aspects of their "linguistic repertoires" manifest a tacit understanding of various literary forms.

Lee therefore advocates that teachers incorporate "cultural data sets" from students' everyday lives. She also instructs teachers to have their students bring favorite hip hop lyrics to class before they introduce the formal curriculum. In the classroom, students are prompted to engage in a group discussion about the lyrics and how they incorporate factors such as symbolism, irony, and character analysis. Teachers then make connections to the knowledge students already possess, with respect to standard literary genre analysis. This is accomplished by modeling the use of such analyses and then scaffolding for students to do likewise. Once this process is fully actualized, students are instructed to apply these analyses to the formal curriculum subject matter, such as *The Canterbury Tales* or *Macbeth*. Generally speaking, there were discernible improvements in students' classroom engagement, story comprehension, and quality of written assignments.

Implications of Culture in Academic Settings

We don't mean to imply that all schooling contexts need to be infused with cultural factors, as if those existing contexts are currently empty cultural vessels. This is far from the case. However, certain real-life experiences, fundamental themes, subjects, and genres have always been more greatly privileged in the academic settings of America's classrooms. Moreover, we're not suggesting that we need to replace individualism and competition, which have come to dominate the cultural landscapes of schools that serve a preponderance of Black children (Ellison, Boykin, Towns, & Stokes, 2000). Instead, the schools' cultural-themed contexts need to be diversified so that a fuller range is used. If teachers make explicit links between the material and performance strategies with popular culture data sets and conventional canons, and if they center the learning process more proactively on the diversity of students' experiences, then students can eventually become more adaptively flexible in the application of their talents, skills, and effort.

The implication, again, is not that we must only use communalism, popular culture, or specific neighborhood-based examples to help Black or other minority children to learn. If we pluralize the cultural conditions under which teaching and learning transpire, then we can maximize the possibility that a greater number of students—from a wider range of backgrounds— will be more fully engaged and responsive to the increasingly higher learning demands they will be expected to meet in the 21st century (Delpit, 1995; Hale, 2004).

Chapter Summary

Two intersubjectivity factors were presented in this chapter: meaning- ful learning and culture. Research shows that both have great promise for enhancing student engagement and gap-closing academic outcomes. With respect to meaningful learning, heightened results obtain when students' personal values and interests are taken into account and when their personal experiences are reflected in the curriculum. The positive effects of making learning relevant to students' own experiences and interests come from link- ing new material and skills to what students already know. Furthermore, when the personal interests and experiences are those of low-income Black and Latino students, they are less likely to be already included in the cur- riculum. Therefore, infusing such experiences very likely has gap-closing consequences.

Similar arguments can be made about cultural matters. Culture has been long advanced as an explanation for why gaps exist in the first place. Never- theless, when culture is viewed as a student asset, its infusion into teaching and learning contexts potentially has a positive impact on the academic per- formance of disenfranchised students of color. As implied in this summary and elsewhere in this book, matters of culture have had a controversial his- tory in accounting for academic outcomes. Because of this, great effort was taken to address the problems of cultural explanations and the ways these problems can be transcended. Although concerns for overgeneralizations, negative stereotypes, and essentialism (i.e., seeing culture as a fixed, even innate, attribute of an individual or group) are legitimate, there are ways to construe culture that also seek to avoid these legitimate worries.

A more proactive view of culture and cultural differences posits that behavior is overdetermined and thus may arise from a number of sources. Cultural variation should not be understood strictly in terms of race or ethnicity or in terms of unique expressions for a given identified group. However, certain behaviors, values, or expressions of interest may arise because they have been cultivated in the experiences to which a given person has been prominently exposed. This would happen by virtue of that person's participation in a given cultural community—a community of people who have emphasized these behaviors, values, and interests in the course of their daily lives, through intergenerational traditions, contact with significant cultural agents in the community, group identification or affiliation, or the society at large.

Culture also has multiple dimensions. For example, it can refer to adaptation to local circumstances (functional culture); to interests in certain popular culture forms, such as music or movies (expressive culture); or to certain foundational cultural themes (fundamental culture). By incorporating certain and diverse functional, expressive, or fundamental cultural inclinations of students into teaching and learning contexts—especially for those whose cultural inclinations have been traditionally ignored or underappreciated—we can build upon or create assets in the service of promoting increased achievement and gap-closing outcomes.

Asset-Focused Factors:
Information-Processing Quality

07

An essential aspect of learning and performance processes is the use of effective or adaptive mental operations to accomplish the (academic) task at hand. These operations can take many forms. They can entail

→ Memorizing and recalling factual information, deploying learned procedures, and identifying and recognizing known information.

→ Applying what is already known to understand new information, solve problems, discern the relationships between or among bodies of information, unpack or synthesize information, draw conclusions from evidence or arguments presented, and understand information in increasingly complex ways.

→ Generating new knowledge, applying knowledge gained outside the classroom, developing ways to represent knowledge, acquiring and using strategies for learning, critiquing and evaluating information, and extracting or applying abstract principles.

Higher- or deeper-level learning/performance operations build on more basic operations. Consequently, mastering basic operations is, to some degree, a prerequisite for mastering more complex operations, yet, in practice, basic and more "advanced" operations go hand in hand (National Mathematics Advisory Panel, 2008).

By common acceptance, cognitive scientists generally refer to such operations as forms of information processing. School learning and performance outcomes are certainly linked to the quality of information processing that takes place as students engage with subject matter. Moreover, information-processing quality can be seen in terms of both efficiency and effectiveness. Efficiency refers to accomplishing a task while not unnecessarily wasting time and effort. Effectiveness refers to producing the highest-quality result possible under the circumstances.

Another critical approach to closing achievement gaps is the promotion of acquisition and use of information-processing assets for students of color in academic settings. Fostering these assets requires educators to discern where they exist outside school and help students use them in formal academic settings. When such assets are not yet part of a student's repertoire, educators must directly provide for their acquisition and use both inside and outside school settings.

This chapter deals with what is currently known about efficient and effective forms of information processing and the results of efforts to promote such assets, particularly for minority students from low-income backgrounds.

Research on Cognitive Load and Working Memory

One of the challenges to information-processing efficiency is the natural limitation on how many discrete units of information a person can process or hold in his or her immediate or working memory at a given time. Recent research demonstrates that working memory prowess has a positive impact on academic performance. Welsh, Nix, Blair, Bierman, and Nelson (2010) show that growth in the emergent literacy skills of Black and Latino preschool children from low-income backgrounds is predicted by the extent of their working memory. Elsewhere, Lee, Ng, and Ng (2009) find that working memory prowess not only correlates with accuracy in algebra problem solving for 5th grade children in Singapore (from low- to medium-income backgrounds) but also significantly predicts students' skill with problem representation and constructing viable solution strategies, which are indicative of deep information processing.

There is a danger, though, that our ability to process information is subject to cognitive overload. This matter was first raised more than 50 years ago by George Miller (1956) in a seminal article entitled "The Magical Number Seven Plus or Minus Two." This article synthesized a great deal of data from a variety of existing research programs and concluded that humans are capable of holding between five and nine separate "bits" of information (e.g., numbers, letters, names) in their working memory at a time. Borrowing a term from communication systems theory, he asserted that we have a limited "channel capacity" when it comes to handling information. When we exceed this capacity, performance drops off markedly.

The work of Richard Mayer, among others, has concentrated attention on matters of cognitive load (DeLeeuw & Mayer, 2008; Kirschner, 2002; Mayer, 2004; Mayer, Griffith, Jurkowitz, & Rothman, 2008; Stull & Mayer, 2007). Mayer and his colleagues have posited that there are actually three dimensions to cognitive load: extraneous processing, essential processing, and generative processing. Extraneous processing does not support the task at hand; it does not focus on the learning goal. It is a distracter information source. Essential processing, as the term implies, has to do with the burden inherent in handling information that is essential for accomplishing a task or learning objective. Generative processing speaks to handling the deeper processing levels of material. Thus, it entails, among other things, elaboration or critical thinking about, cognitive restructuring of, and enrichment of the information presented.

In recent years, work has been done on the adverse impact of extraneous processing demands on performance outcomes, which dovetails with the earlier discussion in this book on intersubjectivity. Linnenbrink, Ryan, and Pintrich (1999), working with a sample of undergraduate students, found that when a student experiences negative affect, it adversely affects his or her working memory capacity. Feeling anxious or worrying about the task at hand competes with mental processing space and constricts the attention focused on that task. Attentional resources are compromised; the working memory does not operate at its natural optimum (but inherently limited) capacity. This can also happen when, while working on a task, one's mind is "clouded" with negative thoughts and internal speech about potential failure. Moreover, the same consequences would obtain when one is preoccupied with the physical symptoms of worry, such as accelerated heart rate, sweaty palms, and so on. These researchers found that mastery goals reduce negative affect, which leads to enhanced functioning of working memory. By contrast, performance goals lead to higher negative affect, which in turn leads to decreased functioning of working memory.

Extraneous factors can also come into play when irrelevant information is included in the information array, and this is particularly problematic when the student is not fully adept at separating irrelevant from relevant details and when extraneous information is presented in an interesting or otherwise attention-grabbing fashion (Stull & Mayer, 2007).

Cognitive load is also burdensome for essential processing reasons. Evidence indicates that this burden can be alleviated (and working memory capacity enhanced) when information is redundantly presented across different modalities (Kirschner, 2002)—for example, when information is presented via audio while it is simultaneously displayed on a screen in print. A more common approach to getting beyond cognitive load is through *automatic processing*. The limitations of processing capacity hold for the conscious or deliberate processing of information. Humans process information nonconsciously, and such nonconscious processing does not count against the cognitive load in one's limited mental processing space at a given time. Thus, it is to the advantage of the learner to handle as much basic information as possible through automatic processing. As used in the literature, automaticity refers to the processing of information with little or no mental effort or even full conscious awareness. Automaticity is fostered through repeated opportunities to master basic information. This could be by memorizing basic addition and multiplication facts—in other words, to automatically know (without having to go through the calculation steps) that $5 + 4 = 9$ or that $6 \times 3 = 18$. This can also apply to reading—for example, to facilitate fluency through repeated reading or rapidly decode words without thinking (Dowhower, 1994). In essence, automaticity enhances working memory prowess.

This process of unburdening cognitive load (practice that ultimately leads to automaticity) happens, for example, as we move from novice to skilled drivers. At first, we experience information overload as our channel capacity cannot cope with the multiple, simultaneous information demands at play. We must be cognizant of the speed of the car, the street signs, the traffic lights, other automobiles, steering, the dashboard gauges, and of what is happening in the rear-view mirror and the side-view mirror. Consciously processing all these information units is an overwhelming experience. Yet over time, more experienced drivers handle all of these demands with relative ease, as these information elements are essentially handled automatically—that is, without much conscious processing.

The classic work of Perfetti and Hogaboam (1975) was among the first studies to call attention to the importance of automatic processing. They demonstrated that, for elementary students, automatic decoding is essential for reading. Students who score high on standardized reading tests are faster at pronouncing words—or even pseudowords—than students who score low in reading comprehension. More recently, the work of Cumming and Elkins (1999) added insights on the role of automaticity in the handling of complex mathematics tasks. The sample in this study consisted of 3rd through 6th grade students from heterogeneous backgrounds. The study found that increasing automaticity aided performance on complex math tasks. Students with cognitive loads that were inefficient at processing basic math facts had poorer performance with the complex processing required for problem solving. Frequency of exposure to basic math facts led to increased automatic processing of them, which in turn led to better performance on math problem-solving tasks. Providing students with thinking strategies alone did not facilitate problem-solving performance, but increased automaticity plus the provision of thinking strategies resulted in better problem-solving outcomes.

Although automaticity does occur through repeated exposure to information and rote rehearsal of basic facts, this approach often is not the best way to produce the desired outcomes in more complex problem solving. This is because simply drilling students on multiplication tables (for example) can be dull and tedious and lead to a mechanical, meaningless, and insecure grasp of the information. Many have called for multiple practice opportunities that are situated in subject-matter lessons—practice opportunities that are organically linked or embedded in more substantive learning opportunities.

A case in point comes from the work of Siegler and colleagues (Laski & Siegler, 2007; Siegler & Booth, 2004; Siegler & Ramani, 2008). They found that preschoolers' grasp of the number line—a real or imagined horizontal line that is marked by equally spaced units—is an important ingredient for grasping the fundamentals of arithmetic in elementary school. Many preschool-aged children from low-income backgrounds, however, do not have a solid understanding of the number line. In other words, they have difficulty grasping the concept that if they start at 7 and move up two spaces along the line, then they arrive at 9, or if they start at 7 and move back 4 spaces, they arrive at 3.

Siegler and Ramani (2008) gave low-income children practice with numerical boards—where through spinning a wheel or tossing a pair of dice, they could move a token up or down a designated number of spaces—and found that this practice led to a firmer mastery of the number line, which in turn led to greater skill at number estimation. The initial gap in numerical estimation knowledge that existed between these children and more affluent children was effectively reduced. A more recent study by Ramani and Siegler (2011) further confirmed these findings using numerical board games and extended them to a wider range of math skills (including numerical identification and arithmetic learning).

Research on Text and Problem Structures

In the pursuit of more effective information processing, matters of structure are looming increasingly large as vehicles for gap-closing outcomes. The notion here is that focusing only (or initially) on what is the correct math operation or on word or sentence meanings may not be the ideal way to solve problems or gain an understanding of written text. Discerning the regularities, patterns, and typologies is a better strategy to accomplish the problem-solving or comprehension task at hand.

The term *schema-based instruction* has been used to describe this approach to performance facilitation. The reasoning is that discerning the crucial categories that problems or text elements fit into, and discerning the relationships among these elements, helps learners separate relevant from irrelevant information and use existing knowledge structures more effectively to guide current performance.

A recent representative example of schema-based instruction (and learning) is provided by Jitendra and colleagues (Jitendra et al., 2007). They contrast the more conventional pedagogy of general strategy instruction with schema-based instruction for solving mathematics word problems. To be sure, general strategy instruction is seen as an improvement over the more common and orthodox approach to math instruction where teachers take students through the appropriate math operations and then leave students to independently apply this procedural knowledge in an attempt to solve new word problems. In the case of general strategy instruction, the aim is to get children to follow a general regimen for problem solving. In the study cited above, teachers taught students to use a four-step solution method: reading for understanding, planning a solution strategy, executing that strategy, and checking the answer.

For schema-based instruction, the core skill is the ability to pay attention to key semantic information that cues students into the appropriate category a given problem will typically fall into. This helps students make sense of what the problem is asking them to do. There is a limited number of categories for general classes of problems. For example, with addition and subtraction problems (at the early elementary level), problems are highly likely to fall into one of four categories: change, combine (or group), compare, or equalize. Examples of each are included below:

→ **Change:** Andy has five marbles. He gives three marbles to Nick. How many marbles does Andy have now?

→ **Combine/Group:** Andy has two marbles. Nick has three marbles. How many marbles do they have all together?

→ **Compare:** Nick has five marbles. Andy has two marbles. How many more marbles does Nick have?

→ **Equalize:** Nick has five marbles. Andy has two marbles. How many marbles does Andy have to buy to have as many marbles as Nick?

For schema-based instruction, Jitendra and colleagues had the students follow a different four-step solution strategy: determine the problem type, organize the problem information using a diagram, develop a plan for solution, and solve the problem.

In this investigation (Jitendra et al., 2007), students took part in either a general strategy instruction or a schema-based instruction condition, and problems fell into the change, group, and compare categories only. Students were all 3rd graders who attended a public school that was among the lowest achieving in the entire district. This school was also marked by a large population of students from low-income backgrounds. Half of the students were White, and half were Black or Latino.

Students worked on the normal math curriculum lessons five days a week for seven weeks. Classrooms were randomly assigned to either the schema-based or the general strategy instruction treatment conditions. It was found that students in the schema-based condition significantly outperformed their counterparts in the other condition on a follow-up test that involved math word problems, even though the pretest performance levels for the two groups were equivalent. A maintenance test was administered six weeks after the end of the intervention, and the performance difference was maintained and even became larger. By contrast, students in both conditions improved significantly from pretest to posttest performance in their math computation skills, but the improvement levels were essentially the same. It was also found that students in the schema-based instruction condition substantially outperformed their counterparts on the statewide math assessment test administered that year. Still further, the results indicated that on both the problem-solving test and the statewide math assessment, the differences in performance between the two conditions were greatest for students who initially were the lowest performing. It was also reported that only 2 of the 45 students who participated in the schema-based instruction performed below basic on the statewide math assessment.

Another relevant study was conducted by Williams and colleagues (2005). One notable feature of this study was that it deployed successful comprehension instruction for 2nd grade ethnic minority children from urban environments. Previously, little attention had been given to such pedagogy. What attention had been given focused on narrative text. This study, by contrast, focused on expository text. Given the common claim that children *learn to read* up to the 3rd grade and *read to learn* from the 4th grade on (implying that comprehension becomes a primary focus of instruction during 4th grade) (e.g., Willms, 2006), if comprehension instruction for low-income ethnic minority children can be successfully accomplished before 4th grade, then they will have an advantage in surmounting the so-called 4th grade reading achievement slump.

A focus on early expository reading has its challenges. Narrative texts for young readers can be very linear in structure and concrete in nature. It is difficult to produce expository texts that are similarly structured. As Williams and her colleagues point out, such text often is abstract and includes multifaceted interconnections of ideas. Consequently, they reason that successful comprehension instruction requires practice at discerning the vicissitudes of text structure. The authors identify five major types of expository text structures: description, sequence, compare–contrast, problem–solution, and cause–effect. Indeed, noncontrived expository texts often embody combinations of these structural types. Of these five types, compare–contrast is among the most difficult to grasp. Consequently, Williams and colleagues chose to discern if 2nd grade children could use compare–contrast texts (text structure instruction) to increase their comprehension skills. They didn't choose random 2nd graders, but, rather, they chose those who were most at risk for reading comprehension failure.

Of the children included in this study, 57 percent were Latino and 41 percent were African American. Close to 90 percent of these children were enrolled in the school's free and reduced-price lunch program. Children participated in one of three conditions: a compare–contrast instruction group, a comprehension-instruction group that did not focus on text structure, and a no-treatment control group where children received a normal regimen of reading instruction. Instruction was all carried out by the children's regular classroom teachers. The text passages all required comparing and contrasting features of various pairs of animals. An example of such a paragraph is as follows:

> Frogs and crocodiles are alike: they are cold-blooded. Frogs can jump very far, and they have long sticky tongues. Frogs have smooth skin, but crocodiles have scales. Crocodiles use their sharp teeth to protect themselves. Crocodiles get oxygen from the air. They can't breathe under water. However, frogs get oxygen to breathe from the air and the water.

The ultimate content goal was to classify animals with respect to key categories, such as skin type, oxygen acquisition, and body temperature type (warm- or cold-blooded). There were a total of 15 instructional sessions, and they were conducted at the approximate rate of two per week. For both treatment conditions, a graphic organizer was used to aid comprehension. For the compare–contrast instruction group, the learning aid accentuated comparisons and contrasts. For the comprehension-instruction group, the learning aid helped students organize the information in the text along topical lines. No performance benefits accrued for the no-treatment control group.

Subsequent comprehension tests revealed that students in the compare–contrast instruction group outperformed their counterparts in the comprehension-instruction and no-treatment groups. In fact, there generally was no difference in performance between students in the latter two groups, with respect to posttest comprehension levels. More specifically, students in the compare–contrast group demonstrated superior abilities to summarize information from the teaching sessions. They were also superior in terms of comparing and contrasting features of two animals that had not been paired together during instruction and knowing text content unrelated to animal comparative information (e.g., that frogs have long, sticky tongues).

Finally, there was no difference in vocabulary knowledge between the two treatment groups, but children in both conditions performed better than those in the no-treatment control group. This finding suggests that focusing so heavily on comparative information did not sacrifice students' ability to grasp general content information from the text. Two more recent studies by Williams and her colleagues replicated and extended these basic findings on the benefits of text-structure (compare–contrast) instruction (Williams, Brooke-Stafford, Lauer, Hall, & Pollini, 2009; Williams et al., 2007). The 2007 study extended the findings to a cause–effect text structure. The 2009 study was able to extend the previous findings to a transfer task that contained a text structure unrelated to cause–effect.

In a study by Rubman and Waters (2000), conditions were created to better capture actual classroom learning and discern how representations might play a role in performance outcomes. This study also spoke more directly to matters of the achievement gap. In this study, 3rd and 6th graders classified as "skilled" or "less skilled" readers were evenly divided into two conditions. Half of the students read a story only, and half constructed storyboard representations using cutout figures. (This was done in light of the fact that very young children are not adept at monitoring their own reading comprehension.) It was found that the storyboards strengthened students' understanding of the overall text and of inconsistencies in the stories. This was particularly the case for less skilled readers.

Moreover, the most information-rich stories were also more greatly recalled by students in the storyboard condition. The storyboard process increased students' encoding and memory skills and helped them comprehend the story as a whole, rather than as a set of disconnected ideas and passages. Somewhat more specifically, skilled and unskilled 3rd grade readers performed equally well in the storyboard condition, but this was not the case in the read-only condition where skilled readers outperformed their low-skilled peers. As an example, for students detecting inconsistencies in the storyboard condition, there was a 41 percent increase over baseline in the performance of low-skilled 3rd graders, a 29 percent increase for low-skilled 6th graders, and 21 percent increases for high-skilled 3rd and 6th graders.

At the other end of the age spectrum, a study by Faggella-Luby, Schumaker, and Deshler (2007) demonstrated the superiority of text-structure instruction for secondary students. This study underscored the importance of providing explicit comprehension instruction even in subject-matter courses at the secondary level. In the case of this study, a literature course was targeted, and thus the texts were narrative rather than expository. Narrative text structures typically take different forms, including character(s), precipitating events, goals, conflicts, and resolutions.

This investigation studied 79 9th grade students who were labeled as "at risk," which indicated that these students had performed poorly on the previous year's state achievement tests. Teachers used an embedded story-structure routine to foster story comprehension. There were three phases to this instructional routine: self-questioning, story structure analysis, and summary writing. During self-questioning, queries such as *Who? What?* and *Where?* were posed and addressed relative to structural elements of the story. Story structure analysis consisted of students' filling in a story-structure diagram where they tied story information to its appropriate structural element. Summary writing required students, after reading the story, to summarize it using the structural elements as a framework.

Students were randomly assigned to an embedded story-structure condition or to a comprehension skills condition. For the latter context, focus was on getting students to use three research-based strategies to aid text understanding: one was designed to foster vocabulary knowledge, one guided students to ask and answer questions concerning the information contained or implied in the story text, and one required students to map self-identified critical components in the story and draw relationships among these components.

Daily instruction in both conditions lasted for nine days, and each session lasted either 90 or 120 minutes. There was no difference in story comprehension levels among students in the two conditions on a pretest administered prior to the interventions. Both the embedded story-structure and comprehension skills interventions led to substantially increased comprehension on the follow-up unit comprehension test. However, the improvement was greater for students in the embedded story-structure group.

Other studies have produced comparable results. For example, Low, Over, Doolan, and Michell (1994) determined that students can be taught to use schemas as they solve algebraic word problems. They trained 11th graders to identify whether text information was irrelevant, relevant but not sufficient, or relevant and sufficient for problem solution. Students in this condition outperformed those who received no training or when practice was focused on computation and calculation. Elsewhere, Cook and Mayer (1988) taught college undergraduates how to outline textbook paragraphs linked to how the texts were structured. Learning that the material is organized by categories or in a hierarchy, that there is a sequential structure akin to a flow chart, or that comparisons and contrasts are relevant led to increased understanding and recall of scientific text material.

Research on Effective Strategies and Skills

Another highly promising arena within the information-processing domain concerns prompting or directly teaching students to use critical-thinking, problem-solving, or learning strategies to promote enhanced academic outcomes. The line of reasoning here is that such strategies are crucial and valuable yet are not ones that students—especially low-income ethnic minority students—typically use in formal learning settings. These students may actually be using such strategies in informal settings outside school, but the links or routes to their usage in school have not been established, and most students fail to recognize that these tactics are already in their learning arsenal. Moreover, the direct teaching of and regular practice with such strategies is rarely if ever done (Connor, Morrison, & Petrella, 2004). This state of pedagogical affairs, given the evidence to be presented in this section, needs to be rectified.

Adaptive learning strategies have their impact in large measure because they lead to deeper processing of the subject matter. They take students beyond rote memorization of facts, beyond knowing the "right" answer, and beyond mastering what is literally on the printed page. It helps students recognize what they should actually do with the facts, why the right answer is correct, and what can be inferred from information on the printed page.

The benefit of such an instructional approach can be gleaned from a recent investigation by Crosnoe and colleagues (2010). They found that in classrooms that promote inference-based learning techniques (i.e., activities that require students to reason, solve problems, create, evaluate, or engage in deductive reasoning), low-math-achieving students (the majority of whom were ethnic minority) improved their math achievement outcomes more steeply from 3rd to 5th grade than did average and high-achieving students (who were predominantly White). However, this gap-closing result occurred only when these classrooms also fostered teacher–student relationship quality, and it did not occur in classrooms that primarily manifested "basic skills" instruction (i.e., activities that require students to come up with *yes* or *no* responses or responses that are either correct or incorrect).

Deep processing implies

→ Restructuring material into a more incisive knowledge representation.
→ Incorporating information into a higher-order knowledge structure.
→ Breaking information down into smaller units.

One of the more actively researched areas for deep processing is referred to as cognitive elaboration. Here, the focus is on going beyond *yes/no* or *true/false* answers, beyond bubbling in multiple-choice responses, and beyond providing simple dates and names as answers. Instead, the focus is on enabling students to justify their answers, to provide more thoughtful and reflective answers, and to recognize their role as knowledge producers (and not simply knowledge consumers).

One of the defining studies of cognitive elaboration was done by Rickards and Hatcher (1977). They first administered a reading diagnostic test to a sample of White, middle-class 5th graders. Based on the results, a subset of students was classified as either "good" or "poor" at reading comprehension, and these students were chosen to take part in the project. Students read an 800-word passage, and after every two paragraphs, they were asked a question that required rote recall of information from the passage, or they were asked a question that required placing factual information into conceptual categories, or they received no question at all.

"Good comprehenders" were consistently superior at recalling central information. However, "poor comprehenders" recalled more information when they were prompted by questions that required greater elaboration than mere rote memorization. Furthermore, when they were asked about ancillary, more nuanced passage information with questions that prompted for elaboration, poor comprehenders performed as well as good comprehenders, regardless of which condition the good comprehenders had been in.

Pressley and colleagues (Pressley et al., 1992) conducted an extensive review of the research literature through the 1980s and concluded that posing questions does not yield beneficial academic results by itself. The questions must lead to deep processing—to reflective, inferential, and comparative processing of information. Moreover, this cannot be a passive learning process. When a question is posed, if students receive the answer from teachers or other students, then achievement is negatively affected. On the other hand, in response to questions, when students provide self-generated explanations to others, achievement is positively affected.

Why is this the case? Pressley and colleagues reason that students who explain their rationale have to clarify, organize, and transform the material. In doing so, they are more likely to discern gaps in their own knowledge and pursue routes to eliminate those gaps. When the receiver of this information doesn't grasp the explanation, students must work even harder to represent the information adequately, which generally leads to new or better examples. This line of reasoning sheds light on the findings that, in cooperative pairs, students who explain learn more than those who just listen and check for errors (Dansereau, 1988) and that tutors learn more than tutees (Allen, 1976). Having to justify or elaborate one's answers clearly has beneficial academic effects.

King (1991, 1992, 1998) has been influential in the domain of cognitive elaboration. Her work verifies that comprehension and recall are more pronounced when students are required to elaborate on material, which typically entails adding details, clarifying an idea, applying an analogy, and so on. Moreover, King's research concurs that self-elaborations are more beneficial than those that originate with the teacher or textbook. King has proposed the notion of a guided student-generated questioning strategy, which has proven effective across the age span. Students are provided with a set of generic question stems that are independent of subject-matter content. Examples of such stems are as follows:

What is another example of ...?

What would happen if ...?

What are the strengths and weaknesses of ...?

What is the difference between ... and ...?

Do you agree or disagree with ...? Support your answer with evidence. (King, 1992, p. 113)

Students are then taught how to apply these questions to the lesson at hand. King proposed a specific learning structure to direct the guided questioning strategy—students pose questions independently and then pair up and alternate asking and answering questions with a partner. Students are induced to go beyond rote memorization. This strategy leads to higher-quality representation of the relevant material, to deeper understanding, and of course to greater pathways for recall of information. It has been deployed successfully with a variety of learning formats, including lecture presentation; peer-guided, individual-guided, and unguided small-group discussions; and unguided independent review. Across the various usages of the technique, results have consistently shown that it leads to better recall and comprehension.

It should be noted that, typically, students do not spontaneously ask one another or themselves questions. Moreover, when groups are prompted to ask questions that are not encased in the guided questioning process, they tend to ask recall rather than "critical thinking" questions. Matters of autonomy are at play here. The technique leads to student ownership of questions and answers—in other words, students own their own learning process. Efficiency in learning also comes into play. Students are actually in a better position than their teachers to recognize their own knowledge gaps. Nevertheless, they have to gain experience at "tuning in" to such gaps (relative to their prior knowledge) and being prepared to acknowledge that these gaps exist in the first place. Related to the direct teaching of generic questioning and explanation skills is the direct teaching of specific academic skills or learning strategies that are often indexes of academic performance. Examples include explicitly teaching comprehension skills, vocabulary skills, or strategies for making inferences. Unfortunately, there has been a paucity of such efforts in the field at large, especially for young children.

As a case in point, Hamman, Berthelot, Saia, and Crowley (2000) conducted an extensive observational study on the extent of various instructional approaches found in middle school classrooms. They observed teachers' instructional techniques and classified them according to four types: quizzing, coaching, interacting, and directing. *Coaching* is the term they use to capture strategy instruction, *quizzing* is about asking students questions, *interacting* is about having a positive interaction focus, and *directing* entails a standard teacher-control focus (i.e., lecturing and providing task-related information).

The findings revealed the incidence of directing, interacting, quizzing, and coaching was 60, 36, 22, and 9 percent, respectively (there was some overlap in cataloging the categories). Even when coaching occurred, it took the form of telling students about the cognitive processes they would go through while accomplishing a task. For example: "I'm going to describe for you how I figured out the perimeter when that little corner is missing. I'll show you how to figure out the answer using other information sources since the specific information is not presented." Rarely was it manifested as actually explaining the processes involved or having students practice the strategies the teacher presented. Somewhat more recently, Parker and Hurry (2007) deployed similar methods and documented a similar trend at the elementary level. They found that quizzing and directing were most often observed. In the infrequent occurrences when coaching was attempted, it took the form of teacher-modeled strategies employed by (for example) skilled readers. On the whole, teachers did not make these strategies explicit or have students engage in substantive strategy practice.

In recent years, however, work has been done that highlights the effectiveness of explicitly teaching students how to execute cognitive learning strategies. One noteworthy example is the work of Connor, Morrison, and Petrella (2004), who point out that approximately one-third of U.S. students fail to read proficiently by the 4th grade. They argue that this can be rectified to a large degree if we explicitly teach young children strategies for effective comprehension. They cite a previous study by Connor, Morrison, and Katch (2004), which showed that 1st grade children who began the year with low decoding skills showed improvement when teachers provided them with explicit decoding instruction (e.g., to heighten phonological awareness). This is significantly more effective than activities such as sustained silent reading. The most effective sequence is to begin with teacher-directed instruction early in the school year and gradually relinquish responsibility for learning to students. Connor, Morrison, and Petrella (2004) followed up with the same cohort of students, who were now in the 3rd grade.

For this study, there were 73 3rd graders, and 25 percent of the sample was Black. Black students in this study generally had lower word recognition, vocabulary, and reading comprehension scores than their White counterparts. Overall, it was generally observed that instruction for this cohort tended to be child managed.

Indeed, fewer than 20 minutes per day, on average, were devoted to explicit, teacher-managed instruction. Of that, less than one minute was devoted to explicit teaching of comprehension strategies. It was also found that when child-managed instruction was enacted, there was less growth in reading comprehension. However, students who started out as good readers actually showed a slight growth in reading comprehension in predominantly child-managed classrooms. Moreover, explicit, teacher-managed reading strategy instruction was particularly beneficial for poor readers.

Another study of note was conducted by Biemiller and Boote (2006). Their study stands out because it is one of the very few that systematically tackled the direct teaching of vocabulary skills to young children. As the researchers point out, vocabulary knowledge—that is, word meaning knowledge—is distinct from comprehension, yet vocabulary skill is a strong predictor of reading comprehension. Clearly, it is very difficult to comprehend text if you don't know the meaning of the words in the text, but early primary grades in the United States include virtually no vocabulary instruction. The presumption is that word-decoding proficiency should precede vocabulary learning.

Biemiller and Boote also note that the absence of vocabulary pedagogy is particularly problematic for low-income ethnic minority students. Unfortunately, few guidelines exist for what constitutes effective vocabulary instruction. Even the esteemed National Reading Panel Report (National Institute of Child Health and Human Development, 2000) concluded that, as of its writing, there was little or no systematic evidence for what good vocabulary instruction should be.

Biemiller and Boote point out that children with limited vocabularies in the 3rd grade are highly vulnerable to long-term problems with reading comprehension. Unfortunately, if increasing vocabulary size does not become a priority in classrooms that serve low-income children of color, then such growth will be determined by out-of-school experiences, which are likely to privilege children from more affluent backgrounds. Moreover, Biemiller and Boote note that during the elementary school years, the average child adds a minimum of 840 root word meanings per year. Yet students in the lowest quartile in reading achievement add only approximately 570 words per year. Thus, the gap widens over time, affecting comprehension and, down the line, the learning of content-based material in secondary schools.

Just like the learning of many other academic skills, vocabulary instruction would seem to be best accomplished in specific, concrete task contexts, rather than by giving children word definitions to memorize. On the contrary, Biemiller and Boote posit that effective vocabulary instruction should involve syntactic cues, given in the context of interesting narratives and with brief verbal explanations linked to those narratives. The best approach is, therefore, an instructional intervention that combines repeated reading of interesting text with the interspersal of direct explanations, followed by students subsequently encountering these words in other contexts. When repeated readings are linked to word meaning explanations, reading comprehension gaps are effectively closed among students from preschool through 4th grade.

For their own work, they studied a sample of students in kindergarten, 1st, and 2nd grade. Students were described as coming from working-class backgrounds, and approximately 50 percent were English language learners.

In one study, the methodology called for the manipulation of two key factors: number of repeated readings of the target text (two versus four) and whether word meaning instruction was provided or not. All books were age-appropriate narrative fiction. Word meaning instruction in this study was essentially "stop and tell" the meaning of a given word. The vocabulary sessions were all conducted by the regular classroom teachers who worked with the whole class. Comprehension was not measured in this study—only word meanings. It was found that repeated reading alone led to a 12 percent gain over baseline in word knowledge, whereas a 22 percent gain was obtained when repeated reading was augmented with word meaning instruction. In this study, children received either two or four trials of repeated reading. The increase in repeated readings was only beneficial overall for kindergarten students, and it was beneficial for 1st graders in the noninstruction condition only.

In a second study, certain modifications to the study design were made. All interventions were done with four repeated readings. Students were taught approximately 60 percent more words in each session. Word meaning review sessions were also interspersed. A transfer test was added to discern word meaning knowledge in a new verbal context (i.e., a new text with the same words). There was also a six-week delayed test of word meanings. In this study, with the improved teaching regimen, a 41 percent increase in word knowledge was obtained. Also, delayed recall was at least as good as immediate recall. Moreover, the enhanced effect extended to the transfer test as well.

In a related vein, research during the last two decades has shown that direct instruction for making inferences can be beneficial for facilitating reading comprehension, particularly for young and struggling readers. Inferences with respect to reading have to do with drawing conclusions about events in text that are not explicitly described. Children routinely draw inferences in their everyday experiences outside school; they fill in gaps in information about events where such information is not literally present. However, no effort is made in school to explicitly induce learners to use such skills in the context of formal classroom reading exercises.

In one telling study, Hansen (1981) provided practice with two different ways of making inferences to a group of "average" 2nd grade students from diverse socioeconomic backgrounds. Across a five-week period, students either practiced making inferences about assigned text passages or received a five-week prereading regimen of inferential thinking strategy training. This training consisted of several segments in which students

1. Discussed questions that drew on their own prior experiences, which were pertinent to the impending story.
2. Answered those questions.
3. Discussed what story characters might do in similar settings.
4. Offered their own hypotheses of what might happen.
5. Repeated steps 1–4.
6. Discussed the advantage of this approach to reading.

It was found that all students (regardless of the preparatory instruction they had received) demonstrated equal growth of inferential reading comprehension skills. Intriguingly, all students also showed increased literal comprehension.

These findings prompted Hansen to pursue a follow-up investigation (Hansen & Pearson, 1983), which sought to extend the previous investigation in three notable ways. First, it combined prereading thinking strategy training and practice with inference questions that were tied to the text. Second, classroom teachers deployed this method over a five-week period during regular reading instruction. Third, the study focused on 4th grade students from diverse socioeconomic backgrounds who were either "good" or "poor" readers. (Poor readers were defined as students who were one year below grade level in their reading achievement scores.) This was contrasted with a control condition where teachers followed the instructions in the basal reading program's teacher manual.

It was found that inference comprehension levels for poor readers were substantially better when they received inference training. (These students scored 50 percent higher than poor readers in the control condition.) Among good readers, there was no difference in their inference comprehension as a function of the two conditions. To underscore these findings, the performance of good readers was twice the level achieved by poor readers in the control condition. Thus, the comprehension gap between good and poor readers was cut in half in the training condition, relative to the control condition.

A similar pattern of findings was obtained by Oakhill and Yuill (1996). Here, elementary students received seven 30-minute training sessions in inference making, and they were given experience at generating questions that could be answered based on text information. Poor readers improved their comprehension levels with this intervention, whereas good readers did not. In a study by Winne, Graham, and Prock (1993), 24 low-achieving 3rd through 5th graders were given nine training sessions where they answered an inference question about a passage and five additional questions that related to other informational aspects of the passage. These other aspects related to factors such as problem statement, spurious but seemingly relevant information, and irrelevant descriptive details. There were two conditions for training. In one condition, the six questions were posed, and feedback was given about the correct answers to these questions. Students had to independently determine which processes were involved. In the other condition, students were given explicit feedback that explained the relevant processes and critical facts for gathering information about the problem. Both conditions improved comprehension, but the feedback condition proved to be more effective.

Chapter Summary

This chapter dealt with matters of information-processing quality. As such, it identified research on aspects of cognitive functioning (e.g., memory, problem solving, and thinking and learning processes) that, when enriched or made more explicit for students, can lead to more learning involvement and enhanced gap-closing outcomes.

Reducing the load placed on students' working memory, by providing multiple practice activities, can produce achievement benefits. Essentially, the more students can process information automatically (rather than deliberately or consciously), the more efficiently they can learn, because they can handle or address more overall information at a given time. In addition, information can be more effectively processed when students are taught to discern patterns or regularities in the problems or texts they are expected to master. This has been referred to as schema-based instruction. When students become more adept at discerning such schemas, long-term educational advantages can be accrued, and they can even transcend the academic year in which students first acquired the relevant skill. These benefits are found for Black and Latino students from 2nd grade through high school.

Moreover, directly teaching critical-thinking, problem-solving, and learning strategies has achievement-boosting effects, as does encouraging students to elaborate on their answers and responses. Such approaches to teaching and learning help students process information on a deeper level; students are more prepared to deal with learning tasks with more mental effort and in less shallow ways. As such, students are able to move beyond the literal information and infer or extrapolate other pertinent information. Unfortunately, as is the case with other effective gap-closing approaches, direct strategic or elaboration-prompting teaching is conspicuous by its absence in our nation's schools—particularly in formal classroom settings that serve low-income Black and Latino students.

Part II Summary

In the previous chapters, we made the case that to proactively and successfully address the achievement gap, we must realize the attendant complexity and bring systematic, empirical evidence to bear in order to chart paths toward solutions. The achievement gap can be indexed in several ways, and, indeed, it is underscored by several other gaps as well. These include disparities dealing with attainment, opportunity, and preparation, among others.

The achievement gap itself is at least three-dimensional. There is the gap among certain ethnic minority groups and their White counterparts. There is the gap between U.S. students and their counterparts in certain Asian and European countries. There is also the looming gap between the knowledge and skills that students currently possess and what they will require for the future. This multidimensional achievement gap challenge may seem daunting, but the research and evidence presented in Part II of this book provides a path for success in meeting present and future demands.

Key to this success is a focus on the promotion and enhancement of student engagement. Evidence seems to confirm that increases in academic learning and achievement are very likely to be preceded by the promotion and sustained enhancement of student engagement. Moreover, certain adaptive learning orientations (or guiding functions) and certain classroom dynamics (or asset-focused factors) are particularly instrumental in promoting or directing the requisite levels of engagement that lead to the desired outcomes. When we refer to assets, the notion is to depart from the conventional preoccupation with minority students' deficits and deficiencies and instead concentrate on the personal, social, cultural, experiential, and intellectual capital that students from diverse backgrounds bring with them into their classrooms. We also need to provide conditions that allow these assets to flourish; when such assets are not readily apparent, we must create them in the course of teaching and learning activities.

Prominent among the guiding functions are self-efficacy, self-regulated learning, and incremental beliefs about intelligence or ability. Among the classroom dynamics are positive teacher–student relationship quality, collaborative learning, mastery classroom goal structures, meaningful learning, cultural significance, and a host of information-processing elements such as automaticity, cognitive elaboration, and strategic and schema-based teaching and learning. Moreover, it would seem to follow that to actualize these asset-focused factors and guiding functions in the service of enhanced three-dimensional engagement requires a departure from the "business as usual" forms of classroom teaching and learning.

According to the evidence reviewed in this volume, in order to close the achievement gap, attention needs to be given to transactional approaches to teaching and learning. Transactional approaches focus on optimizing learning exchanges that occur inside classrooms (and perhaps other learning settings as well) on an ongoing and daily basis, between teachers and students and among students themselves. Capturing the texture and contours of classroom transactions is not necessarily straightforward. Such exchanges do not lend themselves to straightforward oversight or accountability. The manifestations of transactions that maximize learning opportunities may not be obvious to the uninitiated eye. They may be more nuanced, multifaceted, and fluctuating, rather than straightforwardly apparent and static. Indeed, transactional classroom functioning requires changes in what classroom activities look like, and in what teachers and students talk about, think about, act on, and believe in. This is tantamount to changing what Tyack and Tobin (1994) refer to as the very "grammar" of teaching and learning.

Although enhancing what happens inside classrooms may be essential to closing achievement gaps, this is certainly not the entire story. Indeed, multiple pathways to success are necessary, and multiple layers of the schooling enterprise must be taken into consideration. Beyond the classroom, we must attend to the school at large, along with other school-based stakeholders such as school leaders and educational specialists (e.g., counselors). We must examine factors that pertain to families and the surrounding community. We must address district, state, and federal levels of analysis as well. We will focus more on these considerations in Part III.

PART III

Applying
What We Know

As we mentioned in Chapter 1, the release of the most recent NAEP scores serve as a pointed reminder that the United States still has a long way to go in its efforts to close the achievement gap. There is some variation among the states with respect to how their schools and students have performed. In states such as New York, Maryland, Massachusetts, and Georgia, minority students have made significant gains in literacy and math. However, in other states, such as Nebraska, Wisconsin, and Minnesota, the gap has widened even further (Dillon, 2009).

Understanding why some states, districts, and schools are making progress while others are not is critical to understanding what it will take for the nation as a whole to move forward in educating all children. We will discuss some of these lessons in the final chapters of this book.

Though not all policymakers agree, what has become increasingly clear is that doing more of what hasn't worked over the last eight years is unlikely to produce a different set of results. As we previously pointed out, the enactment of No Child Left Behind in 2001 succeeded in focusing the attention of the nation's schools on the need to close the achievement gap. NCLB held schools accountable for student outcomes on the basis of clear academic standards (adopted by the states) through annual assessments administered in the 3rd–8th grades. As a result, greater attention was focused on whether all students were learning in schools throughout the United States. Some states went further and extended testing to lower grades and adopted graduation exit exams that are designed to ensure minimal competency for all high school graduates. These steps have been important for creating a context in which schools can be held accountable for academic outcomes and for raising awareness about the importance of ensuring that all students are learning. However, the measures required by NCLB have not been sufficient to produce real evidence that higher test scores actually mean that student ability has improved. Indeed, there is growing evidence that large numbers of high school students who have passed state exit exams are not prepared for college and, as a result, have been forced to take remedial courses in English and math. A recent national study on state exit exams reveals that several states have actually lowered their academic standards in order to increase the number of students who can pass the tests (Urbina, 2010).

Requiring public reports of test score results by race, NCLB has exposed the lack of focus on educational equity, even though the law does nothing to help schools or districts address the problem. Despite the fact that NCLB was frequently portrayed as a means to ensure that the most impoverished children would be better served by our nation's schools, the law has not led to significant improvements in schools where poor and disadvantaged children are concentrated (with the exception of a few schools and districts).

Results such as these make it hard for even the most ardent proponents of NCLB to claim that the law has achieved its goals or that continued reliance on the strategies it promotes will eventually lead to better results. In most schools that cater to poor children, achievement by any measure is still consistently low, and in many of our largest cities, the majority of schools are still not meeting the educational needs of the children they serve. In May 2010, the National Center for Education Statistics reported that among the nation's high-poverty schools, the average high school graduation rate fell from 86 percent in 2000 to 68 percent in 2008, whereas the rate in low-poverty schools remained about 91 percent. In most major cities across the country, middle-class families refuse to enroll their children in public schools, and dropout rates still hover around 50 percent (and in some cities are even higher) (Bridgeland, DiIulio, & Morison, 2006)—this is the clearest evidence that we, as a nation, are still relegating too many students to an inferior education.

Since its inception, a number of NCLB's critics have claimed that the law was flawed because it was not designed to address the conditions under which children learn. Our research and experience with schools across the country, including those that have made the greatest progress, have led us to believe that this crucial aspect of educational reform must be addressed if sustainable gains in learning are to be made. Put most simply, if we want to bring about significant improvements in learning outcomes for students, we have to do more to address the context in which learning takes place.

This means we must address the learning environment in classrooms and schools; the skills of teachers and the quality of instruction they provide; the specific learning and support strategies that are employed; and the support systems that are put in place outside the classroom, including tutors, mentors, social workers, professional interventions, and a variety of health-related interventions. It also means we must extend learning opportunities for children by expanding access to high-quality after-school and summer programs. At the district level, it means targeting support to "high-need schools" rather than merely labeling them as failing. It means providing clear feedback to principals and teachers about what they can do to improve and providing support to address student needs if they lack the resources. It means coordinating services with nonprofits and other public agencies to help schools respond to the safety, health, and nutritional needs of students. At the state and federal levels, it means adopting policies that make it easier for schools to do their jobs by ensuring universal access to preschool and health care for all children and adopting incentives for highly skilled personnel to be recruited to work within schools that have traditionally struggled to attract talent.

In the final chapters of this book, we provide some detail on the policies that are needed at the local, state, and federal levels to bring effective practices to scale at a wider level and make sustainable reform possible. We want to make it clear that it is possible to make greater progress in closing the achievement gap by abandoning failed strategies, learning from successful schools, and simply doing more of what the research shows is most effective. As reasonable as such an approach might seem, we must be clear that doing what it takes to educate all children will also require considerable political will. Our nation has grown accustomed to the idea that certain schools, especially those that serve poor children of color, are more likely to fail. A lack of urgency to address this issue also suggests that we have come to accept the achievement gap as an unalterable aspect of the American social fabric. We are not so naive as to believe that generating the public will to challenge both sets of beliefs will be easy, but we have good reason to believe that it can be done.

We also want to be explicit in advocating for strategies that contribute to success, because we know there are many educators who are seeking guidance and who genuinely want to create schools where all children are learning—schools where a child's race or class is no longer a predictor for how well he or she might perform. By identifying strategies that have proven successful in closing the gap, we are in a better position to keep all stakeholders accountable for what they do to support learning for all students. Accountability is essential, but only if we have done what it takes to provide educators, students, and parents with the support they need to succeed. Such an approach makes far more sense than holding students and schools accountable by simply issuing reports about their progress (or lack thereof) as we do now in states across the country. Labeling a school as failing or denying students a high school diploma when we know that we have not done the work necessary to help them improve is neither fair nor effective (Haney, 2004). It takes more than pressure or humiliation to improve failing schools. We know that children have no ability to control important aspects of their education (e.g., teacher quality), and we know that many underresourced schools simply lack the capacity to meet the needs of the students they serve. For the first time in our nation's history, we must begin to hold all parties—educators, government, churches, businesses, and families—accountable for the education and well-being of our children.

Why Are Some Schools Making More Progress Than Others?

08

For educators trying to gain traction in their efforts to close the achievement gap, it is important to note that the obstacles they are likely to encounter in high-poverty urban and rural districts will be very different from those in more affluent suburban districts. Generally, the primary challenges confronting districts that serve large numbers of poor children relate to capacity. Are the resources, personnel, and support systems available to provide students with high-quality instruction and create learning environments that foster higher levels of achievement? Do they have the ability to address the basic needs of children—health, housing, and nutrition—that many of their students lack and that invariably have an impact on learning? Can the large, highly politicized urban districts maintain the stability in leadership to follow through on reforms, implement strategies with fidelity and quality control, and attract and sustain the community support that is vital to long-term progress?

The efforts undertaken by Principal Beth Thomas at Kingsview Middle School in Montgomery County, Maryland, exemplify the types of measures employed by schools that are making significant progress in closing the achievement gap. After developing a broad and bold vision for her school, Thomas went a step further—she worked with her staff to identify concrete steps to bring the school's vision to reality. The steps taken by this school were action oriented and measureable, which are important attributes since they then allow for clear guidance on what must be done and accountability to determine whether or not real progress is made. These steps include ensuring that

→ Every student enrolls in at least one above-grade-level course during middle school.

→ All classes are representative of the entire student population.

→ All students and staff have access to technology that is an integral feature of teaching and learning.

→ Professional development and ongoing growth opportunities are available to all staff and are embedded within the school day.

→ Student suspensions decrease in frequency each year.

Moreover, professional development at the school prepared teachers to deliver instruction that emphasized factors such as quality teacher–student relationships, student improvement, cultural relevance, and critical thinking. These are among the gap-closing, asset-focused areas identified in the previous chapters.

It is also the case that the approaches taken at Kingsview work because of the relentless focus on fidelity and quality in implementation. Principal Thomas does not merely admonish her staff with slogans or speak in platitudes about her commitment to academic success; rather, she takes decisive steps to ensure that academic achievement remains the priority of her school, and she keeps everyone focused on learning outcomes. Such commitment explains why schools such as Kingsview are successfully closing the achievement gap while so many others are not.

A close look at the urban districts where the greatest progress has been made in recent years—Atlanta, New York,[1] Norfolk, and parts of San Antonio (Northeast Independent School District) and Houston (Adline Independent School District)—reveals that they have found ways to address many of the obstacles named above. Even though these higher-performing districts still have a long way to go and there is considerable variation in the specific strategies they have implemented in reading and math curricula, professional development, and district management, these districts share important characteristics: stability in leadership, an ability to avoid the political conflicts that often undermine reforms, coherent educational strategies that are implemented with attention to quality control, and data systems that allow them to monitor student and school progress and to intervene early and effectively when expected goals are not obtained. Karin Chenoweth (2007, 2009), an analyst with the Education Trust and the author of two important books on why some schools and districts are successfully closing the gap, provides detailed accounts of the strategies that the most successful districts have used. These strategies will be discussed in greater detail in the section that follows.

The success of urban school districts such as Atlanta, Georgia; Norfolk, Virginia; and others that are making progress in closing the achievement gap is, of course, relative. It is important to recognize that even though most academic indicators are moving in a positive direction, there remain large numbers of students who lag far behind and schools that are struggling to meet student needs. Nonetheless, even the relative success of school districts that serve large numbers of disadvantaged minority students should serve as an example and inspiration to other districts.

Sadly, the number of suburban districts that are also achieving progress is smaller. Montgomery County, Maryland; Abington, Pennsylvania; and Brockton, Massachusetts, stand out because they have made steady progress in reducing academic disparities between affluent White students and more disadvantaged children of color. However, these districts are the exceptions. In many suburban communities where family incomes and per-pupil spending is high, academic disparities remain wide and, far too often, predictable. To understand why some schools have experienced success in closing the achievement gap while far more have not, this chapter presents an analysis of two suburban school districts and the efforts they have made to address racial disparities in academic outcomes. Like many suburban districts, these communities have experienced a recent change in demographics that has drawn attention to racial disparities in achievement patterns and forced district personnel to reexamine traditional approaches. In contrast to many urban and rural districts, the two districts we examine have ample resources and serve relatively affluent, highly educated communities. Nevertheless, one district has made significant progress in reducing the achievement gap, whereas the other has not. We present these two cases in the hope that by drawing attention to the particular approaches that have been used and the divergent results that have been obtained, educators, policymakers, parents, and others will gain an understanding of the factors that contribute to success in one setting and paralysis in another. By drawing attention to what works and why, we may also gain a clearer sense of what it might take to create schools where the race and socioeconomic status of a child no longer predict how well he or she will perform in school.

A Tale of Two Districts

In recent years, suburban school districts located in the inner ring of metropolitan areas have become far more diverse and racially integrated than urban or rural school districts (Orfield & Lee, 2006). To those familiar with the development of suburban communities, many of which were created in the aftermath of World War II, this demographic shift might come as a surprise. After all, many suburban communities were populated as a direct result of "White flight" from cities during the 1950s and 1960s. Attracted by the prospect of owning a single-family home (with a federally subsidized mortgage), many middle-class White families sought to escape urban neighborhoods and schools that had increasing numbers of Black and Latino students (Gans, 1995). Today, many of these suburban schools are among the most integrated in the nation (Civil Rights Project, 2009).

The "browning of the suburbs" started slowly in the 1970s and picked up steam in the 1990s as many middle-class Black and Latino families followed the same path as the middle-class Whites who preceded them. As was true in the past, life in the suburbs symbolized a clear and deliberate step toward upward mobility and fulfillment of the American Dream; life in the suburbs seemed to hold the promise of escape from the crime, pollution, and overcrowding of the inner city. Most important, the move to suburbia also held the promise that the children of upwardly mobile minority professionals would be able to attend well-run, racially integrated schools. For many, this prospect meant that the American Dream would no longer be deferred.

Unfortunately, it is now clear that many suburban school districts are struggling in their efforts to educate Black and Latino students. In fact, throughout the country, the achievement gap is often even more pronounced in suburban school districts, and the likelihood that minority children will be tracked into low-ability or special education classes is substantially greater. It is also not uncommon to find suburban schools that are nominally integrated but segregated within. Despite the fact that many of these school districts have a track record of success and send large numbers of students (most of whom are White and affluent) to colleges and universities, wide racial disparities in academic achievement are more often than not the norm (Noguera & Wing, 2006).

Because they are often more diverse and challenged by persistent disparities in student achievement, many suburban schools are faced with both top-down and bottom-up pressure to find ways to address the achievement gap. NCLB and state-level accountability measures impose top-down pressure in that they compel district and school leaders to show evidence of Annual Yearly Progress (AYP) in the achievement of historically underachieving students. Simultaneously, district leaders are increasingly faced with pressure from minority parents and community organizations that seek to hold them accountable for the low performance of these students. In the face of such pressures, the leadership in suburban districts typically cannot offer superficial solutions or excuses. In many cases, the minority parents they serve are too savvy and well organized to be easily put off. As a result, suburban district leaders are forced to develop new strategies to address the achievement gap and demonstrate real evidence that those strategies are working.

Although the factors that contribute to the achievement gap are similar for most districts, there are clear differences in the policies and practices that districts have used and in the commitment they have shown to address disparities. Not surprisingly, some districts have made more progress and shown greater resolve in closing the achievement gap than others. In 2006 and 2007, Noguera and his colleagues (Sealey-Ruiz, Handville, & Noguera, 2008) led a research effort in two suburban school districts in the New York City metropolitan area. Prior to this research, both districts had undertaken a variety of measures to reduce disparities in student achievement. Despite their efforts, neither had experienced the level of improvement necessary to meet the requirements and goals of NCLB or to assuage the demands of the local community for better performance. In an effort to understand why past efforts had failed, and concerned that public frustration was growing, the two districts sought assistance.

Over the course of two years—one year in each district—extensive research was carried out to uncover the factors that contributed to the persistence of racial disparities in student achievement. The research included a set of recommendations for changes in policies and practices that were intended to help reduce academic disparities and close the racial achievement gap. In subsequent years, it became clear that one district was making substantially greater progress than the other. The findings suggest that even though both districts continued to exhibit racial disparities in student achievement, there were clear differences in the strategies they used to close the gap and in the institutionalization of policies and practices that would enable them to sustain progress in reducing disparities. The district names used below are pseudonyms.

Gardenville

From the beginning, educational leaders in Gardenville acknowledged that their concern about the achievement gap developed largely in response to growing political pressure from groups of disgruntled parents. Long recognized for its cultural, ethnic, and religious diversity, Gardenville takes pride in the fact that it was one of the first communities in the United States to voluntarily integrate its public schools. However, the district experienced White flight during the 1980s and 1990s, and the racial balance shifted. Although the elementary schools remained relatively diverse (approximately half White and half minority), the secondary schools became largely minority (over 75 percent). By the time this research commenced in the 2005–06 school year, the district had 5,500 students (down from 9,000 in 1978). Black students constituted almost half of the student population (48.7 percent), followed by Latinos (21.2 percent), Whites (18.8 percent), and Asians (10.9 percent). Although the community was relatively affluent—average home values exceeded $450,000 and median family income was $74,903 in 2005—racial disparities in achievement were pervasive, and overall achievement was relatively low for a community with such high per-pupil spending (the district was in the top 10 percent of the state).

At the time research began, the most common explanation offered by district administrators for the achievement gap was that it was caused by the presence of a large number of low-income minority students who were attending the district's schools illegally (by using false addresses to claim residence). Although they had no evidence to support this claim, many asserted that if the district could invest in private investigators to identify children who were illegally enrolled, then there would be a significant rise in test scores. This claim was proven false, but it still served as a formidable obstacle to getting teachers and administrators to move beyond blaming children and parents for low achievement. This was especially evident in the surveys and interviews that were conducted with educators, who reported that the quality of their work was fine and that it was up to parents to do something to improve student achievement outcomes.

In addition to controversies related to the cause of low student achievement, there was considerable pressure in the community over local property taxes. In 2006, per-pupil spending in Gardenville was $14,320—one of the highest rates in the state. However, approximately 40 percent of families in the town did not enroll their children in the district's public schools. With a large percentage of voters (particularly those without children enrolled in the public schools) resentful over the heavy tax burden created by the cost of public education, and still others dissatisfied by low levels of student achievement among Black and Latino students, Gardenville district leaders found themselves under attack in an increasingly untenable situation.

Riverview

Riverview is a small town with an equally rich history and a racially and eth-nically diverse population. During the 1970s, there were a series of race riots at the high school, which many attributed to the sudden increase in Black student enrollment. Even as relations improved and tensions decreased, memory of past conflicts informed much of the discourse about the importance of creating equitable schools. Beginning in the 1990s, Riverview experienced another wave of dramatic demographic change as the number of Latino families moving into the community substantially increased. Latinos moving into Riverview came from a variety of backgrounds (e.g., Dominican, Mexican, Central American), and there is evidence that the population is composed of both documented and undocumented students. Although the school seemed to handle the change in its ethnic population far better than in the past, it struggled to find ways to respond to the academic and social needs of its changing student population. This was the primary reason given by the district leadership for examining the factors behind its persistent gaps in student achievement.

Like Gardenville, the Riverview school district benefited from a tax base that generated a relatively high rate of revenue to the district (per-pupil spending in 2007 was $19,054). Riverview, however, is far from a mono-lithic community, and household incomes range from $53,549 to $127,274. Neighborhoods in the community were highly segregated, which contributed to a high degree of race and class segregation at the elementary level. How-ever, because it has only two middle schools and one high school, Riverview's secondary schools are far more integrated.

To address racial imbalance in its schools, the district adopted an integra-tion plan in the 1980s that relied heavily on parental choice and magnet schools to promote voluntary integration. The plan seems to have worked to some degree, and the district has received national recognition for its academic accomplishments. For three years (2003–2006), Riverview High School was ranked as one of the top 100 high schools in the country by *U.S. News & World Report*. Despite these accolades, district leaders were fully aware that not enough of their Black and Latino students were meeting the district's high educational standards. Having acknowledged the disparities that existed, Riverview made closing the achievement gap a top district priority. Unlike Gardenville, closing the achievement gap in Riverview was seen as a matter of pride. According to the superintendent, "We think we have great schools, and we believe it is our mission to educate all of the students we serve. We are willing to do whatever it takes to close these gaps in student achievement, and I am personally willing to make tough decisions if that's what it takes to get the job done."

Although the data collected from Riverview did not identify it as an unqualified success story, many of the strategies that were used show promise and are worthy of emulation by other districts interested in addressing the achievement gap. Most important, the lessons learned from the relative success of Riverview, especially when juxtaposed to the reform paralysis experienced by Gardenville, should prove enlightening to researchers, policymakers, and educational leaders who seek to understand what it takes to narrow gaps in student achievement.

Race and Achievement in School

Not surprisingly, disparities in student achievement are reflected in graduation rates. In 2005, one-third of all Gardenville high school graduates received alternative diplomas because they were not able to pass the state's mandatory exit exam. These students were disproportionately Black and Latino males, and many had been categorized as special education students. A large number of the students who received alternative diplomas were student athletes on the football and basketball teams, and it was rumored that many had been placed in easier classes so they could remain academically eligible to participate in the sports program. In Gardenville, few educators acknowledged the lower achievement of minority males as a school problem. Instead, they cited negative peer and family influences as the cause for the high rates of failure.

In Riverview, there was a significant difference in the graduation rates for different racial groups. Whereas White students had a four-year graduation rate of 97 percent, Black students had a four-year graduation rate of only 64 percent, and Latinos fared only slightly better at 68 percent. Administrators searched for the cause of and solution to these disparities. They rejected the idea that something was wrong with the students, and they were willing to experiment with interventions they hoped would improve outcomes. One of the strategies they chose was a 9th grade study skills class, which was created in response to evidence that revealed high failure rates were concentrated among minority students in that grade. The district's willingness to adopt strategies to address uneven academic results was one of the primary reasons why Riverview made progress in its efforts to close the achievement gap.

During the 2005–06 school year, White and Asian students in Gardenville were overrepresented in 4th grade gifted-and-talented courses, but Black and Latino students were considerably underrepresented. Among 4th grade students, 19.2 percent of White students and 16.7 percent of Asian students were placed in gifted-and-talented courses, compared to only 5.7 percent of Black students and 3.9 percent of Latino students. Similar patterns were evident in other parts of the school district. For example, in the high school, White students were substantially more likely to be enrolled in advanced courses than were minority students. Over 70 percent of students in honors and advanced placement courses were White, even though Gardenville High School was only 16 percent White. As might be expected, students enrolled in these classes obtained higher grades and SAT scores, and they were more likely to be admitted to highly ranked colleges and universities. At the other end of the spectrum, Black and Latino students were overrepresented in remedial and special education courses, and very few of these students matriculated to four-year colleges after graduation.

Persistent patterns of racial disparities in achievement and course enrollment were a constant source of controversy and concern in Gardenville. In focus group interviews, Black parents expressed dissatisfaction with the inequitable access to the district's top courses for their children, and several parents complained that their students were discouraged from enrolling in rigorous courses. One parent explained her frustration in this way: "Even though my son tested into gifted classes when he was in the third grade,

I had to fight to get him placed. The teachers said he lacked the maturity. Please! He was a third grader. He excelled in the gifted classes once I fought to get him in. Why should we have to fight so hard?"

Similar frustrations were expressed by minority parents at the high school level. Although Gardenville High School offers open enrollment to advanced classes, students of color reported that they felt discouraged from enrolling in honors courses. In surveys conducted with high school students, 65 percent of Black students reported that they were not encouraged to take challenging courses, and 62 percent stated that they did not feel supported by their teachers. This lack of minority students in advanced courses was confirmed by classroom observations and other data on student performance. Data revealed that most students of color were enrolled in general education classes regarded by students as "easy" and "unchallenging." As was true at the elementary level, this form of tracking generated considerable criticism from minority parents. One high school parent said, "Classes are rigorous if you're in honors; but if not, the kids are not being challenged. My elder daughter was in mostly honors classes, and she regularly had three hours of homework. My son is in basic classes, and he never has homework. Even if he's not ready for advanced work, why are the expectations so low?" Such frustration was widespread among minority parents in Gardenville and contributed to a political climate that was at times racially polarized and acrimonious on matters pertaining to student achievement.

There were similar racial disparities in the composition of gifted, honors, and advanced placement classes in Riverview, but the degree of imbalance was not as pronounced. In the elementary schools, White students composed 74 percent of the students who were enrolled in gifted classes, but they were barely over half of the total student population. Similarly, Black and Latino students in the high school composed 16 percent and 18 percent, respectively, of the students in advanced courses, but they were 24 percent and 28 percent, respectively, of the total. Clear patterns of an achievement gap between students enrolled in advanced placement (AP) and non-AP courses were revealed. During the 2006–07 school year, Black and Latino students were the most underrepresented population in the advanced math classes.

After controlling for achievement, Black and Latino students were nearly 10 and 13 percent *less* likely than White and Asian students to take and pass the state math exam in the 8th or 9th grade. Approximately half of all Black and Latino students reported they would attend two- or four-year colleges after graduation, yet more than 82 percent of White students and 100 percent of Asian students made similar assertions. For the high school state math exam, Black and Latino students had mean scores below 72 (out of a maximum 100), whereas White and Asian students had mean scores of 86.

Despite these disparities, minority parents and students in Riverview did not express the same degree of anger or frustration as did parents in Gardenville. The difference appeared to be related to the sense that district officials were willing to work with them to address issues of access. When asked whether he felt his children were being encouraged to take college prep courses, the response of one father was indicative of the general consensus: "The teachers at Riverview go out of their way to help our kids. They will stay after school to offer tutoring, and they will call home if they are concerned about something. My daughter is a senior this year, and she is applying to colleges now. Her counselors have been very helpful in explaining how to apply, in helping her sign up for the SAT, and in taking her on tours of colleges. I feel she is being well prepared for college, and I am glad because I can't help her myself since I never went to college."

This is not to suggest that addressing tracking and the racial disparities it fosters is not important in Riverview. Riverview's highest-performing high school students performed 16–26 percent better on state achievement measures than did students in lower-level classes. They were also estimated to be 48 percent more likely to pass the exams required for a diploma with advanced designation and 38 percent more likely to report that they would attend a four-year college after graduation.

In Riverview, the effect of being on the advanced academic track was positive and significant, even after controlling for a student's prior achievement. An examination of all students who were in the 11th grade during the 2005–06 school year revealed that more than 70 percent of White students and 100 percent of Asian students took at least one AP or college-level course, but only 45 percent of Latino students and 28 percent of Black students took one of these courses. Less than half of the Black and Latino students passed the exams required for the state's high honors diploma, compared with 84 percent of White students. For the second tier advanced designation diplomas, 23 percent of Black students and 11 percent of Latino students qualified, compared to 63 percent of White students.[2]

However, as was true for their parents, students of color in Riverview were also less likely than students in Gardenville to report feeling discouraged to take challenging courses. Only 18 percent of minority students at Riverview High School reported that they felt discouraged from enrolling in honors or advanced placement courses, and 78 percent reported that they felt supported by their teachers. Students consistently referred to their teachers as "helpful," "encouraging," or "a person I can count on and trust," and they often described the school's administrators as "people who look out for us and want the best for us."

Unlike in Gardenville, where conversations about tracking often degenerated into blame and accusations over racism between parents and administrators, Riverview district administrators sought to find other ways to promote college access for students who were unable to handle advanced placement courses. For example, as a way to address the lack of diversity in the high school's advanced placement courses, Riverview administrators worked with a local college to offer a variety of college credit–bearing courses to attract Black and Latino students. Some of the courses focused on African American and Latino history and culture and were aimed specifically at recruiting Black and Latino students. Additionally, this initiative offered other courses in math, science, foreign languages, and history. Consistently, there were more minority students enrolled in these classes than in the high school's advanced placement courses. Such efforts significantly increased the number of minority students who were succeeding academically and matriculating to college from Riverview High School.

Efforts to Close the Achievement Gap

The study of these two districts revealed strong connections between the way educational leaders address learning conditions and academic placement procedures, and whether or not the racial achievement gap is widening or closing. In Gardenville, there was a distinct tendency among teachers and administrators to blame students and parents for low minority student achievement and to rationalize low achievement as the product of low-income students who were enrolled illegally. In Riverview, there was greater willingness to accept responsibility for changing student outcomes and little desire to question the right of students to enroll in district schools.

Prior to this research, Riverview had established mentoring programs for Black and Latino male students at the middle and high school levels to address the social marginalization these students claimed they experienced in school and the higher rates of academic failure that were common among them. Riverview also introduced other reforms, including block scheduling and advisory groups, which were intended to change the context for teaching and learning and provide students with a greater degree of personal support. By all appearances, these efforts had a positive impact on the achievement of Black and Latino students and contributed to support for the district among minority students and their parents, most of whom expressed confidence that the district was genuinely trying to meet their needs.

By contrast, data from surveys and focus groups revealed that Gardenville was mired in a debate over who was to blame for low student achievement. It was even claimed that the decision to support research on the achievement gap was made not as a sincere effort to identify the causes of underachievement or embrace recommendations on the actions that needed to be taken but to convince parents that the district was doing *something*. Even after the research resulted in a number of practical suggestions for short-, medium-, and long-term strategies that could be used to reduce the achievement gap, school board members and administrators were unable to develop a plan to ensure that these recommendations were implemented. They remained stuck in discussions over who should be blamed for persistent disparities.

The experiences of these two suburban school districts should serve as a sobering reminder of why it is so difficult to bring about concrete progress in the effort to close the achievement gap. Despite their stated commitments to educate all students, and despite the considerable resources at their disposal, these two districts experienced dramatically different degrees of success. Riverview continues to make steady, incremental progress in closing the achievement gap, yet Gardenville is not. In both districts, wide disparities that correspond to students' race and class backgrounds persist, and it appears likely that the gap will not close entirely in the near future. Nevertheless, Riverview is gradually becoming a district that consistently produces a significant number of high-achieving students of color; there has been a steady increase in the representation of minority students in gifted, honors, and advanced placement classes. Such signs of progress are important. As patterns of success and failure change in Riverview, stereotypes about the connection between racial identity and student achievement are being shattered. The vast majority of students at Riverview High School reported that they did not think certain racial groups were inherently smarter than others or did not belong in advanced classes. Such responses suggest that attitudes about the relationship between race and intelligence are evolving and may lead to even greater progress in the future.

Suburban school districts faced with similar challenges can learn from the experiences of these two districts. In Riverview, deliberate steps have been taken to reduce disparities in student achievement. These include restructuring academic programs and providing additional support to students in need. Through concrete actions, such as increasing minority students' access to rigorous courses, improved mentoring and counseling for students regarded as "at risk" for failure, and increased stakeholder involvement in school-related reforms, Riverview has demonstrated its serious commitment to closing the gap.

Some of these actions pose risks. By targeting certain groups of students for mentoring or additional academic support, the district runs the risk of stigmatizing those it wants to help. One could easily infer that if students need extra help, it must be because they are not as smart or capable.

Similarly, by creating support groups for Black and Latino males, the district risks contributing to racial segregation within the school, a practice that may inadvertently contribute to a deterioration in race relations. These risks are not minor, and districts that seek to learn from the experiences of Riverview should be mindful that there is a long history of educational programs that were intended to help students (e.g., special education and many Title I programs) having the opposite effect. This is why it is so important for districts to collect data and evaluate the interventions they implement to help students. Quality control is essential, as is concrete evidence that those students who are targeted for support are actually being helped.

The experience of Gardenville is also instructive, even if for a different reason. Learning from the failure and paralysis that characterize ongoing discussions over what to do about the achievement gap is important because the mistakes made there are not unique. To a large degree, the inability to achieve progress in Gardenville can be attributed to an unwillingness to confront the ways in which the structure or culture of schools contributes to racial disparities. Educators in Riverview have embraced the challenge of closing the achievement gap and have been willing to confront obstacles that stymie student progress as they search for ways to improve learning conditions. Sadly, in Gardenville, there continues to be a debate over who should be blamed for low achievement—lazy students, biased teachers, or uninvolved parents. Aside from the hostility that such accusations generate, this debate prevents all stakeholders from focusing on what they must each do to take responsibility for changing academic outcomes.

Educational leaders in Gardenville have addressed the achievement gap largely as a response to political pressure from a community that is increasingly dissatisfied with the quality of its public schools. Although these leaders would like to reduce the pressure they are under, they lack a clear commitment to address the complex educational issues that stand in the way of change. The mere fact that so many teachers and administrators continue to blame minority students and parents for low achievement is the clearest sign that they have not yet begun to accept responsibility for addressing the obstacles to achievement. The first step in such a process would be a willingness to respond to the question of what they might do differently with respect to the ways in which they are sorting and labeling students, the way they are teaching them, and the way they have organized their schools. Unlike in Riverview, where this type of introspection and critical analysis is widely embraced, there is tremendous reluctance in Gardenville to evaluate the strategies and programs they have implemented to boost student achievement. The community remains paralyzed in a fruitless debate while relatively simple measures (e.g., offering a college advising day) are ignored. Even in the face of empirical evidence that shows how racial disparities are produced and maintained, educational leaders in Gardenville were not able to take action.

These two cases also remind us that educational efforts to reform schools and raise student achievement cannot be viewed separately from political issues related to race and achievement or from questions of leadership accountability. Several researchers have found that political and ideological attitudes toward the presence of minority students and their families influence how these students are treated in school (Lipman, 1998; Meier, Stewart, & England, 1989). In communities where White educators lament demographic change and are unconcerned when students of color remain stuck in low-level courses, progress in raising achievement and reducing disparities is rarely forthcoming (Wheelock, 1992). By contrast, possibilities for positive change are encouraged in schools and communities where students of color are welcomed and challenged and where educational leaders willingly accept responsibility for making sure that all students receive a good education.

The experience of these two school districts also demonstrates why educational leaders must openly address the highly politicized nature of the relationship between race and student achievement. District leaders must convince their teachers, students, and other community stakeholders that increasing the achievement of Black and Latino students is not only possible but also necessary, and it will not come at the expense of high achievement among White students. To accomplish this, district leaders must move their communities beyond the all-too-common tendency to perceive educational equity as a zero-sum scenario in which efforts to address the needs of struggling students come at the expense of high-achieving White students. When this occurs, racial polarization and incrimination often stymie efforts to promote change (Noguera & Wing, 2006). By contrast, districts and communities that directly confront the challenge of racial disparities, combined with a clearly articulated and fully funded intervention strategy, are more likely to experience tangible gains for their students. The ability of educators to accomplish this will ultimately determine whether progress is made in closing the nation's racial achievement gap.

Learning from Schools and Districts That Are Closing the Gap

For the sake of preserving the anonymity of Gardenville and Riverview, their real names were not used. This practice is standard, but it limits the ability of educators to learn from the successes and mistakes of others. Despite the fact that many schools and districts have experienced failure and frustration in their efforts, there are some places where real progress is being made. These districts deserve to be named, known, and studied because they provide proof that it can be done.

University Park Campus School—Worcester, MA

Located in one of the poorest neighborhoods of Worcester, the University Park Campus School (UPCS) serves 231 students in grades 7–12, and each cohort is randomly selected by lottery. The school demographics closely match those of the community, with 7.4 percent of the students identified as Black and 40.3 percent identified as Latino. Moreover, the school identifies nearly 78 percent of the student population as low income.

The majority of students enter 7th grade at UPCS nearly two grade levels behind in reading and math, and they largely come from families in which no one has attended college (Conley, 2010). Despite these hurdles, the school is steadfast in its mission to prepare every student for college. To achieve this ambitious goal, UPCS employs a focused curriculum taught at high levels, with the goal of providing students with a firm base of core academic knowledge as they move into high school (Chenoweth, 2007). The school also uses teaching strategies and academic support services to ensure that each student receives the support needed to learn and achieve. At UPCS, academic rigor is not used as an excuse to allow students to flounder. Rather, students are actively supported through instructional strategies designed to meet their needs and through individualized support systems. In this way, each student has the opportunity to meet the high expectations and standards set by the school.

Since its inception, UPCS has distinguished itself as a school that is capable of producing high-achieving students of color, and it continues to build upon its initial success. From the 2005–06 through 2008–09 school years, UPCS improved student performance with dramatic increases in the number of students at the "advanced" and "proficient" levels and decreases in the number of students at the "needs improvement" level (see Figure 8.1).

In 2009, over 90 percent of UPCS students scored at the "advanced" or "proficient" level on the 10th grade state English language arts and mathematics tests on their first try, and the remaining students reached proficiency on subsequent attempts (see Figure 8.2).

FIGURE 8.1 ⟶ MCAS 10TH GRADE ENGLISH LANGUAGE ARTS

	2006	2007	2008	2009
Advanced	23%	19%	28%	42%
Proficient	43%	57%	56%	55%
Needs improvement	34%	24%	16%	3%
Failing	0%	0%	0%	0%

⟶ MCAS 10TH GRADE MATHEMATICS

	2006	2007	2008	2009
Advanced	40%	62%	78%	71%
Proficient	26%	29%	9%	24%
Needs improvement	31%	10%	13%	5%
Failing	3%	0%	0%	0%

MCAS = Massachusetts Comprehensive Assessment System

Source: Massachusetts Department of Elementary & Secondary Education, 2009. Retrieved from http://profiles.doe.mass.edu/state_report/mcas.aspx

FIGURE 8.2 ⟶ 2009 MCAS 10TH GRADE ENGLISH LANGUAGE ARTS
BY RACE/ETHNICITY

	PROFICIENT	ADVANCED	AT OR ABOVE PROFICIENT
Hispanic	50%	43%	93%
White	62%	38%	100%
Low income	56%	40%	96%

⟶ 2009 MCAS 10TH GRADE MATHEMATICS BY RACE/ETHNICITY

	PROFICIENT	ADVANCED	AT OR ABOVE PROFICIENT
Hispanic	21%	71%	92%
White	69%	31%	100%
Low income	72%	20%	92%

MCAS = Massachusetts Comprehensive Assessment System

Source: Massachusetts Department of Elementary & Secondary Education, 2009. Retrieved from
http://profiles.doe.mass.edu/state_report/mcas.aspx

In addition to displaying high levels of achievement, UPCS students also graduate at rates that are substantially higher than the national average. In 2008, the school had a 93.9 percent graduation rate, with 90.9 percent of Latino students, 92.6 percent of Black students, and 93 percent of low-income students graduating.[3]

It should be pointed out that UPCS has an advantage that many public high schools do not have—a partnership with a major college, Clark University in Worcester. Clark provides support for curriculum development, professional development for teachers, college advising for students, and administrative support for the school leadership. Instead of pointing to this partnership as a reason why the results obtained may not be replicable, the question we should ask is why doesn't every college have a partnership with a local school? The United States has thousands of excellent colleges and universities. Many of these are located in communities where the local schools that train their future students are floundering. Doesn't it make sense to follow the lead set by UPCS and Clark and build strong partnerships across the country? Why isn't this happening already?

Steubenville City School District—Steubenville, OH

Steubenville City School District has a diverse student body of 2,227, with 29 percent of the students identified as Black and 13.9 percent identified as Multiracial. Moreover, the school district identifies nearly 60 percent of the student population as economically disadvantaged.

Over the past 10 years, the district has made great strides in closing the achievement gap. From 1998 to 2009, the number of students who reached or exceeded the state's proficiency levels in reading and math has risen, with Black and Multiracial students nearly closing the achievement gap at some grade levels. This trend is most apparent when looking at students' performance on the 4th grade state reading and mathematics test. In 1998–99, there was at least a 10-point difference in the percentage of Black and White students who were at or above proficiency. By 2008–09, not only had the level of Black and White student performance increased in the district, but the achievement gap between the groups had all but disappeared (see Figures 8.3 and 8.4). Currently, the vast majority of students in this district are achieving at or above proficiency in reading, writing, and mathematics.

The Steubenville City School District has established itself as a high-achieving school district. It stands out among schools serving similar groups of students, as well as among all schools in Ohio. According to its 2008–09 district report card, Steubenville City School District's students outperformed students in similar school districts and the state as a whole on Ohio's 3rd–8th grade assessments (see Figure 8.5).

According to Education Trust, much of the district's success is due to its commitment to a coherent, districtwide curriculum and a keen focus on teaching (Education Trust, 2009). The performance of each student is monitored closely, teachers receive professional development that is tailored to enable them to become more effective at meeting learning needs, and schools have systems in place to intervene early when students are not making progress. These are all strategies that show up repeatedly in the research literature as essential for student success. The difference is that in Steubenville City School District, educators implement these strategies with considerable attention to how they are carried out at the classroom level. Quality control

FIGURE 8.3 ---→ PERCENTAGE OF 4TH GRADE STUDENTS AT OR ABOVE
PROFICIENCY IN READING (BY RACE/ETHNICITY)

	98–99	99–00	00–01	01–02	02–03	03–04	04–05	05–06	06–07	07–08	08–09
Black	70.7%	75.5%	56.7%	77.1%	77.8%	84.7%	86.2%	80.5%	84.0%	83.7%	97.7%
Multiracial	—	82.4%	81.8%	75.0%	50.0%	87.0%	92.3%	92.0%	91.6%	95.0%	96.6%
White	81.1%	86.1%	67.6%	85.3%	90.3%	86.2%	98.5%	89.9%	97.8%	91.4%	93.7%

---→ PERCENTAGE OF 4TH GRADE STUDENTS AT OR ABOVE
PROFICIENCY IN MATHEMATICS (BY RACE/ETHNICITY)

	98–99	99–00	00–01	01–02	02–03	03–04	04–05	05–06	06–07	07–08	08–09
Black	67.3%	59.2%	56.7%	73.9%	65.0%	81.4%	86.2%	91.3%	78.0%	85.7%	97.6%
Multiracial	—	88.3%	81.8%	81.3%	41.6%	77.3%	84.7%	84.0%	79.2%	85.0%	96.5%
White	79.3%	75.9%	76.9%	90.5%	82.7%	86.1%	91.1%	94.3%	91.1%	87.8%	92.3%

Source: Ohio Department of Education, 2009. Retrieved from www.ode.state.oh.us

is more likely when there is a willingness to evaluate and use data to monitor the effectiveness of practices that are used. Though this might seem obvious, this kind of careful approach to implementing instructional support systems is often missing in schools.

P.S. 124 Osmond A. Church—New York, NY

P.S. 124 Osmond A. Church in Ozone Park (a neighborhood of Queens) currently serves a diverse population of 1,100 students from prekindergarten through 8th grade. Of these students, 36 percent are Black, 21 percent are Latino, and 40 percent are Asian or Native Hawaiian. Moreover, 97 percent of the student body qualifies for free or reduced-price lunch. Although schools with these demographic characteristics are often expected to produce low student outcomes, Osmond A. Church defies these expectations with a majority of students reaching proficiency on state assessments (see Figure 8.6).

This high level of success is equally shared among all students. A look at students' performance on 4th grade English language arts and mathematics exams reveals that Osmond A. Church has been particularly successful at

FIGURE 8.4 ⟶ PERCENTAGE OF 4TH GRADE STUDENTS AT OR ABOVE PROFICIENCY IN READING (BY RACE/ETHNICITY)

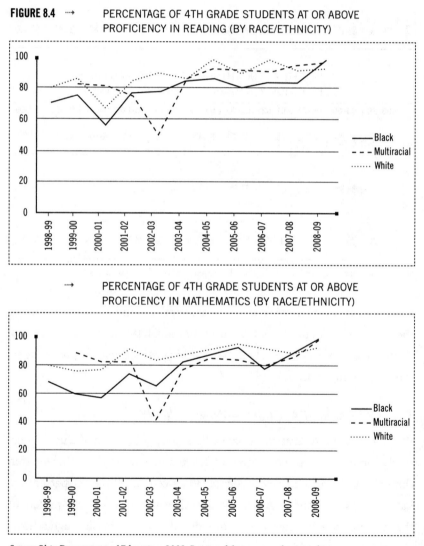

⟶ PERCENTAGE OF 4TH GRADE STUDENTS AT OR ABOVE PROFICIENCY IN MATHEMATICS (BY RACE/ETHNICITY)

Source: Ohio Department of Education, 2009. Retrieved from www.ode.state.oh.us

maintaining the high performance levels of its students of color (see Figure 8.7).

Chenoweth (2009) points out that this high level of student success was not always the norm; in 2000, fewer than half of the students were able to meet the New York State standards, and the school was considered to be

FIGURE 8.5 ⇢ STEUBENVILLE DISTRICT READING PROFICIENCY

	PROFICIENT	ACCELERATED	ADVANCED	AT OR ABOVE PROFICIENT
Black (non-Hispanic)	48.8%	26.4%	13.4%	88.6%
Multiracial	38.6%	30.3%	13.1%	82.0%
White (non-Hispanic)	36.9%	32.7%	20.9%	90.5%
Economically disadvantaged	43.2%	28.2%	14.5%	85.9%

⇢ STEUBENVILLE DISTRICT WRITING PROFICIENCY

	PROFICIENT	ACCELERATED	ADVANCED	AT OR ABOVE PROFICIENT
Black (non-Hispanic)	47.7%	40.6%	0.8%	89.1%
Multiracial	42.9%	35.7%	0.0%	78.6%
White (non-Hispanic)	33.6%	53.5%	3.9%	91.0%
Economically disadvantaged	43.2%	39.9%	1.2%	84.3%

⇢ STEUBENVILLE DISTRICT MATHEMATICS PROFICIENCY

	PROFICIENT	ACCELERATED	ADVANCED	AT OR ABOVE PROFICIENT
Black (non-Hispanic)	42.6%	27.5%	18.2%	88.3%
Multiracial	40.0%	20%	20.7%	80.7%
White (non-Hispanic)	30.6%	26.1%	32.2%	88.9%
Economically disadvantaged	36.4%	27.9%	21.5%	85.8%

Source: Ohio Department of Education, 2009. Retrieved from www.ode.state.oh.us

failing. With the help of a comprehensive school grant and a commitment to help all students learn to become educated citizens, the school leadership was able to implement successful programs and practices that ultimately improved the achievement of all students.

FIGURE 8.6 ⟶ PERCENTAGE OF STUDENTS THAT SCORED AT OR ABOVE LEVEL 3 IN ENGLISH LANGUAGE ARTS

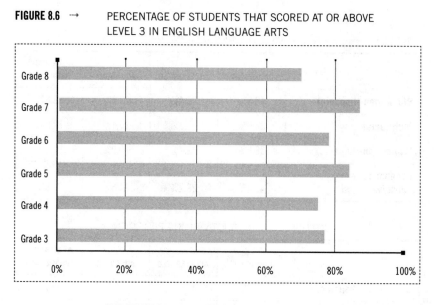

⟶ PERCENTAGE OF STUDENTS THAT SCORED AT OR ABOVE LEVEL 3 IN MATHEMATICS

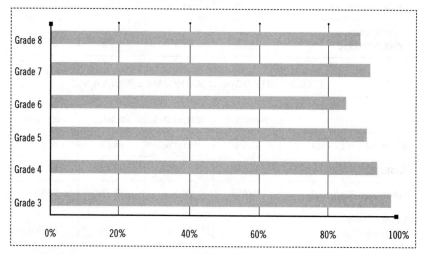

Source: New York State Education Department, 2009. Retrieved from www.p12.nysed.gov/irs/ela-math/

As is true for students in other successful schools, students at Osmond A. Church are achieving at higher levels not because they are special but because careful attention has been paid to creating learning conditions in which academic success is more likely. This is ultimately the only way to close the achievement gap. Because many students come from poor and disadvantaged backgrounds, the school has developed partnerships with community-based social service agencies that help respond to the nonacademic (i.e., social, emotional, and psychological) needs that invariably have an impact on learning. They also provide enriched learning opportunities after school to extend learning time in ways that are most likely to make a difference. This holistic approach to educating "disadvantaged" students makes it possible for Osmond A. Church to beat the odds and for its students to achieve at levels commensurate with those obtained by more affluent children.

FIGURE 8.7 ⟶ PERCENTAGE OF 4TH GRADE STUDENTS THAT SCORED AT OR ABOVE LEVEL 3 IN ENGLISH LANGUAGE ARTS (BY RACE/ETHNICITY)

	2005–2006	2006–2007	2007–2008
All students	82%	67%	75%
Black	80%	74%	74%
Latino	—	—	78%
Economically disadvantaged	82%	67%	75%

⟶ PERCENTAGE OF 4TH GRADE STUDENTS THAT SCORED AT OR ABOVE LEVEL 3 IN MATHEMATICS (BY RACE/ETHNICITY)

	2005–2006	2006–2007	2007–2008
All students	85%	91%	94%
Black	87%	90%	91%
Latino	—	—	90%
Economically disadvantaged	88%	91%	94%

Source: New York State Education Department, 2009. Retrieved from www.p12.nysed.gov/irs/ela-math/

These schools show us that even though there aren't simple solutions to closing the achievement gap, a great deal can be done to create conditions where the learning needs of all students are met. In fact, extracting lessons from successful schools should serve as the basis for state and federal policy. Too often, school reforms have been based on "silver bullet" solutions: phonics-based literacy, small schools, technology, and so on. The failure of these reforms should serve as the most pointed reminder that there are no easy answers and that school success always requires several ingredients to come together simultaneously with strong leadership, parent involvement, student engagement, and high levels of teacher efficacy. When the strategies embraced overlook these issues, the lofty promises of school reform are rarely achieved. By learning from successful schools, we provide educators with clear examples of what it actually looks like when the right ingredients come together. We also make it very clear that, under the right conditions, *all* children can achieve.

What Can We Do to Close the Gap?

09

In Chapter 8, we pointed out that efforts to address the achievement gap are likely to encounter very different kinds of obstacles in low-income urban and rural districts than they are in middle-class suburban districts. In the former, the primary obstacles to producing higher achievement among students and improved performance among schools are broadly related to the capacity of schools to meet students' needs. In the latter, the obstacles to higher achievement for all students are related to what we can call the politics of equity—the tendency of schools to prioritize the needs of the most privileged and affluent students, which often comes at the expense of other, more disadvantaged students. In this final chapter, we describe some of these obstacles and what policymakers at the local, state, and federal levels can do to address them.

We also pay heed to the systematic empirical research reviewed in Chapters 3–7: the most promising, most effective classroom-based practices that, if well implemented, can very likely lead to gap-closing learning opportunities for low-income children of color. At the same time, these practices also hold promise for raising academic performance for virtually all students and adequately preparing them for the rigors, realities, and future responsibilities of the 21st century.

Rethinking Assessment

Whether intended or not, many educators report that one of the effects of NCLB on schools is that it narrows the focus on student test scores. This makes sense; test scores are the basis for holding students and schools accountable, and under the accountability systems that states have developed to rate and rank schools, tests scores serve as the primary currency of evaluation. In New York, Chicago, Los Angeles, and a growing number of other cities, test scores are also used to determine whether a school should be closed (Zeleny, 2010). U.S. Secretary of Education Arne Duncan has called for states to use test scores to judge teacher performance and to award raises based on students' state exam performance (CBS News, 2009).

For all of these reasons, many schools have become preoccupied with finding strategies to raise scores. This has created a boon for test preparation firms such as Kaplan and McGraw-Hill, whose profits have soared as schools desperately look for strategies to raise test scores (Milner, 2004–05). It has also led to a growing number of cases in which educators have been accused and found guilty of cheating and altering the results of state exams. In addition, there is clear evidence that several states have simply lowered their standards in order to increase the number of students who pass and are deemed proficient on state exams.[1]

Numerous critics have objected to overreliance on test scores as a means to gauge student performance. Former U.S. Assistant Secretary of Education Diane Ravitch has argued that the excessive emphasis on testing promoted by NCLB has led to a gross distortion of our nation's approach to education (Ravitch, 2010). She and others point out that raw scores often do not reveal other dimensions of learning and academic performance that are important to promoting higher levels of achievement. For example, oral presentation, discursive writing, and a variety of problem-solving skills are often inadequately measured on standardized tests that rely on multiple-choice questions (Meier, 2001). Important social skills, such as the ability to work in groups, deliver public presentations, and deliberate thoughtfully over complex issues typically cannot be assessed on standardized exams. Most important, for the results of tests to have validity, there must be some assurance that students are in fact prepared for the test, both by ensuring that students are exposed to a curriculum that covers the material on the exam and by guaranteeing access to competent instructors who can teach that material. Despite the reliance on standardized tests, no state has devised a way to ensure that these basic conditions are met.

Finally, most assessment experts agree that the primary value of a test should be to provide diagnostic feedback on the learning needs of students to both teachers and students. For this to happen, teachers have to be provided with the results of assessments at the beginning of the school year so the information can be used to guide instruction and learning interventions. In most states, this does not occur. Instead, tests are typically administered in the spring, and the results are not released to schools until the end of the school year and students have been assigned to new teachers. Even when students are tested more frequently, training on how to analyze and use the test results to modify instruction and meet student needs is not consistently provided.

To the degree that test scores accurately gauge student learning, the scores reveal how much students have learned or mastered with respect to what they have been exposed to at a given point in time. However, we must always maintain a healthy degree of skepticism when we analyze the results of standardized tests and *not* assume that a score constitutes an accurate measure of intellectual ability. Scores do not tell us why a student performed at a particular level. Was the student motivated to do his or her best? Some children are known to race through standardized tests, filling in bubbles without even looking at questions. Did the student experience fatigue because he or she didn't get enough sleep the night before? Is there a crucial gap in the student's learning (e.g., he or she can't read sufficiently in English) that has not been addressed and that might affect performance? Was the teacher effective in covering the material on the exam and helping students prepare? None of these questions negate the potential value of using standardized assessments to gauge student learning, but if we want to respond to the learning needs of our students, we need more information than a single test can provide.

This does not mean that testing is necessarily harmful or that assessment cannot be used as a tool for gauging academic progress. When used effectively, assessments can help guide interventions and provide teachers with information on how to tailor instruction to support students. Former U.S. Secretary of Education Rod Paige points out that we can effectively eliminate the achievement gap if we stop testing, simply because we would no longer know how well students are doing (Paige & Witty, 2010). There is some validity to this point, because without the benefit of assessments and other accountability measures, we would have no way of knowing how well students are being served. However, it is important for educators to remember that assessment is only a tool, not a panacea. When combined with other indicators—attendance, graduation rates, SAT and ACT scores, the number of students in remedial courses in college—school districts can obtain a reliable indication of how well they are preparing their students. If assessment results are used to devise constructive responses, rather than punish, apply pressure on, or humiliate students, educators can also learn what might be done to bring about greater progress. It would be foolhardy and irresponsible to call for an abolition of testing because of the way standardized tests have been misused, but it would be negligent not to address the inappropriate and unfair ways in which standardized tests are presently being used in states and school districts throughout the country.

Current research makes a persuasive case that much of our attention should be focused on enhancing students' behavioral, affective, and cognitive engagement inside the classroom and on a daily basis. Engagement should be appreciated as a precursor to measurable achievement. If we have not secured greater student engagement, we should not expect discernible changes in tested achievement. Instead of narrowly focusing on assessment, we should instead be focusing much more on high-quality instruction. What is good teaching, and how do we make sure that more students have access to teachers who are able to meet their learning needs? This is really the critical issue, because it is good teaching—rather than testing—that leads to higher levels of academic performance. Therefore, we should support good teaching that encourages students to think critically and independently. We should ask ourselves, "How do we encourage teaching that creates stimulating and inspiring classrooms, where students engage in problem solving and use their creativity and imagination to address interesting and important subjects, and where teachers push students to continue learning long after the exam is over?" Unfortunately, educational policy largely ignores these needs and instead remains fixated on high-stakes standardized tests. As a consequence, there are far too many schools and classrooms where students are bored by passive learning and where conformity and regurgitation are the primary objectives of performance.

The problems that arise when schools narrowly focus on test preparation were clearly evident in 2002 when we conducted research at several high schools in Boston. That year marked the beginning of Massachusetts's implementation of a high-stakes exit exam, one that all high school students were required to pass before the end of the academic year. To show that the state meant business, students who failed the exams would be denied diplomas, regardless of their course grades during high school. Schools had several years to prepare students for the high-stakes exam, but by the fall of 2001, it was already clear that several high schools in Boston and other urban districts were in serious trouble. Several high schools were faced with the prospect of losing as many as half of their seniors because these students had already failed the exam on two previous occasions.

In response to this possibility, many schools placed at-risk students in double-period test-preparation courses in math and literacy. These courses were designed to provide students with test-taking skills and expose them to the material that would be covered. However, the results of a two-year study on high school reform revealed that many of the teachers of these test-prep courses were either unqualified or incapable of teaching the material (many were in fact substitute teachers) (Noguera, 2004). This study also revealed, through an examination of transcripts, that many students at risk for failure lacked the basic skills necessary to pass the exam. Based on their 8th grade test scores and academic work, it was clear that many of these students were unable to read or write at the 9th grade level, either because they were illiterate in English or simply because they had been allowed to progress through school without learning to read. Low literacy levels was a serious problem because the exam was geared toward students who could read (at least minimally) at a 9th grade level, and the test-prep classes offered at the high schools offered no instruction in reading.

Similarly, most of the students vulnerable for failure in math had never taken courses that exposed them to the content covered on the exam.[2] In six out of ten high schools studied, half or more of the seniors failed the Massachusetts Comprehensive Assessment System and were denied diplomas. Across the state, approximately 6,000 students failed the test the first time (Coleman & Vishnane, 2003). Approximately one-third of those students were special education students with individualized educational plans. Another one-third were English language learners who either had not been in the United States long enough or simply had not learned enough English to pass the exam. The final one-third were students from struggling school districts in cities with long histories of failure, such as Lawrence, Springfield, Mount Holyoke, and Boston. Although all of these students were allowed to retake the exam over the summer, the fact that many had already failed three times made it unlikely that they would choose to take it again.

When confronted with the pressures generated by high-stakes exams, it is understandable that schools feel compelled to adopt test-prep strategies such as the ones used in Boston. However, research on schools that successfully close the gap shows that there is another way. The alternative almost always involves the development of a long-term, comprehensive approach that aims to provide students with an enriched learning environment and systematically trains teachers to meet the learning needs of their students. For example, to improve student performance at Brockton High School in Massachusetts, teachers focused on literacy in all subjects; over time, racial disparities in student achievement began to disappear. According to a *New York Times* article on the school: "The first big step was to go back to basics, and deem that reading, writing, speaking and reasoning were the most important skills to teach. They set out to recruit every educator in the building—not just English, but math, science, even guidance counselors—to teach those skills to students.... Teachers helped students understand what good writing looks like, and began devoting faculty meetings to teaching department heads how to use rubrics" (Dillon, 2010b).

Similar strategies are being used in districts such as Montgomery County, Maryland; Orange County, Florida; and Aldine Independent School District in Houston, Texas. These districts have made steady progress in closing the achievement gap, and a wide variety of strategies have been deployed to boost student achievement. Other districts should learn from the strategies these districts (and others) have used to increase student success. Despite the challenges created by the misuse of testing, these districts exhibit clear signs that progress can be made in educating all students regardless of their backgrounds.

Building the Capacity of High-Poverty Schools

In districts that serve large numbers of poor children in urban and rural areas, developing the capacity of schools involves many things, including providing the staff with appropriate training, implementing effective intervention strategies, and obtaining the resources necessary to meet student needs. For example, if a school serves large numbers of English language learners or children with learning disabilities, it might have to do what Edison Elementary in Portchester, New York, has done—ensure that all staff (as opposed to a few specialists) receive training in language acquisition and provide services that support students and families (Martin, Fergus, & Noguera, 2009). Similarly, schools that serve children who lack adequate nutrition or health care must develop partnerships with social service agencies and clinics. A case in point is P.S. 188 on the Lower East Side of Manhattan, where partnerships with local hospitals and nonprofit agencies have made it possible for social workers, nurses, and even dentists to deliver services to students in need. This has made it possible for teachers to focus exclusively on what they know best: teaching in response to the academic needs of their students.[3]

These are not new ideas, of course, but rarely have both approaches been combined. Full-service schools, Beacon schools, community schools, and other schools that provide necessary social services have been around for many years (Comer, 1988). However, no city or state has taken this idea to a scale that ensures all students who need such services actually receive them. More important, relatively few schools have combined a social service strategy with a well-thought-out academic enrichment strategy. For several years, Yale psychiatrist James Comer championed this combined approach, and schools where his model was successfully implemented obtained impressive results (Ramirez-Smith, 1995). Today, the Comer model is rarely mentioned by policymakers as a viable approach. Instead, a new, much more expensive version—the Harlem Children's Zone, developed by Geoffrey Canada—has been acclaimed by politicians as an ideal model (Tough, 2008).

The Harlem Children's Zone, like other full-service models, is based on the recognition that for schools that serve large numbers of poor children to succeed, they have to attend to both the academic and social needs of children. Put most simply, capacity building involves doing whatever it takes to obtain the resources and create the conditions to meet and respond to student needs. This is precisely what is being done by the small but significant number of high-performing/high-poverty schools throughout the country (Chenoweth, 2009; Education Trust, 2002). Some, but not all, of these are charter schools; many others are public schools led by resourceful and entrepreneurial principals who in many cases are successful at writing grants and attracting private resources to support their schools. Increasingly, the strategies these schools employ are well known: They provide their teachers with ongoing, site-based professional development to ensure that they have a significant number of highly trained personnel (Darling-Hammond, 2010). They ensure that their facilities are safe, attractive, and equipped with appropriate technology (Bloom, Thompson, Unterman, Herlihy, & Payne, 2010). They provide a well-rounded curriculum that includes the arts, sports, and extended learning opportunities after school (Waldfogel & Lahaie, 2007). They develop social support systems to respond to the health, nutritional, and emotional needs of disadvantaged children (Dryfoos, 1993). Perhaps most important, they develop strong partnerships with the parents and communities they serve (Blankstein & Noguera, 2004).

Though currently small, the number of high-performing/high-poverty schools is growing. Although these schools may not have eliminated the achievement gap, their relative success in raising achievement serves as proof that it is possible to provide a greater number of children with high-quality education than we are currently doing. Chenoweth (2007) presents several case studies of schools that are raising the achievement of Black and Latino students. She explains that there is no singular approach that makes it possible for schools to succeed. They simply must do whatever it takes to meet the educational and social needs of the children they serve. She writes, "I have become convinced that there is no one single factor that is at the core of a successful school. That is, there is not one structure, or one curriculum, or one set of policies and procedures that, if every school in the country were to adopt it, would transform them into high-achieving schools. Schools are complex organisms that can't be changed that easily. Over and over, the teachers and principals in these schools told me, 'There is no magic bullet'" (p. 213).

Chenoweth's finding that there is no single approach that works to educate disadvantaged children is both reassuring and disturbing. It is reassuring in that it reminds us that achieving success is not merely a matter of attracting extraordinary teachers or principals or of using a particular curriculum or instructional strategy. Ordinary people who are committed and dedicated to their work can get the job done. However, this finding is also disturbing because it suggests that such results should be possible for a greater number of schools. Chenoweth explains that exceptional schools differentiate themselves from "run-of-the-mill schools" in that "the adults in [exceptional] schools expect their students to learn, and work hard to master the skills and knowledge to teach those students" (2007, p. 226).[4] What does this tell us about the large number of schools where children are not achieving or performing at high levels? What makes it possible for a small number of schools to take all of these actions and succeed when so many others fail?

At the heart of Chenoweth's analysis is her identification of the way in which these exceptional schools position themselves relative to the students and parents they serve. They view the schools they work in as part of the community, and they envision their role as educators to be one of acting in solidarity with parents to overcome obstacles to learning. These educators understand that poverty creates numerous challenges for children, but this pragmatic recognition does not negate their assumption that all students can achieve at high levels if given the opportunity and exposure. Instead, awareness of the challenges that children face compels the educators who serve them to devise strategies that mitigate, and in some cases even overcome, those obstacles. Good intentions may be important but are not enough. Indeed, several evidence-based, gap-closing strategies have been identified earlier in this volume, and these are convergent with the suggestions offered in Chenoweth's work.

This compels us to ask a basic question: Why is it that highly effective schools and districts continue to be the exception? Why haven't state and local governments implemented strategies to develop the capacity of schools in impoverished communities, and why hasn't the federal government done more to help schools create conditions that are essential for learning? These important questions must be answered if we are to bring about sustained improvement in the nation's schools. Until we can find ways to generate the will to hold elected leaders and their appointees accountable for doing what it takes to educate poor children, schools in impoverished urban and rural communities will remain mired in a cycle of failure.

Overcoming Zero-Sum Scenarios in Suburbia

Sadly, there has been relatively little progress in closing the achievement gap in most suburban school districts across the country, even though many are well endowed with resources and enjoy high per-pupil spending. In many suburban schools, disparities in student achievement that correspond to the racial and socioeconomic backgrounds of children are pervasive and entrenched. In such communities, the obstacles to educating all children are generally unrelated to capacity and resource constraints. More often than not, they are political in nature and relate to the attitudes and beliefs of educators and broad segments of the community toward the children who underachieve.

Compelled by NCLB to do more to raise the achievement of students who have historically lagged behind academically, many suburban districts have had their weaknesses and flaws exposed. As discussed in Part I, even those schools that have been successful with privileged children and have affluent and highly educated parents are typically less successful with minority students, English language learners, and children with special needs. As demonstrated through the examples of suburban Gardenville and Riverview (Chapter 8), the inability to meet the learning needs of underachieving students is largely due to the unwillingness of leadership to adopt approaches proven to be effective. Why is this so? It is primarily due to a widely held perception of a zero-sum scenario—efforts to meet the needs of students who are behind are too often regarded as harmful to the interests of high-achieving, affluent children.

Even though most district leaders claim they would like to be more successful in meeting the educational needs of underachieving students, powerful political pressures make implementing reforms difficult in many of their districts. Opposition to policies and practices that might make it possible for districts to reduce academic disparities—such as reducing tracking, expanding access to rigorous subjects such as algebra and physics, and providing academic support so privileged students are not set up for failure—often comes from the parents of high achievers. Too often, these parents fear that such reforms will lower standards and diminish the quality of education that their children receive. Occasionally, such opposition can also come from veteran teachers who resent being asked to teach those whom they regard as low achievers or from community members and even students who feel threatened by the implementation of strategies to further equity in outcomes. Unless district leaders are able to overcome this opposition, so they can meet the needs of both high and low achievers, gaps in achievement may never be closed, because the opportunity to learn has not been fully extended to all students.

Reducing the Dropout Rate by Transforming Failing Schools

Since his appointment as secretary of education, Arne Duncan has made lowering the dropout rate a national priority. Threatening tough action, he has called on superintendents to shut down approximately 5,000 so-called dropout factories. Similarly, President Obama used his inauguration as an opportunity to draw attention to the dropout issue, calling on dropouts to remember, "When you drop out you not only give up on yourself but your entire community and country. We need you to stay in school and pursue your education" (Obama, 2009).

Although shutting down failing schools should be considered an option when all other strategies have proven unsuccessful, we should follow the lead forged by turnaround schools across the country and implement strategies that have proven effective at reversing failure. For example, P.S. 12 in the Brownsville section of Brooklyn was labeled a school in need of improvement (SINI) by the State of New York in 2006. By the spring of 2009, P.S. 12 was removed from the list as over 60 percent of its students were performing above proficiency on state assessments (Chapman, 2010). The school principal, Nyree Dixon, requested transfers for one-third of her teachers whom she regarded as either incompetent or unwilling to change. (State law allowed for up to 50 percent of teachers to be transferred.) She also asked her best math and literacy teachers to serve as instructional coaches. These veterans were asked to work in their colleagues' classrooms to provide ongoing professional development, model lessons, and regular feedback. Finally, Dixon forged a strong partnership with parents to increase their support for the school and for their children at home. It is important to note that this improvement occurred in a school where over 95 percent of the children qualified for free and reduced-price lunch and in a neighborhood characterized by high levels of poverty and crime. Dixon didn't change *whom* she served; she changed *how* they were served.

Closing the Preparation Gap

A vast body of research has shown that the achievement gap between middle-class and poor children, as well as among racial groups, is present long before kindergarten (Rothstein, 2004b). A significant number of studies have shown that, with the support of high-quality early childhood learning opportunities, it is possible to make significant progress in reducing these gaps (e.g., Azzi-Lessing, 2009; Crane & Barg, 2003). Research has also shown that when children who attend Head Start programs are compared to children from similar backgrounds who do not, the Head Start children are not only more successful in school but also more likely to graduate from high school and attend college (Azzi-Lessing, 2009). Longitudinal research carried out in Oklahoma, the state that has gone to the greatest lengths to provide universal access to high-quality early childhood education programs, has shown that children who attend Head Start are also more likely to be employed, earn higher incomes, and avoid prison during adulthood than children who are not enrolled (Lamy, Barnett, & Jung, 2005).

Given what we know about the benefits of preschool and early childhood education, we should ask ourselves why our nation has not done more to get poor children into such programs. If we were serious about closing the achievement gap, why should we wait until students enroll in kindergarten to address the problem when research suggests that high-quality learning experiences during infancy would be far more effective (Rothstein, 2004b)? Research by Jack Shonkoff, director of the Center on the Developing Child at Harvard University, has shown that important changes occur within a child's brain from birth to age three. If children are placed in stressful environments or do not receive proper stimulation during this period, their brains will be less likely to experience the kind of cognitive development that is essential to learning in later years (Committee on Integrating the Science of Early Childhood Development, 2000).

Few could disagree that addressing the "preparation gap" by expanding access to quality preschool makes sense. The reason why many poor children lack this opportunity has more to do with the unwillingness of state and federal governments to invest in such services than it does with the credibility of existing research. Expanding access to high-quality early childhood programs would be costly, but it is far more cost-effective to invest in preschool than to try to address learning deficits that show up later in life. Unfortunately, our nation has generally not been very good about taking a proactive approach to complex social issues.

In the absence of thoughtful and far-reaching social policy on early childhood education, districts that want to do something about the preparation gap should consider taking steps on their own to address the problem. Of course, what can be done is contingent upon the availability of resources. However, some responses, such as starting an early reading program aimed at new mothers at pediatric hospitals, can be done at low cost, and such programs have been shown to increase the likelihood that parents will read to their children during infancy (Brazelton & Sparrow, 2006). Similarly, it may be possible to invite the educators who work at local preschools to attend district-run professional development workshops so they receive the benefits of formal training. As the children enrolled in these community-based programs will eventually attend the local public schools, it makes sense to reach out to those educators, many of whom receive no training in early childhood education.

Adopting "Opportunity to Learn" Standards

Setting high academic standards for schools and students is important but relatively easy to do. The harder, yet more effective, strategy is to adopt and implement standards that create optimal conditions for learning. This means ensuring that all children, regardless of where they live, have access to high-quality schools. According to education policy expert Linda Darling-Hammond, this is exactly what countries such as South Korea, Singapore, Finland, and others have done (and obtained higher academic performance from their students than the United States has done) (Darling-Hammond, 2010). It is also what federal, state, and local government policies in the United States must strive to achieve.

The Schott Foundation and a number of other civil rights organizations have begun calling for "opportunity to learn" standards (Schott Foundation, 2009). The adoption of such standards would go a long way toward improving the quality of education in low-income communities and ensuring that all children, regardless of their race, socioeconomic status, or neighborhood or state in which they reside, would receive a high-quality education. Of course, such a change in policy would require a significant amount of political will, but it is worth noting that there is compelling logic behind such an approach. We have safety standards for airports, highways, prescription drugs, food, and water. In each case, the government regulates the provision of services and holds providers accountable for quality. To date, no state has adopted standards for schools to which it holds itself accountable. However, the adoption of these standards would be a good first step to reducing the number of poor children in underresourced, inferior schools.

Public education is by far the most accessible and democratic institution in the United States. All students have the right to a public education, regardless of their race, income, religion, gender, sexual orientation, or legal status (the courts have ruled that even undocumented immigrants have a right to a public education). Nevertheless, there is no guarantee that the education they receive will be equal. In fact, throughout the United States, public schools exhibit a high degree of inequality that is fostered by both inequities in per-pupil spending and the personal resources that families provide. Throughout the country, school funding policies are characterized by an allocation gap; we typically spend the most on children from the wealthiest families, and we spend the least on children from the poorest families (Reed, 2001). In most states, schools receive the majority of their funding from local property taxes. As a consequence, poor communities typically have fewer resources to spend on their public schools. This imbalance in resources contributes to profound inequity between schools, especially in communities where poverty is concentrated and the poor are isolated. It also contributes to a situation that Kozol (1992) has called "savage inequalities"—unsuitable learning environments that increase the likelihood of failure. The public funds that support public education play a major role in determining teachers' salaries, the condition of facilities, and the overall quality of education that children receive—all of which dramatically affect students' "opportunity to learn."

Closing or at least reducing the opportunity to learn gap is essential if disparities in achievement are to be lessened. We should not be surprised to find that disadvantaged students who attend inferior schools do not perform as well as affluent students who attend schools with abundant resources. Inequality in school funding, combined with a pervasive and growing inequality in income and wealth, creates an environment that makes closing the achievement gap challenging. It is unreasonable to expect that poor children will do as well as middle-class children if we ignore these inherent disadvantages and pretend to promote equity by holding all students to a common set of academic standards.

Opportunity gaps are perpetuated by two related aspects of inequality: inequities that are directly related to children's backgrounds and school practices that reinforce and often exacerbate inequity. Private tutors, computers, summer camp, music lessons, sports, and much more are available to children fortunate enough to have been born into families with the means to obtain these services. By contrast, poor children often lack access to many of the basic ingredients necessary for healthy social development—safety, good nutrition, and emotional and psychological support (Neher, 1991). Rothstein argues that we could actually raise student achievement without ever touching schools if we simply made sure that all students had access to a dentist, had an eye exam, and had lead paint removed from their homes (Rothstein, 2004b).

A recent international study by UNICEF found that among the 25 wealthiest nations, the United States ranked 24th on a wide variety of indicators related to child health, education, and well-being (UNICEF, 2002). One-fifth of all children in the United States come from families with incomes below the poverty level, and many of these children experience chronic hunger (Fass & Cauthen, 2006). It is not surprising that many of these children do not excel in school, given that so many of their basic needs are not being met. Indeed, there is a vast body of research that hungry, sick, and homeless children likely will not do very well in school (e.g., Bryk, Sebring, Allensworth, Luppescu, & Easton, 2010; Rothstein, 2004b).

We cannot separate a child's educational needs from his or her social welfare. One thing that schools can do in this respect is make sure that disadvantages related to children's socioeconomic backgrounds are not exacerbated in school. They can do this by avoiding practices that effectively deny poor children the opportunity to learn. For example, it is a common practice in many schools to assign the most effective teachers to the highest-achieving students and the least experienced and effective teachers to the neediest students. This typically happens because school and district leadership is unwilling or too timid to insist that there be fairness in teacher assignments and because the parents of high-achieving students refuse to allow teachers of questionable competence to teach their children. By contrast, poor parents are more likely to trust those in authority and defer to the decisions they make. A substantial body of research (see Chapters 3–7) has shown that improving the quality of instruction is the most effective way to boost student achievement.

There are numerous other ways in which schools shortchange poor children and contribute to the perpetuation of the achievement gap. Here are two common examples. First, schools use special education and English as a second language (ESL) classes as a place to put children who require additional support, but they often do not monitor the performance of those students to ensure that they receive high-quality instruction and are making academic progress. Unfortunately, this is a common practice in many schools, especially when there are no advocates on staff for students with special learning needs. When run by competent, well-trained teachers, high-quality interventions can ensure that the learning needs of vulnerable students are met. However, administrators must be vigilant about maintaining quality and doggedly monitor academic outcomes and classroom practices to ensure that programs designed for students with special learning needs do not become "dumping grounds" that further marginalize the students they were designed to help.

Second, schools succumb to the tendency to punish the neediest and lowest-performing students disproportionately. In most schools, there is a direct correspondence between the achievement gap and the discipline gap—poor, Black, Latino, and low-achieving students are typically the most likely to be punished in school (Gregory, Skiba, & Noguera, 2010). Most often, such students are punished (for disruptive and defiant behavior) by removal from the classroom or suspension, ostensibly to ensure that others have the chance to learn. Although order and safety are essential prerequisites for learning, schools must link their disciplinary practices to their educational goals. It is often the case that students who are behind academically and disconnected from learning are also more likely to act out (Noguera, 2008).

The same is true for a broad range of "high-need" students: children in foster care, who reside in group homes, or who are abused or neglected at home. Suspending these students for misbehavior effectively denies them the opportunity to learn, and it does little to teach them how to behave appropriately or address the factors that motivate their problematic behavior. The fact that schools typically punish the same students over and over again is a clear sign that such measures are not effective at changing student behavior. The ultimate goal of discipline should be to help students learn how to regulate their behavior so they become self-disciplined. It is important for schools not to tolerate or condone antisocial behavior, but they must also work harder at creating a positive learning environment in which respect and an ethical culture reinforce the attitudes and behavior they seek to promote (Noguera, 2003). For this to happen, schools must be open to using alternative forms of punishment that focus on developing character; promoting prosocial values, ethics, and norms; and maintaining a connection to learning.

Promoting School Choice and Charters

There is a growing consensus among policymakers that school choice can serve as an effective way to promote reform. Choice typically refers to a system that allows parents to choose which school their children will attend, rather than have the decision based on the neighborhood in which the family resides. Increasingly, choice has also become associated with competition among charter and traditional public schools. School choice is generally regarded as a good idea, as long as there are many high-quality schools to choose from and a commitment to maintaining some degree of diversity with respect to race and socioeconomic status (so poor and minority children are not concentrated in the worst schools). Unfortunately, in many communities that have enacted choice plans, this has not been the case. Well-organized and informed parents do their best to gain access to the best schools, and, invariably, those parents who are least informed and confronted with the greatest challenges are left out. Racial segregation in schools has been on the rise, and in many parts of the country, charter schools are even more segregated than public schools (Orfield & Lee, 2006). A substantial body of research shows that when poor children are concentrated in particular schools, raising achievement becomes more challenging (Barton & Coley, 2010; Bryk et al., 2010; Jencks et al., 1972; Orfield & Lee, 2006). Furthermore, in most choice systems, it's not parents but schools that actually do the choosing. The better schools are often able to screen students and limit enrollment, and because of high demand, they can be selective about whom they choose. Those who are not chosen often end up attending lower-quality public schools with fewer resources.

Several, but certainly not all, charter schools have demonstrated considerable success in educating poor children. In New York, charter schools administered by the State University of New York have consistently outperformed similar schools in the communities where they are located (Charter Schools Institute, 2010). The success of the SUNY charter schools has been credited to the rigorous review policies that are applied to the schools and the firm accountability standards that are maintained. If similar quality-control measures can be adopted elsewhere, charter schools should be supported as a means to increase the supply of good schools available to poor children. However, they must also serve high-need children (i.e., children with learning disabilities and English language learners). Charter schools must be held accountable for attrition and not be allowed to dismiss or discourage students who are more difficult to teach. If such policies were enacted by state governments, charter schools might serve as models of innovation and provide concrete examples to traditional public schools of what is possible.

Evaluating Teachers Based Upon Student Performance and Peer Evaluation

Addressing the effectiveness of teachers must be an essential part of education reform in this country. A vast body of research has demonstrated that among the many variables influencing student achievement (e.g., parental support, peer influences, student motivation), the quality of instruction that students receive may be the most important because it is potentially the most easily altered (Darling-Hammond & Richardson, 2009; Good, 1987; Silva, 2010). Teacher effectiveness can be enhanced through improved professional development. Instruction can also be supplemented by the effective use of technology to personalize learning and after-school programs that reinforce the learning that occurs during the school day. In most schools that have experienced a significant turnaround in performance, considerable emphasis was placed on strategies to improve the quality of teaching (Smith, 2007).

The powerful connection between excellent teaching and higher levels of student learning seems obvious. However, this does not mean that judging and rewarding teachers on the basis of test scores is necessarily a good idea. Since the enactment of NCLB, many schools have adopted scripted curricula intended to tightly control instruction and ensure that students will be prepared for annual state exams. Such an emphasis is understandable, given that schools are increasingly judged on the basis of student test scores. However, several studies have shown that an exclusive focus on testing has led to a narrowing of the curriculum and heavy emphasis on test preparation in large numbers of schools, and these tendencies are having a damaging effect on teaching and learning (Haney 2004; Irvine 2003; King, 2005).[5] The tendency to narrow the focus of the curriculum and deemphasize the cultivation of higher-order thinking skills, which are more difficult to assess, will undoubtedly increase if student test scores continue to be used to evaluate and reward teachers. Such an approach could also discourage teachers from working in high-need schools or with academically challenged students, for whom it may be more difficult to produce measurable gains in test scores.

As researchers who have studied these issues for many years, we recognize that it is essential for teachers to focus on evidence that their students are learning. However, it makes more sense for districts to focus on direct observation of teachers and provide training tailored to their specific needs than to rely largely on student test scores to evaluate teacher performance. A small (but statistically significant) number of districts have used peer mentoring and evaluation as strategies to promote effective teaching (Goldstein, 2010; Goldstein & Noguera, 2006). These schools that employ peer evaluation have removed a larger number of ineffective teachers than did those schools that rely upon administrators (who often are not trained in the subject matter) to conduct evaluations. Such an approach, when combined with ongoing, site-based professional development and subject-matter coaching, has considerable promise and should be encouraged. It is also important for school districts to create incentives, including increased pay, to attract teachers with a history of success in high-need schools and classrooms. If such a strategy were combined with lower class sizes and extended learning opportunities after school and during the summer, it is possible that we could see major gains for a vast number of struggling students.

Critics frequently charge that, in some school districts, teachers' unions have obstructed reform because they resist attempts to grant greater flexibility in how teachers are assigned and because they make it difficult to remove ineffective and negligent teachers. This claim is frequently exaggerated; otherwise, one would expect to find that in the states where unions are weakest, educational performance is highest. In fact, the opposite tends to be true (Eberts & Stone, 1987; McDonnell & Pascal, 1988). There are examples in some school districts of policies advocated by teacher unions that have been obstacles to improvement. In specific areas where this is the case, unions must recognize that intransigence only undermines the credibility and stature of the teaching profession. When unions make it difficult to remove ineffective teachers, it hurts not only students but also hardworking, conscientious teachers. Nonetheless, as it seems likely that teacher unions will be around for many years to come, it would be wise to find ways to collaborate with them, devise peer-review programs, and use the negotiation process to push for greater flexibility in teacher assignments. Given the evidence provided earlier in this volume, it also seems wise to broaden the criteria for *teaching* (rather than *teacher*) effectiveness to include the nurturance of student engagement and development of strategies that enhance students' adaptive learning postures and focus on students' assets.

Changing the Paradigm to Educate All Students

Educational institutions must perform two parallel and, at times, contradictory functions. First, schools must pass on the knowledge and skills acquired by previous generations so a new generation of students will be able to perform the tasks required to function in the modern world. This includes basic skills in literacy and numeracy, as well as more advanced skills in science, mathematics, and other subjects. This type of training is essential if we are to prepare young people for jobs in areas that are critical to the performance of our economy and if we are to ensure that there will be an adequate number of doctors, engineers, teachers, and other professionals to serve societal needs in the future.

However, in addition to preparing students to meet the needs of the present, schools must also devise strategies to respond to the problems of the future. This includes challenges inherited from previous generations (e.g., infectious diseases, budget deficits, climate change) and a host of new problems that have yet to materialize. For example, who would have anticipated that longer life spans would become a burden on our health care and social service systems or that the end of the Cold War would be followed by a global war on terrorism? The need to prepare today's students for an uncertain future compels schools to find ways to nurture students' creativity, imagination, and problem-solving skills so they will have the intellectual ability to respond to the formidable challenges they will likely face. For example, unless we are going to abandon postindustrial cities such as Detroit, Cleveland, and Buffalo, future generations must find ways to make these cities economically viable. Similarly, if climate change continues unabated, future generations will have to devise ways to respond to the related environmental, political, and economic crises. In the face of such challenges, old forms of knowledge will undoubtedly be inadequate. New ideas, technology, and approaches will be needed if we are to contend with unknown challenges of the future and achieve some form of progress.

In essence, the first function of education is aimed at preparing young people to transition into society as it is, whereas the second function must provide students with the tools and intellectual foundation they will use to transform society into what we hope it will become. The first function is inherently conservative. It emphasizes passing on existing knowledge and skills so that young people can be successfully assimilated into the workforce. The second function is inherently more progressive, because it aims at deliberately preparing young people to become agents of innovation and change.

Realistically, schools must carry out both functions. If we ignore the practical need that students have for skills that will enable them to participate fully in our society, they will be unable to compete for jobs or understand what is expected of them in order to participate as informed citizens in our democracy. However, if we ignore the need to cultivate creativity and problem solving, then subsequent generations will be unable to contend with the formidable array of problems they will inherit and that will arise in the future.

John Taylor Gatto, a former Teacher of the Year for New York City (1989, 1990, and 1991) who received the same honor from New York State in 1991, is now a renowned author, acclaimed for his creative insights about teaching and education. In his most recent book (2005), he suggests that many of the most influential inventors and entrepreneurs did not receive training that was responsible for their contributions in school. In fact, he contends that their contributions frequently occurred in spite of school, rather than because of it. He argues that schools often rely on strategies that stifle creativity and innovation because they emphasize conformity and obedience. Gatto calls for six policy changes that should foster the kind of learning environments that will prepare students for the uncertainties of the 21st century. These include

1. A shift away from a content-based curriculum to one that focuses on helping students develop independent learning strategies.
2. A shift away from external rewards and threats to a focus on cultivating the intrinsic motivation to learn and self-discipline.
3. A greater emphasis on teaching children how to communicate and collaborate with others.
4. The need to focus on preparing students to respect human rights and democracy by practicing such principles within schools.
5. Greater use of technology to personalize learning for students and to empower students to control the pace at which they learn.

6. Greater tolerance for variations in learning styles and motivation and less emphasis on conformity. (Gatto, 2005)

Gatto writes, "Look… at the seven lessons of school teaching—confusion, class position, indifference, emotional and intellectual dependency, conditional self-esteem, surveillance—all of these lessons are prime training for permanent underclasses, people deprived forever of finding the center of their own special genius.… Over this time the training has shaken loose from its own original logic: to regulate the poor." He goes on to say, "Can you imagine a school where children challenged prevailing assumptions? Or worked alone without guidance? Or defined their own problems? It would be a radical contradiction of everything we've been conditioned to expect schools to do" (p. 42).

To many policymakers, Gatto's critique of education and his calls for change can easily be dismissed as impractical and idealistic. This is because educational policy is primarily premised on a lack of trust—in teachers who are seen as incompetent and lazy, in public schools that are frequently described as undermining the economic competitiveness of U.S. society, and in parents who are seen as failing to raise their children properly. When a lack of trust is combined with a lack of political will to undertake the social reforms necessary to reduce inequality, we end up with educational policies that are overly punitive and narrowly focused on teaching basic skills. For several years, international comparisons have shown that educational performance in the United States is lagging steadily behind that of other nations (Darling-Hammond, 2010; Schmidt et al., 2001). It is increasingly clear that we cannot afford to continue to pursue the same educational policies that have left us with dropout rates as high as 50 percent in most of our major cities (Bridgeland, DiIulio, & Morison, 2006). We must find a way to carry out important social functions that are essential to the well-being and progress of society. If not, we will be in serious trouble.

Until there is an alternative institution, we will have to rely primarily on public schools to produce the next generation of scientists, researchers, artists, and politicians. We cannot afford to leave it to chance that a generation of innovators will emerge and be able to solve the vast number of problems they will face. Instead, we must find ways to increase the possibility that schools can be places where critical thinking and problem-solving abilities are nurtured, where good teaching can flourish, and where the pursuit of knowledge is recognized as inherently important. For this to happen, we will undoubtedly have to change the paradigm that has served as the framework for most educational practices and policies for the last hundred years.

One of the major reasons why the achievement gap was not addressed in the past was because it was assumed that intelligence was largely an innate property, rooted in the genetic endowments of children. This assumption about the biological basis of intelligence not only influenced attitudes toward the education of children of color but also informed educational practices for all children. It led schools to rely on a variety of strategies aimed at measuring aptitude and academic potential and to devise a variety of means to sort students based on these measures. Historically, schools carried out these tasks by identifying students with talent and potential early, employing a variety of strategies to assess intelligence and acumen, and then grouping students based on their presumed potential (Boykin, 2000). Today, such sorting practices are common and widespread, even as we proclaim concern about educating all children.

Interestingly, although NCLB is rooted largely in the old paradigm of schooling, it requires schools to produce evidence that all children, regardless of their backgrounds, are learning. To meet the requirements of the law, schools have to adopt a new paradigm—one that compels them to devise new ways to cultivate talent and ability. By identifying the achievement gap as a problem and framing it as one that schools have a moral imperative to address, NCLB forced U.S. schools to confront an issue that required them to take a new approach and adopt a new paradigm.

If we are going to make greater progress in educating all children, then we must ensure that all students have an equal opportunity to learn. If we are to succeed in making sure that all students receive an education that prepares them for the present and the future, then we must enact policies that actively promote educational equity and foster critical and innovative thinking, intrinsic motivation, creativity, and problem solving. A commitment to equity will also force schools to adopt educational practices that allow them to take responsibility for student outcomes, evidence of mastery, and conditions that foster effective teaching and higher levels of learning.

Jencks and colleagues (1972) argue that Americans are generally comfortable with the principle of equal opportunity, but they tend to be divided over the question of equality in results. If genuine progress is to be achieved in educating all children, then what is needed is a complete change in direction. The United States needs a new policy agenda for education that will make it possible for schools to play a central role in ongoing efforts to rebuild the U.S. economy. The Obama administration has been clear about its determination to expand access to high-quality early childhood and after-school programs and to end the federal obsession with using standardized testing as the exclusive tool for evaluating the performance of schools. The question now is how these general values and goals can be translated into policy.

As the federal government contemplates what it will do to address the challenges confronting our nation's schools, it will need to understand that the problems cannot be solved by a few sweeping reforms (i.e., Race to the Top, increasing the number of charter schools, forcing states to evaluate teachers on the basis of student test scores) or major investments in a few discrete initiatives. New approaches to educating children and managing schools and districts are necessary to enact the changes in educational outcomes that the nation so desperately needs. From finding ways to break the cycle of poverty to devising new strategies to generate employment in cities where the manufacturing sector has collapsed, the federal government (and others) will need a bold new strategy for reforming public education if the nation is to move forward.

Considering Other Paradigm-Changing Issues and Their Policy Implications

Let evidence be our guide. We must let the most successful, systematic, and replicable evidence guide implementation of schooling practices. Too often, what gets implemented in the name of school reform or improvement is what sounds good or looks good. An evidence-based approach is one that draws on the research literature for what works, as well as for why and how it works. Beyond the research literature, though, we must also make sure that the evidence is gathered with fidelity and supported by data-driven instruction, adequate and appropriate preparation, high-quality instruction, and students who are engaged. When this is not the case, it is critical that appropriate adjustments are made.

Pay attention to classroom transactions and dynamics. In spite of dictates and directives that are passed down from the federal government to the state to the local district to the individual school, the nexus of the educational process takes place inside classrooms, on an ongoing basis, between teachers and students and among students themselves. Whatever is done inside classrooms to maximize these daily learning opportunities must be the ultimate focus of attention. Consequently, the policies and practices at each level should be actualized with this ultimate goal in mind.

Focus on assets. In a related vein, it is also crucial that we pay attention to and highlight an asset-focused framework. With respect to individual classrooms, this means we must build on the personal, social, cultural, experiential, and intellectual assets that students from diverse backgrounds bring with them, provide conditions that allow these assets to flourish, and, when such assets are not readily apparent, create them for students in the course of teaching and learning activities. As mentioned at the beginning of Chapter 5, these assets can consist as examples of one's interests, preferences, motivations, passions, attitudes, beliefs, identities, prior and emerging experiences, knowledge, understandings, skills, or competencies. The asset-focused strategies that were laid out, and whose effectiveness is documented across Chapters 5–7, are positioned well to capitalize on such existing and emerging assets and create them if necessary. Moreover, when the guiding functions/adaptive learning postures described and documented in Chapter 4 are manifested, they serve as crucial assets as well.

Educate the whole child. Although standardized achievement testing is important, and there is a definite need for universal metrics with which we can measure the progress our schools are making in educating children, we cannot slip into letting "the testing tail wag the educational dog." To be sure, youth from marginalized backgrounds need to perform better on tests, but to move them from the social margins and prepare them for the rigors, realities, and responsibilities of the 21st century, we must also focus on the whole child. We must encourage our students to see themselves as good students, good readers, and budding scientists. We must heighten their social and emotional competence, in addition to their self- or collective efficacy. We must get them to be active agents in their own learning processes. They must believe that they can become smarter or better learners if they are willing to put forth greater effort. They must also see their education as meaningful to their lives—personally, socially, and culturally—and understand how their experiences connect with what they learn in school and, in turn, how what they learn in school can be put to practical benefit in their lives, in their communities, and for the good of society at large. Finally, they must also have optimism about their educational futures.

Seek multiple pathways to success. We must move away from a "sorting paradigm" to one that focuses on cultivating high levels of talent (Boykin, 2000; Boykin & Ellison, 2009). Given the arguments of this book, it is clear that we must overdetermine success to foster this talent. That is, we must establish multiple pathways, all of which are evidence based, that can lead to successful, gap-closing outcomes. Among these are classroom-based factors, to be sure, but they must also include leadership and organizational functions, academic support activities, student services, and parent and community engagement. All of these pathways, as for any learning context, should be imbued with activities that promote engagement, support adaptive learning postures, and have an asset focus. With teachers in particular, it is clear that a one-shot workshop approach to professional development is woefully insufficient (Darling-Hammond & Richardson, 2009). After any workshop, there should be follow-up, job-embedded support activities that include constructive feedback, coaching, and classroom demonstrations. In addition, teachers should form professional learning communities that further sharpen and deepen their skills at delivering high-quality instruction (Wood, 2007).

A Concluding Comment

As we've stated repeatedly throughout this book, policymakers must recognize that our educational troubles are inextricably related to the deep and profound inequalities that characterize most aspects of modern U.S. society. We must create a social safety net for children, and we must expand access to excellent schools so that all children have the opportunity to achieve their potential. As immigration is unlikely to fade as an issue (Clark, 1998; Pew Center, 2011), the federal government must also find ways to ensure that schools can meet the learning needs of documented and undocumented children, so that those who cross our borders do not become an underclass trapped in low-wage jobs.

A broader and bolder approach to education is needed to achieve success and bring about sustainable reform in public education. Such an approach must be rooted in the recognition that children need to be well fed, healthy, and intellectually challenged in order to thrive and achieve. Educators, policymakers, parents, and students throughout the country must demand such an educational environment if we have a hope of creating the schools our children need and deserve. The effort to promote equity and close the achievement gap is consistent with the basic promise of public education in the United States—schools should function as the equalizers of opportunity (Sizer, 1984). No matter how difficult and elusive it may be, the goal of closing the achievement gap remains one that we must pursue if schools are to remain viable as public institutions.

Notes

Chapter 1

1. We choose to use *Black* rather than *African American* to identify students of African descent because *Black* includes students of African and Caribbean heritage. In many school districts, data on student performance do not draw distinctions within racial groups based on immigration status or national origin.
2. Several national leaders, including Presidents Bush and Obama, Chancellor of New York City Public Schools Joel Klein, and Secretary of Education Arne Duncan, have referred to education as the civil rights issue of the 21st century. However, none of these individuals has spelled out what this means with respect to who the opponents of educational rights are or how these rights will be won.
3. It has become increasingly common to blame teacher unions for the lack of progress in improving student achievement. See, for example, Thomas and Weingart (2010).
4. The NAEP long-term trend assessment uses "scale anchors" to define particular performance levels. The reading performance levels are as follows: (150) Carry out simple, discrete reading tasks, (200) Demonstrate partially developed skills and understanding, (250) Interrelate ideas and make generalizations, (300) Understand complicated information, and (350) Learn from specialized reading materials.
5. The lowest performance level reported in the 9-year-old NAEP LTT is 150, and the highest performance level is 250.
6. The lowest performance level reported in the 13-year-old NAEP LTT is 200, and the highest performance level is 300.
7. The NAEP long-term trend assessment uses "scale anchors" to define particular performance levels. The mathematics performance levels are as follows: (150) Simple arithmetic facts, (200) Beginning skills and understandings, (250) Numerical operations and beginning problem solving, (300) Moderately complex procedures and reasoning, and (350) Multistep problem solving and algebra.
8. Although there may appear to be a numerical difference in the size of the achievement gap between two years, these differences may not be statistically significant. When two numbers are not statistically significant from each other, they are, for all intents and purposes, equal to each other. Difference in NAEP sample sizes may account

for wide ranges of numbers that appear to differ from one another, but they are not statistically different.

9. There are only two ways that Black and Latino student achievement can meet the levels of achievement of their White peers. The first way is for Black and Latino student achievement to increase while White student achievement decreases, remains constant, or increases at a slightly slower rate. The second way is for White student achievement to decline while Black and Latino student achievement increases, remains constant, or at the very least decreases at a slower rate.

Chapter 2

1. For example, prior to 1980, Latinos were classified as Whites on the U.S. Census. This made it difficult to address the common practice of segregating Latino students throughout the Southwest and in California.

2. We are not implying that the physical differences associated with race—skin color, hair texture, and so forth—are irrelevant; rather, we are arguing that the social significance associated with these differences varies over time. For a discussion on how phenotype and the physical characteristics associated with race relate to the idea that race can be regarded as a social construct, see Fergus (2004).

Chapter 8

1. New York City was regarded as one of the best-performing urban districts in the nation until the state of New York recalibrated the rankings associated with test score results; as a result, large numbers of students were reclassified as deficient and in need of remediation.

2. This does not suggest that the students who did not pass the regents exams were ineligible to graduate, since the local diploma option was available for those students. Students who earned a regents diploma, however, were more competitive applicants for college admission than students earning local diplomas.

3. Conley (2010) notes that even though UPCS has a high college attendance rate, its college-bound graduates often need additional supports to sustain their level of success at the college level.

Chapter 9

1. The most recent example of test score inflation is in New York. In July 2010, David Steiner, the commissioner of education, reported that a review of the state's exams by an assessment expert revealed that the thresholds set by the state to determine student proficiency had been set too low and needed to be recalibrated. As a result of the modifications, thousands of students who had been designated as proficient and on grade level in literacy and math were reclassified as being in need of remediation (Medina, 2010).

2. The state exam used in Massachusetts is widely regarded as one of the most challenging in the nation (Chenoweth, 2009). To be fully prepared, students need to have taken and passed Algebra and Geometry by 10th grade. At most high schools in Boston in 2002, fewer than 25 percent were prepared in this way.

3. Despite serving an impoverished student population where over 95 percent qualify for free and reduced-price lunch, P.S. 188 has received an *A* on the district ratings. Its former principal, Barbara Slatin, credits its many partnerships with health and social service agencies for this extraordinary success.

4. According to Chenoweth (2007), exceptional schools teach their students; do not teach to the state tests; have high expectations of their students; know what the stakes are; embrace and use all of the data they can get their hands on; use data to focus on individual students, not just groups of students; constantly reexamine what they do; embrace accountability; make decisions on what is good for kids, not what is good for adults; use school time wisely; leverage as many resources from the community as possible; expand the time students—particularly struggling students—have in school; do not spend a lot of time disciplining students, in the sense of punishment; establish an atmosphere of respect; like kids; make sure that the kids who struggle the most have the best instruction; have principals who are a constant presence; recognize that while the principals are important leaders, they are not the only leaders; pay careful attention to the quality of the teaching staff; provide teachers with time to meet so they can plan and work collaboratively; provide teachers with time to observe one another; think seriously about professional development; assume they will have to train new teachers more or less from scratch and carefully acculturate all newly hired teachers; have high-quality, dedicated, and competent office and building staff who feel they are part of the educational mission of the school; and are nice places to work.

5. Several studies and news reports on school districts have found that schools are narrowing the curriculum to increase the amount of time that students spend on subjects that will be tested. Several of these reports cite examples where subjects such as social studies, music, art, physical education, and even science have been given less time and attention, as a result of the increased focus on test preparation in math and literacy. For more information, see Dillon (2006) and Jennings (2006).

References

Allen, B., & Boykin, A. (1991). The influence of contextual factors on Afro-American and Euro American children's performance: Effects of movement opportunity and music. *International Journal of Psychology, 26*(3), 373–387.

Allen, B. A., & Butler, L. (1996). The effects of music and movement opportunity on the analogical reasoning performance of African American and White school children: A preliminary study. *Journal of Black Psychology, 22*(3), 316–328.

Allen, V. (1976). The helping relationship and socialization of children: Some perspectives on tutoring. In V. Allen (Ed.), *Children as teachers* (pp. 9–26). New York: Academic Press.

Ames, C. (1992). Classrooms: Goals, structures, and student motivation. *Journal of Educational Psychology, 84*(3), 261–271.

Ames. C. A. (1990). Motivation: What teachers need to know. *Teachers College Record, 91*(3), 409–421.

Anand, P. G., & Ross, S. M. (1987). Using computer-assisted instruction to personalize arithmetic materials for elementary school children. *Journal of Educational Psychology, 79*(1), 72–78.

Anyon, J. (2005). *Radical possibilities: Public policy, urban education, and a new social movement.* New York: Routledge.

Aronson, J., Fried, C., & Good, C. (2002). Reducing the effects of stereotype threat on African American college students by shaping theories of intelligence. *Journal of Experimental Social Psychology, 38*, 113–125.

Assor, A., Kaplan, H., & Roth, G. (2002). Choice is good, but relevance is excellent: Autonomy-enhancing and suppressing teacher behaviours in predicting student's engagement in school work. *British Journal of Educational Psychology, 72*(2), 261–278.

Azzi-Lessing, L. (2009). Quality support infrastructure in early childhood: Still (mostly) missing. *Early Childhood Research & Practice, 11*(1).

Baker, J. A. (1999). Teacher–student interaction in urban at-risk classrooms: Differential behavior, relationship, quality, and student satisfaction with school. *The Elementary School Journal, 100*(1), 57–70.

Balfanz, R., & Byrnes, V. (2006). Closing the mathematics achievement gap in high-poverty middle schools: Enablers and constraints. *Journal of Education for Students Placed at Risk, 11*(2), 143–159.

Bandura, A. (1977). Self-efficacy: Toward a unifying theory of behavioral change. *Psychology Review, 84*(2), 191–215.

Bandura, A. (1986). *Social foundations of thought and action: A social cognitive theory.* Englewood Cliffs, NJ: Prentice Hall.

Bandura, A. (1993). Perceived self-efficacy in cognitive development and functioning. *Educational Psychologist, 28*(2), 117–148.

Bandura, A. (1994). Self-efficacy. In V. S. Ramachaudran (Ed.), *Encyclopedia of human behavior* (vol. 4, pp. 71–81). New York: Academic Press.

Banks, J. (1981). *Multi-ethnic education.* Needham Heights, MA: Allyn & Bacon.

Barbarin, O. (2002). The Black–White achievement gap in early reading skills: Familial and sociocultural context. In B. Bowman (Ed.), *Love to read: Essays in developing and enhancing early literacy skills of African American children* (pp. 1–15). Washington, DC: National Black Child Development Institute.

Barton, P. E., & Coley, R. J. (2010). The Black–White achievement gap: When progress stopped. Princeton, NJ: Educational Testing Service. Available: http://www.ets.org/Media/Research/pdf/PICBWGAP.pdf

Biemiller, A., & Boote, C. (2006). An effective method for building meaning: Vocabulary in the primary grades. *Journal of Educational Psychology, 98*(1), 44–62.

Blackwell, L. A., Trzesniewski, K. H., & Dweck, C. S. (2007). Implicit theories of intelligence predict achievement across an adolescent transition: A longitudinal study and an intervention. *Child Development, 78*(1), 246–263.

Blankstein, A., & Noguera, P. A. (2004). Reclaiming the promise of public education: The will is the way for schools where failure is not an option. *School Administrator, 61*(5), 31.

Bloom, B. (1971). *Mastery learning.* New York: Holt, Rinehart, & Winston.

Bloom, B. (1981). *All our children learning.* New York: McGraw-Hill.

Bloom, H. S., Thompson, S. L., Unterman, R., Herlihy, C., & Payne, C. F. (2010). *Transforming the high school experience: How New York City's new small schools are boosting student achievement and graduation rates.* New York: MDRC.

Bodovski, K., & Farkas, G. (2007). Mathematics growth in early elementary school: The roles of beginning knowledge, student engagement, and instruction. *The Elementary School Journal, 108*(2), 116–130.

Boekaerts, M., & Cascallar, E. (2006). How far have we moved toward the integration of theory and practice in self-regulation? *Education Psychology Review, 18*(3), 199–210.

Boekaerts, M., Pintrich, P. R., & Zeidner, M. (2000). *Handbook of self-regulation.* San Diego, CA: Academic Press.

Bombardieri, M. (2005, January 17). Summers' remarks on women draw fire. *Boston Globe.*

Bonilla-Silva, E. (2002). We are all Americans! The Latin Americanization of racial stratification in the USA. *Race and Society, 5*(1), 3–16.

Borman, G., & Overman, L. (2004). Academic resilience among poor and minority students. *Elementary School Journal, 104*(3), 177–195.

Boykin, A. W. (1983). The academic performance of Afro-American children. In J. Spence (Ed.), *Achievement and achievement motives* (pp. 321–371). San Francisco: Freeman.

Boykin, A. W. (1986). The triple quandary and the schooling of Afro American children. In U. Neisser (Ed.), *The school achievement of minority children* (pp. 57–93). Hillsdale, NJ: Lawrence Erlbaum.

Boykin, A. W. (2000). The talent development model of schooling: Placing students at promise for academic success. *Journal of Education for Students Placed at Risk, 5*(1–2), 3–25.

Boykin, A. W., & Allen, B. A. (2003). Cultural integrity and schooling outcomes. In P. Pufall & R. Unsworth (Eds.), *Rethinking childhood* (pp. 104–120). New Brunswick, NJ: Rutgers University Press.

Boykin, A. W., & Cunningham, R. (2001). The effects of movement expressiveness in story content and learning context on the analogical reasoning performance of African American children. *Journal of Negro Education, 70*(1–2), 72–83.

Boykin, A. W., & Ellison, C. (1995). The multiple ecologies of Black youth socialization: An Afrographic analysis. In R. L. Taylor (Ed.), *African-American youth: Their social and economic status in the United States* (pp. 93–128). Westport, CT: Praeger Press.

Boykin, A. W., & Ellison, C. (2009). The talent quest model and the educating of African American children. In H. Neville, B. Tynes, & S. Utsey (Eds.), *Handbook of African American psychology* (pp. 237–254). Thousand Oaks, CA: Sage.

Boykin, A. W., Lilja, A., & Tyler, K. (2004). The influence of communal vs. individual learning context on the academic performance in social studies of grade 4–5 African Americans. *Learning Environments Research, 7*(3), 227–244.

Boykin, A. W., Tyler, K. M., & Miller, O. A. (2005). In search of cultural themes and their expressions in the dynamics of classroom life. *Urban Education, 40*(5), 521–549.

Brand, B. R., Glasson, G. E., Green, A. M. (2006). Sociocultural factors influencing students' learning in science and mathematics: An analysis of the perspectives of African American students. *School Science and Mathematics, 106*(5), 228–236.

Braun, H. I., Wang, A., Jenkins, F., & Weinbaum, E. (2006). The Black–White achievement gap: Do state policies matter? *Education Policy Analysis Archives, 14*(8). Retrieved on September 5, 2008, from http://epaa.asu.edu/epaa/v14n8/v14n8.pdf

Brazelton, B., & Sparrow, J. (2006). *Touch points*. New York: A. Merloyd Lawrence Books.

Bridgeland, J. M., DiIulio, J. J., & Morison, K. B. (2006). *The silent epidemic: Perspectives of high school dropouts*. Washington, DC: Civic Enterprises.

Bryk, A. S., & Schneider, B. (2003). Trust in schools: A core resource for school reform. *Educational Leadership, 60*(6), 40–44.

Bryk, A. S., Sebring, P. B., Allensworth, E., Luppescu, S., & Easton, J. Q. (2010). *Organizing schools for improvement: Lessons from Chicago*. Chicago: University of Chicago Press.

Burchinal, M. R., Peisner-Feinberg, E., Pianta, R., & Howes, C. (2002). Development of academic skills from preschool through second grade: Family and classroom predictors of developmental trajectories. *Journal of School Psychology, 40*(5), 415–436.

Byrnes, J. (2003). Factors predictive of mathematic achievement in white, black, and Hispanic 12th graders. *Journal of Educational Psychology, 95*(2), 316–326.

Byrnes, J. P., & Miller, D. C. (2007). The relative importance of predictors of math and science achievement: An opportunity–propensity analysis. *Contemporary Educational Psychology, 32*(4), 599–629.

Camahalan, F. (2006). Effects of a metacognitive reading program on the reading achievement and metacognitive strategies of students with cases of dyslexia. *Reading Improvement, 43*(2), 77–93.

Carlassare, E. (1994). Essentialism in ecofeminist discourse. In C. Merchant (Ed.), *Key concepts in critical theory: Ecology* (pp. 220–234). Atlantic Highlands, NJ: Humanities Press.

Casteel, C. (1997). Attitudes of African American and Caucasian eighth grade students about praises, rewards and punishments. *Elementary School Guidance and Counseling, 31*(4), 262–272.

CBS News. (2009, May 5). 5000 failing schools to close.

Chan, K.S.L., & Moore, P. J. (2006). Development of attribution beliefs and strategic knowledge in years 5–9: A longitudinal analysis. *Educational Psychology, 26*(2), 161–185.

Chapman, B. (2010, December 10). Brownsville P.S. 12 fighting to save afterschool tutoring program. *New York Daily News*, p. 16.

Charter Schools Institute. (2010). *Comparison of charter school performance by authorizer*. Albany, NY: Charter Schools Institute, State University of New York.

Chatterji, M. (2006). Reading achievement gaps, correlates, and moderators of early reading achievement: Evidence from the early childhood longitudinal study (ECLS) kindergarten to first grade sample. *Journal of Educational Psychology, 98*(3), 489–507.

Chenoweth, K. (2007). *It's being done: Academic success in unexpected schools.* Cambridge, MA: Harvard Education Press.

Chenoweth, K. (2009). *How it's being done: Urgent lessons from unexpected schools.* Cambridge, MA: Harvard Education Press.

Chirkov, V. I., Ryan, R. M., Kim, Y., & Kaplan, U. (2003). Differentiating autonomy from individualism and independence: A self-determination theory perspective on internalization of cultural orientations and well-being. *Journal of Personality and Social Psychology, 84*(1), 97–110.

Civil Rights Project. (2009). *U.S. school segregation on the rise.* Los Angeles: UCLA.

Clark, W. (1998). *The California cauldron.* New York: Guilford Press.

Cohen, G. L., Garcia, J., Apfel, N., & Master, A. (2006). Reducing the racial achievement gap: A social-psychological intervention. *Science, 313*(5791), 1307–1310.

Coleman, S., & Vishnane, A. (2003, November 14). Racial gap widens on MCAS. *Boston Globe,* p. 7.

Comer, J. P. (1988). Educating poor minority children. *Scientific American, 259*(5), 24–30.

Committee on Integrating the Science of Early Childhood Development. (2000). *From neurons to neighborhoods: The science of early childhood development.* Washington DC: National Academies Press.

Conley, D. T. (2010). *College and career ready: Helping all students succeed beyond high school.* San Francisco: Jossey-Bass.

Connor, C. M., Morrison, F. J., & Katch, L. E. (2004). Beyond the reading wars: Exploring the effect of child-instruction interactions on growth in early reading. *Scientific Studies of Reading, 8*(4), 305–336.

Connor, C. M., Morrison, F. J., & Petrella, J. N. (2004). Effective reading comprehension instruction: Examining child × instruction interactions. *Journal of Educational Psychology, 96*(4), 682–698.

Cook, L. K., & Mayer, R. E. (1988). Teaching readers about the structure of scientific text. *Journal of Educational Psychology, 80*(4), 448–456.

Cordova, D. I., & Lepper, M. R. (1996). Intrinsic motivation and the process of learning: Beneficial effects of contextualization, personalization, and choice. *Journal of Educational Psychology, 88*(4), 715–730.

Cosby, B., & Poussaint, A. (2007). *Come on, people: On the path from victims to victors.* Nashville, TN: Thomas Nelson.

Crane, J., & Barg, M. (2003, April). Do early childhood intervention programs really work? *Coalition for Evidence-Based Policy.* Available: http://www.evidencebasedprograms.org/static/pdfs/Do%20Early%20Intervention%20Programs%20Really%20Work7.pdf

Cremin, L. A. (1988). *American education: The metropolitan experience, 1876–1980.* New York: HarperCollins.

Crosnoe, R., Morrison, F., Burchinal, M., Pianta, R., Keating, D., Friedman, S. L., & Clarke-Stewart, K. A. (2010). Instruction, teacher–student relations, and math achievement trajectories in elementary school. *Journal of Educational Psychology, 102*(2), 407–417.

Cumming, J. J., & Elkins, J. (1999). Lack of automaticity in the basic addition facts as a characteristic of arithmetic learning problems and instructional needs. *Mathematical Cognition, 5*(2), 149–180.

D'Ailly, H. H., Simpson, J., & MacKinnon, G. E. (1997). Where should "you" go in a math compare problem? *Journal of Educational Psychology, 89*(3), 562–567.

Dansereau, D. F. (1988). Cooperative learning strategies. In C. E. Weinstein, E. T. Goetz, & P. A. Alexander (Eds.), *Learning and study strategies: Issues in assessment, instruction, and evaluation* (pp. 103–120). Orlando, FL: Academic Press.

Darling-Hammond, L. (2004). Standards, accountability, and school reform. *Teachers College Record, 106*(6), 1047–1085.

Darling-Hammond, L. (2007). The flat Earth and education: How America's commitment to equity will determine our future. *Educational Researcher, 36*(6), 318–334.

Darling-Hammond, L. (2010). *The flat world and education: How America's commitment to equity will determine our future.* New York: Teachers College Press.

Darling-Hammond, L., & Richardson, N. (2009). Teaching learning: What matters? *Educational Leadership, 66*(5), 46–55.

Davidman, L., & Davidman, P. (1994). *Teaching with a multicultural perspective.* White Plains, NY: Longman.

Davis-Dorsey, J., Ross, S. M., & Morrison, G. R. (1991). The role of rewording and context personalization in the solving of mathematical word problems. *Journal of Educational Psychology, 83*(1), 61–68.

De La Paz, S. (2007). Managing cognitive demands for writing: Comparing the effects of instructional components in strategy instruction. *Reading & Writing Quarterly, 23*(3), 249–266.

DeLeeuw, K. E:, & Mayer, R. E. (2008). A comparison of three measures of cognitive load: Evidence for separable measures of intrinsic, extraneous, and germane load. *Journal of Educational Psychology, 100*(1), 223–234.

Delpit, L. (1988). The silenced dialogue: Power and pedagogy in educating other people's children. *Harvard Educational Review, 58*(3), 280–298.

Delpit, L. (1995). *Other people's children: Cultural conflict in the classroom.* New York: New Press.

Dessauer, C. (2011, March 8). The last lessons of Jerry Weast: A question and answer session with the retiring superintendent of Montgomery County Public Schools. *Bethesda Magazine.*

Dillon, S. (2006, March 26). Schools cut back on subjects to push reading and math. *New York Times,* p. 11.

Dillon, S. (2009, July 14). Racial gap widens. *New York Times,* p. 1.

Dillon, S. (2010a, March 13). Obama calls for major change in education law. *New York Times,* p. A1.

Dillon, S. (2010b, September 27). 4,100 students prove 'small is better' rule wrong. *New York Times,* p. A1.

DiPerna, J. C., Lei, P.-W., & Reid, E. E. (2007). Kindergarten predictors of mathematical growth in the primary grades: An investigation using the Early Childhood Longitudinal Study–Kindergarten cohort. *Journal of Educational Psychology, 99*(2), 369–379.

Dowhower, S. L. (1994). Repeated reading revisited: Research into practice. *Reading and Writing Quarterly, 10*(4), 343–358.

Dryfoos, J. G. (1993). Schools as places for health, mental health, and social services. *Teachers College Record, 94*(3), 540–567.

Duster, T. (2003). *Backdoor to eugenics.* New York: Routledge.

Dweck, C. S. (1999). *Self-theories: Their role in motivation, personality, and development.* Philadelphia: Psychology Press.

Dweck, C. S. (2007). The perils and promises of praise. *Educational Leadership, 65*(2), 34–39.

Dweck, C. S., & Leggett, E. L. (1988). A social-cognitive approach to motivation and personality. *Psychological Review, 95*(2), 256–273.

Early Childhood Longitudinal Study (ECLS: K–Third Grade). (2004) Washington, DC: U.S. Department of Education, National Center for Education Statistics.

Eberts, R. W., & Stone, J. A. (1987). Teacher unions and the productivity of public schools. *Industrial and Labor Relations Review, 40*(3), 354–363.

Edmonds, R. (1986). Characteristics of effective schools. In U. Neisser (Ed.), *The school achievement of minority children: New perspectives* (pp. 93–104). Hillsdale, NJ: Lawrence Erlbaum.

Education Trust. (2002). *Dispelling the myth revisited: Preliminary findings from a nationwide analysis of high-flying schools.* Washington, DC: Author.

Education Trust. (2009). *Achievement, attainment, and opportunity: How well is your state performing?* Washington, DC: Author. Available: www.edtrust.org

Elliot, A. J., & Harackiewicz, J. M. (1996). Approach and avoidance achievement goals and intrinsic motivation: A mediational analysis. *Journal of Personality and Social Psychology, 70*(3), 461–475.

Ellison, C. M., Boykin, A. W., Towns, D. P., & Stokes, A. (2000). Classroom cultural ecology: The dynamics of classroom life in schools serving low-income African American children (Report No. CRESPAR-R-44). East Lansing, MI: National Center for Research on Teacher Learning.

Ellison, C. M., Boykin, A. W., Tyler, K. M., & Dillihunt, M. L. (2005). Examining classroom learning preferences among elementary school students. *Social Behavior and Personality, 33*(7), 699–708.

Epstein, J. (1994). Theory to practice: School and family partnerships lead to school improvement and school success. In C. Fagnano & B. Werber (Eds.), *School, family, and community interactions: A view from the firing lines* (pp. 39–54). Boulder, CO: Westview Press.

Faggella-Luby, M. N., Schumaker, J. S., & Deshler, D. D. (2007). Embedded learning strategy instruction: Story-structure pedagogy in heterogeneous secondary literature classes. *Learning Disability Quarterly, 30*(2), 131–147.

Farkas, G. (2004). The black–white test score gap. *Contexts, 3*(2), 12–21.

Fass, P. (1989). *Outside in.* New York: Oxford University Press.

Fass, S., & Cauthen, N. (2006). Who are America's poor children? Washington, DC: National Center on Children in Poverty. Available: http://nccp.org/publications/pub_684.html

Fast, L. A., Lewis, J. L., Bryant, M. J., Bocian, K. A., Cardullo, R. A., Rettig, M., & Hammond, K. A. (2010). Does math self-efficacy mediate the effect of the perceived classroom environment on standardized math test performance? *Journal of Educational Psychology, 102*(3), 729–740.

Fergus, E. (2004). *Skin color and identity formation: Perceptions of opportunity and academic orientation among Mexican and Puerto Rican youth.* New York: Routledge.

Ferguson, R. (1998). Teachers' perceptions and expectations and the black–white test score gap. In C. Jenkins & M. Phillips (Eds.), *The black–white test score gap* (pp. 273–317). Washington, DC: Brookings Institution Press.

Ferguson, R. (2003). Teachers' perceptions and expectations and the black–white test score gap. *Urban Education, 38*(4), 460–507.

Ferguson, R. (2007). *Toward excellence with equity.* Cambridge, MA: Harvard University Press.

Ferguson, R. (2010). *How high schools become exemplary: Ways that leadership raises achievement and narrows gaps by improving instruction in 15 public high schools.* Cambridge, MA: Harvard Kennedy School of Government.

Fine, M., Weis, L., Powell, L. C., & Mun Wong, L. (Eds.). (1997). *Off white: Readings on race, power, and society.* New York: Routledge.

Fischer, C. S., Hout, M., Sánchez Jankowski, M., Lucas, S. R., Swidler, A., & Voss, K. (1996). *Inequality by design: Cracking the bell curve myth.* Princeton, NJ: Princeton University Press.

Fordham, S. (1988). Racelessness as a factor in Black students' school success: Pragmatic strategy or Pyrrhic victory? *Harvard Educational Review, 58*(1), 54–84.

Fredericks, J. A., Blumenfeld, P. C., & Paris, A. H. (2004). School engagement: Potential of the concept, state of evidence. *Review of Educational Research, 74*(1), 59–109.

Fredrickson, G. (1981). *White supremacy.* New York: Oxford University Press.

Friedel, J. M., Cortina, K. S., Turner, J. C., & Midgeley, C. (2010). Changes in efficacy beliefs in mathematics across the transition to middle school: Examining the effects of perceived teacher and parent goal emphases. *Journal of Educational Psychology, 102*(1), 102–114.

Fuchs, S. (2005). *Against essentialism: A theory of culture and society.* Cambridge, MA: Harvard University Press.

Gans, H. J. (1995). *The war against the poor: The underclass and antipoverty.* New York: BasicBooks.

García, S. B., Wilkinson, C. Y., & Ortiz, A. A. (1995). Enhancing achievement for language minority students: Classroom, school and family contexts. *Education and Urban Society, 27*(4), 441–462.

Gatto, J. T. (2005). *Dumbing us down: The hidden curriculum of compulsory schooling.* New York: New Society Publishers.

Gay, G. (2000). *Culturally responsive teaching: Theory, research, and practice.* New York: Teachers College Press.

Ginsburg-Block, M., Rohrbeck, C., Lavigne, N., & Fantuzzo, J. W. (2008). Peer-assisted learning: An academic strategy for enhancing motivation among diverse students. In C. Hudley & A. E. Gottfried (Eds.), *Academic motivation and the culture of school in childhood and adolescence* (pp. 247–273). New York: Oxford University Press.

Glazer, N., & Moynihan, D. (1963). *Beyond the melting pot.* Cambridge, MA: MIT Press.

Goldstein, J. (2010). *Peer review and teacher leadership: Linking professionalism and accountability.* New York: Teachers College Press.

Goldstein, M. J., & Noguera, P. A. (2006, March 25). Designing for diversity: How educators can incorporate cultural competence in programs for urban youth. *In Motion.* Available: http://www.inmotionmagazine.com/er/pn_mg_div.html

González, N., Andrade, R., Civil, M., & Moll, L. (2001). Bridging funds of distributed knowledge: Creating zones of practices in mathematics. *Journal of Education for Students Placed at Risk, 6*(1–2), 115–132.

González, N., Moll, L., & Amanti, C. (Eds.). (2005). *Funds of knowledge: Theorizing practice in households, communities, and classrooms.* Mahwah, NJ: Lawrence Erlbaum.

Good, C., Aronson, J., & Inzlicht, M. (2003). Improving adolescents' standardized test performance: An intervention to reduce the effects of stereotype threat. *Journal of Applied Developmental Psychology, 24*(6), 645–662.

Good, T. L. (1987). Two decades of research on teacher expectations: Findings and future directions. *Journal of Teacher Education, 38*(4), 32–47.

Gould, A. (1981). *The mis-measure of man.* New York: Norton.

Graham, S., & Golan, S. (1991). Motivational influences on cognition: Task involvement, ego involvement, and depth of information processing. *Journal of Educational Psychology, 83*(2), 187–194.

Greenwood, C. R. (1996). Research on the practices and behavior of effective teachers at the Juniper Gardens Children's Project: Implications for the education of diverse learners. In D. Speece & B. K. Keogh (Eds.), *Research on classroom ecologies: Implications for inclusion of children with learning disabilities* (pp. 39–68). Hillsdale, NJ: Lawrence Erlbaum.

Greenwood, C. R., Carta, J. J., Kamps, D., & Hall, E. V. (1988). The use of ClassWide peer tutoring strategies in classroom management and instruction. *School Psychology Review, 17,* 258–275.

Greenwood, C. R., Delquadri, J., & Carta, J. J. (1997). *Together we can! Classwide peer tutoring to improve basic academic skills.* Longmont, CO: Sopris West.

Greenwood, C. R., Delquadri, J. C., & Hall, R. V. (1989). Longitudinal effects of classwide peer tutoring. *Journal of Educational Psychology, 81*(3), 371–383.

Greenwood, C. R., Dinwiddie, G., Bailey, V., Carta, J. J., Dorsey, D., Kohler, F. W., Nelson, C., Rotholz, D., & Schulte, D. (1987). Field replication of classwide peer tutoring. *Journal of Applied Behavioral Analysis, 20*(2), 151–160.

Gregory, A., Skiba, R., & Noguera, P. (2010). The achievement gap and the discipline gap: Two sides of the same coin? *Educational Researcher, 39*(1), 59–68.

Griffith, J. (2002). A multilevel analysis of the relation of school learning and social environments to the minority achievement in public elementary schools. *Elementary School Journal, 102*(5), 353–366.

Guthrie, J., Coddington, C., & Wigfield, A. (2009). Profiles of reading motivation among African American and Caucasian students. *Journal of Literacy Research, 41*(3), 317–353.

Guthrie, J., Hoa, L. W., Wigfield, A., Tonks, S. M., Humenick, N. M., & Littles, E. (2007). Reading motivation and reading comprehension growth in the later elementary years. *Contemporary Educational Psychology, 32*(3), 282–313.

Guthrie, J., McRae, A., & Klauda, S. (2007). Contributions of concept-oriented reading instruction to knowledge about interventions for motivations in reading. *Educational Psychologist, 42*(4), 237–250.

Guthrie, J. T., Wigfield, A., Barbosa, P., Perencevich, K. C., Taboada, A., Davis, M. H., Scafiddi, N. T., & Tonks, S. (2004). Increasing reading comprehension and engagement through concept-oriented instruction. *Journal of Educational Psychology, 96*(3), 403–423.

Guthrie, J. T., Wigfield, A., Metsala, J. L., & Cox, K. E. (1999). Motivational and cognitive predictors of text comprehension and reading amount. *Scientific Studies of Reading, 3*(3), 231–256.

Gutman, L. M. (2006). How student and parent goal orientations and classroom goal structures influence the math achievement of African Americans during the high school transition. *Contemporary Educational Psychology, 31*(1), 44–63.

Hacker, A. (1992). *Two nations: Black and White, separate, hostile, unequal.* New York: Scribner.

Hale, J. E. (2004). How schools shortchange African American children. *Educational Leadership, 62*(3), 34–37.

Hamman, D., Berthelot, J., Saia, J., & Crowley, E. (2000). Teachers' coaching of learning and its relation to students' strategic learning. *Journal of Educational Psychology, 92*(2), 342–348.

Hamre, B. K., & Pianta, R. C. (2001). Early teacher–child relationships and the trajectory of children's school outcomes through eighth grade. *Child Development, 72*(2), 625–638.

Hamre, B. K., & Pianta, R. C. (2005). Can instructional and emotional support in the first-grade classroom make a difference for children at risk of school failure? *Child Development, 76*(5), 949–967.

Haney, W. (2004). Analyses of Texas public school enrollments and other data: Expert report concerning the case of *West Orange-Cove v. Alanis*. Unpublished research paper.

Hansen, J. (1981). The effects of inference training and practice on young children's reading comprehension. *Reading Research Quarterly, 16*(3), 391–417.

Hansen, J., & Pearson, P. D. (1983). An instructional study: Improving inferential comprehension of good and poor fourth-grade readers. *Journal of Educational Psychology, 75*(6), 821–829.

Harackiewicz, J. M., Barron, K. E., & Elliot, A. J. (1998). Rethinking achievement goals: When are they adaptive for college students and why? *Educational Psychologist, 33*(1), 1–21.

Harackiewicz, J. M., Barron, K. E., Pintrich, P. R., Elliot, A. J., & Thrash, T. M. (2002). Revision of achievement goal theory: Necessary and illuminating. *Journal of Educational Psychology, 94*(3), 638–645.

Herrnstein, R., & Murray, C. (1994). *The bell curve: Intelligence and class structure in American life*. New York: Free Press.

Hilliard, A. (2003). No mystery: Closing the achievement gap between Africans and excellence. In T. Perry, C. Steele, & A. Hilliard (Eds.), *Young, gifted, and black: Promoting high achievement among African-American students* (pp. 131–165). Boston: Beacon Press.

Hinnant, J. B., O'Brien, M., & Ghazarian, S. R. (2009). The longitudinal relations of teacher expectations to achievement in the early school years. *Journal of Educational Psychology, 101*(3), 662–670.

Hollins, E. R., King, J. E., & Hayman, W. C. (Eds.). (1994). *Teaching diverse populations: Formulating a knowledge base*. Albany, NY: State University of New York Press.

Horner, S. L., & O'Connor, E. A. (2007). Developing self-regulation within the reading recovery context. In S. L. Horner & E. A. O'Connor (Eds.), *Helping beginning and struggling readers and writers to develop self-regulated strategies. Special issue of Reading and Writing Quarterly, 23*(1), 97–109.

Hughes, J., & Kwok, O. (2007). Influence of student–teacher and parent–teacher relationships on lower achieving readers' engagement and achievement in the primary grades. *Journal of Educational Psychology, 99*(1), 39–51.

Hughes, J. N., Luo, W., Kwok, O., & Loyd, L. (2008). Teacher–student support, effortful engagement, and achievement: A 3-year longitudinal study. *Journal of Educational Psychology, 100*(1), 1–14.

Hurley, E. A., Allen, B. A., & Boykin A. W. (2009). Culture and the interaction of student ethnicity with reward structure in group learning. *Cognition & Instruction, 27*(2), 121–146.

Hurley, E., Boykin, A., & Allen, B. (2005). Communal versus individual learning of a math estimation task: African American children and the culture of learning contexts. *The Journal of Psychology, 139*(6), 513–527.

Ignatiev, N. (1991). *How the Irish became white*. New York: Routledge.

Iruka, I. U., Burchinal, M., & Cai, K. (2010). Long-term effect of early relationships for African American children's academic and social development: An examination from kindergarten to fifth grade. *Journal of Black Psychology, 36*(2), 144–171.

Irvine, J. J. (1990). *Black children and school failure: Policies, practices and prescriptions*. Westport, CT: Greenwood Press.

Irvine, J. J. (2003). *Educating teachers for diversity: Seeing with a cultural eye*. New York: Teachers College Press.

Jencks, C., & Phillips, M. (Eds.). (1998). *The black–white test score gap*. Washington, DC: Brookings Institution Press.

Jencks, C., Smith, M., Acland, H., Bane, M. T., Cohen, D., Gintis, H., Heyns, B., & Michelson, S. (1972). *Inequality: A reassessment of the effect of family and schooling in America*. New York: BasicBooks.

Jennings, J. (2006). *How NCLB has undermined the curriculum*. Washington, DC: Center of Education Policy.

Jiobu, R. M. (1988). *Ethnicity and assimilation*. Albany, NY: State University of New York Press.

Jitendra, A. K., Griffin, C., Haria, P., Leh, J., Adams, A., & Kaduvetoor, A. (2007). A comparison of single and multiple strategy instruction on third grade students' mathematical problem solving. *Journal of Educational Psychology, 99*(1), 115–127.

Jussim, L., Eccles, J., & Madon, S. J. (1996). Social perception, social stereotypes, and teacher expectations: Accuracy and the quest for the powerful self-fulfilling prophecy. *Advances in Experimental Social Psychology, 29*, 281–388.

Kagan, S. (1992). *Cooperative learning*. San Clemente, CA: Kagan Cooperative Learning.

Kaplan, A., Gheen, M., & Midgley, C. (2002). Classroom goal structure and student disruptive behaviour. *British Journal of Educational Psychology, 72*(2), 191–212.

Kaplan, A., & Maehr, M. L. (1999). Achievement goals and student well-being. *Contemporary Educational Psychology, 24*(4), 330–358.

Katznelson, I., & Weir, M. (1985). *Schooling for all: Class, race, and the decline of the democratic ideal.* New York: BasicBooks.

Kelly, S. (2007). Classroom discourse and the distribution of student engagement. *Social Psychology of Education, 10*(3), 331–352.

Kelly, S. (2008). Race, social class, and student engagement in middle school English classrooms. *Social Science Research, 37*(2), 434–448.

Kelly, S., & Turner, J. (2009). Rethinking the effects of classroom activity structure on the engagement of low-achieving students. *Teachers College Record, 111*(7), 1665–1692.

King, A. (1991). Effects of training in strategic questioning on children's problem-solving performance. *Journal of Educational Psychology, 83*(3), 307–317.

King, A. (1992). Facilitating elaborative learning through guided student-generated questioning. *Educational Psychologist, 27*(1), 111–126.

King, A. (1998). Transactive peer tutoring: Distributing cognition and metacognition. *Educational psychological review, 10*(1), 57–74.

King, J. (Ed.). (2005). *Black education: A transformative research and action agenda for the new century.* Mahwah, NJ: Lawrence Erlbaum.

Kirp, D. (1982). *Just schools.* Berkeley, CA: University of California Press.

Kirschner, P. A. (2002). Cognitive load theory: Implications of cognitive load theory on the design of learning. *Learning and Instruction, 12*(1), 1–10.

Kozol, J. (1992). *Savage inequalities: Children in America's schools.* New York: Harper Perennial.

Kurtz-Costes, B., Ehrlich, M. F., McCall, R., & Loridant, C. (1995). Motivational determinants of reading comprehension: A comparison of French, Caucasian-American, and African-American adolescents. *Applied Cognitive Psychology, 9*(4), 351–364.

Ladd, G. W., Birch, S. H., & Buhs, E. S. (1999). Children's social and scholastic lives in kindergarten: Related spheres of influence? *Child Development, 70*(6), 1373–1400.

Ladd, G., & Dinella, L. (2009). Continuity and change in early school engagement: Predictive of children's achievement trajectories from first to eighth grade? *Journal of Educational Psychology, 101*(1), 190–206.

Ladson-Billings, G. (1995). Toward a theory of culturally relevant pedagogy. *American Educational Research Journal, 32*(3), 465–491.

Ladson-Billings, G. (2002). But that's just good teaching! The case for culturally relevant pedagogy. In S. J. Denbo & L. M. Beaulieu (Eds.), *Improving schools for African American students: A reader for educational leaders* (pp. 95–102). Springfield, IL: Charles C. Thomas.

Lamy, C., Barnett, W. S., & Jung, K. (2005). *The effects of Oklahoma's early childhood four-year-old program on young children's school readiness.* National Institute for Early Education Research, Rutgers University. Available: http://nieer.org/resources/research/multistate/ok.pdf

Lareau, A. (1989). *Home advantage: Social class and parental intervention in elementary education.* New York: Falmer Press.

Laski, E. V., & Siegler, R. S. (2007). Is 27 a big number? Correlational and causal connections among numerical categorization, number line estimation, and numerical magnitude comparison. *Child Development, 78*(6), 1723–1743.

Ledesma, J. (1995). *Rethinking the model minority thesis* Unpublished paper, University of California, Berkeley.

Lee, C. D. (2001). Is October Brown Chinese? A cultural modeling activity system for under-achieving students. *American Educational Research Journal, 38*(1), 97–141.

Lee, C. D. (2006). Every good-bye ain't gone: Analyzing the cultural underpinnings of classroom talk. *Qualitative Studies in Education, 19*(3), 305–327.

Lee, E. (1995). *Rethinking schools: An agenda for change.* New York: New Press.

Lee, J. (2002). Racial and ethnic achievement gap trends: Reversing the progress toward equity? *Educational Researcher, 31*(1), 3–12.

Lee, J. (2006). *Tracking achievement gaps and assessing the impact of NCLB on the gaps: An in-depth look into national and state reading and math outcome trends.* Cambridge, MA: The Civil Rights Project.

Lee, K., Ng, E. L., & Ng, S. F. (2009). The contributions of working memory and executive functioning to problem representation and solution generation in algebraic word problems. *Journal of Educational Psychology, 101*(2), 373–387.

Lehman, N. (1996). *The big test.* New York: Farrar, Straus, & Giroux.

Lewis, O. (1966). *La vida: A Puerto Rican family in the culture of poverty—San Juan and New York.* New York: Random House.

Liew, J., Chen, Q., & Hughes, J. (2010). Child effortful control, teacher–student relationships, and achievement in academically at-risk children: Additive and interactive effects. *Early Childhood Research Quarterly, 25*(1), 51–64.

Linnenbrink, E. A. (2005). The dilemma of performance-approach goals: The use of multiple goal contexts to promote students' motivation and learning. *Journal of Educational Psychology, 97*(2), 197–213.

Linnenbrink, E. A., & Pintrich, P. R. (2003). The role of self-efficacy beliefs in student engagement and learning in the classroom. *Reading and Writing Quarterly: Overcoming Learning difficulties, 19*(2), 119–137.

Linnenbrink, E. A., Ryan, A. M., & Pintrich, P. R. (1999). The role of goals and affect in working memory functioning. *Learning and Individual Differences, 11*(2), 213.

Lipman, P. (1995). Bringing out the best in them: The contribution of culturally relevant teachers to education. *Theory into Practice, 34*(3), 203–208.

Lipman, P. (1998). *Race, class, and power in school restructuring.* Albany, NY: State University of New York Press.

Lipsitz, G. (2006). *The possessive investment in Whiteness: How White people profit from identity politics.* Rev. and exp. ed. Philadelphia: Temple University Press.

Long, J., Monoi, S., Harper, B., Knoblauch, D., & Murphy, P. (2007). Academic motivation and achievement among urban adolescents. *Urban Education, 42*(3), 196–222.

Low, R., Over, R., Doolan, L., & Michell, S. (1994). Solution of algebraic word problems following training in identifying necessary and sufficient information within problems. *American Journal of Psychology, 107*(3), 423–439.

Lutz, S., Guthrie, J., & Davis, M. (2006). Scaffolding for engagement in elementary school reading instruction. *Journal of Educational Research, 100*(1), 3–20.

Lynch, D. J. (2008). Confronting challenges: Motivational beliefs and learning strategies in difficult college courses. *College Student Journal, 42,* 416–421.

Maheady, L., Mallette, B., Harper, G. F., & Sacca, K. (1991). Heads together: A peer-mediated option for improving the academic achievement of heterogeneous learning groups. *Remedial & Special Education, 12*(2), 25–33.

Maheady, L., Michielli-Pendl, J., Harper, G., & Mallette, B. (2006). The effects of numbered heads together with and without an incentive package on the science test performance of a diverse group of sixth graders. *Journal of Behavioral Education, 15*(1), 25–39.

Maheady, L., Michielli-Pendl, J., Mallette, B., & Harper, G. F. (2002). A collaborative research project to improve the academic performance of a diverse sixth grade science class. *Teacher Education and Special Education: The Journal of the Teacher Education Division of the Council for Exceptional Children, 25*(1), 55–70.

Margolis, H., & McCabe, P. P. (2006). Improving self-efficacy and motivation: What to do, what to say. *Intervention in School and Clinic, 41*(4), 218–227.

Martin, M., Fergus, E., & Noguera, P. (2009). Responding to the needs of the whole child: A case study of a high-performing elementary school for immigrant children. *Reading & Writing Quarterly, 26*(3), 195–222.

Mason, L. H. (2004). Explicit self-regulated strategy development versus reciprocal questioning: Effects on expository reading comprehension among struggling readers. *Journal of Educational Psychology, 96*(2), 283–296.

Mathes, P. G., Howard, J. K., Allen, S. H., & Fuchs, D. (1998). Peer-assisted learning strategies for first grade readers: Responding to the needs of diverse learners. *Reading Research Quarterly, 33*(1), 62–94.

Mathes, P. G., Torgesen, J. K., & Allor, J. H. (2001). The effects of peer-assisted literacy strategies for first-grade readers with and without additional computer assisted instruction in phonological awareness. *American Educational Research Journal, 38*(2), 371–410.

Mayer, R. E. (2004). Teaching of subject matter. In S. T. Fiske (Ed.), *Annual review of psychology* (vol. 55, pp. 715–744). Palo Alto, CA: Annual Reviews.

Mayer, R. E., Griffith, E., Jurkowitz, T. N., & Rothman, D. (2008). Increased interestingness of extraneous details in a multimedia science presentation leads to decreased learning. *Journal of Experimental Psychology: Applied, 14*(4), 329–339.

McDonnell, L. M., & Pascal, A. (1988). *Teacher unions and educational reform.* Santa Monica, CA: The Rand Corp.

McElvain, C. M. (2010). Transactional literature circles and the reading comprehension of English learners in the mainstream classroom. *Journal of Research in Reading,* 33(2), 178–205.

McKown, C., & Weinstein, R. S. (2002). Modeling the role of child ethnicity and gender in children's differential response to teacher expectations. *Journal of Applied Social Psychology, 32*(1), 159–184.

McMaster, K. L., Kung, S., Han, I., & Cao, M. (2008). Peer-assisted learning strategies: A "tier 1" approach to promoting English learners' response to intervention. *Exceptional Children, 74*(2), 194–214.

McWhorter, J. (2000). *Losing the race.* New York: New Press.

Medina, J. (2010, July 28). Standards raised, more students fail tests. *New York Times,* p. 1.

Meier, D. (2001). *Is standardized testing good for education?* Boston: Beacon Press.

Meier, K. J., Stewart, J., & England, R. E. (1989). *Race, class, and education: The politics of second-generation discrimination.* Madison, WI: University of Wisconsin Press.

Middleton, M., & Midgley, C. (1997). Avoiding the demonstration of lack of ability: An under-explored aspect of goal theory. *Journal of Educational Psychology, 89*(4), 710–718.

Miller, G. A. (1956). The magic number seven plus or minus two: Some limits on our capacity for processing information. *The Psychological Review, 63*(2), 81–97.

Miller, S. L. (1995). *An American imperative.* New Haven, CT: Yale University Press.

Milner, B. (2004/2005). Keeping public schools public: Testing companies mine for gold. *Rethinking Schools.* Available: http://www.rethinkingschools.org/special_reports/bushplan/test192.shtml

Mireles-Rios, R., & Romo, L. F. (2010). Maternal and teacher interaction and student engagement in math and reading among Mexican American girls from a rural community. *Hispanic Journal of Behavioral Sciences, 32*(3), 456–469.

Mistry, R. S., White, E. S., Benner, A. D., & Huynh, V. W. (2009). A longitudinal study of the simultaneous influence of mothers' and teachers' educational expectations on low-income youth's academic achievement. *Journal of Youth and Adolescence, 38*(6), 826–838.

Molden, D. C., & Dweck, C. S. (2006). Finding "meaning" in psychology: A lay theories approach to self-regulation, social perception, and social development. *American Psychologist, 61*(3), 192–203.

Montague, M. (2007). Self-regulation and mathematics instruction. *Learning Disabilities Research & Practice, 22*(1), 75–83.

Mooney, E. S., & Thornton, C. A. (1999). Mathematics attribution differences by ethnicity and socioeconomic status. *Journal of Education for Student Placed at Risk, 4*(3), 321–332.

Morrison, K. A., Robbins, H. H., & Rose, D. G. (2008). Operationalizing culturally relevant pedagogy: A synthesis of classroom-based research. *Equity & Excellence in Education, 41*(4), 433–452.

Mucherah, W., & Yoder, A. (2008). Motivation for reading and middle school students' performance on standardized testing in reading. *Reading Psychology, 29*(3), 214–235.

Mueller, C. M., & Dweck, C. S. (1998). Praise for intelligence can undermine children's motivation and performance. *Journal of Personality and Social Psychology, 75*(1), 33–52.

Mullis, I.V.S., Martin, M. O., Gonzalez, E. J., & Chrostowski, S. J. (2004). Trends in International Mathematics and Science Study. Chestnut Hill, MA: TIMSS & PIRLS International Study Center, Boston College.

Murname, R., Willett, J., Bub, K., & McCartney, K. (2006). Understanding trends in the black–white achievement gap during the first years of school. *Brookings Wharton Papers on Urban Affairs, 7,* 97–135.

Murray, C. (2009). Parent and teacher relationships as predictors of school engagement and functioning among low-income urban youth. *Journal of Early Adolescence, 29*(3), 376–404.

National Assessment of Educational Progress (NAEP). (2005). *The nation's report card.* Washington, DC: U.S. Department of Education.

National Center for Education Statistics. (2010). The nation's report card: Trial urban district assessment mathematics 2009. Available: http://nces.ed.gov/nationsreportcard/pubs/dst2009/2010452.asp

National Institute of Child Health and Human Development. (2000). *Report of the National Reading Panel. Teaching children to read: An evidence-based assessment of the scientific research literature on reading and its implications for reading instruction* (NIH Publication No. 00-4769). Washington, DC: U.S. Government Printing Office.

National Mathematics Advisory Panel. (2008). *Foundations for success: The final report of the National Mathematics Advisory Panel.* Washington, DC: U.S. Department of Education.

Navarro, R., Flores, L., & Worthington, R. (2007). Mexican American middle school students' goal intentions in mathematics & science: A test of social cognitive career theory. *Journal of Counseling Psychology, 54*(3), 320–335.

Neher, A. (1991). Maslow's theory of motivation: A critique. *Journal of Humanistic Psychology, 31*(3), 89–112.

Newby, T. J. (1991). Classroom motivation: Strategies of first-year teachers. *Journal of Educational Psychology, 83*(2), 195–200.

Nicholls, J. G., Cheung, P., Lauer, J., & Patashnick, M. (1989). Individual differences in academic motivation: Perceived ability, goals, beliefs, and values. *Learning and Individual Differences, 1*(1), 63–84.

Noe, C. (2004, January 9). Bush decries Democrats' "soft bigotry of low expectations". NewsMax.com. Available: http://archive.newsmax.com/archives/articles/2004/1/9/110923.shtml

Noguera, P. (2003). *City schools and the American dream: Reclaiming the promise of public education.* New York: Teachers College Press.

Noguera, P. (2004). Special topic/Transforming high schools. *Educational Leadership, 61*(8), 26–32.

Noguera, P. (2008, September 2). Creating schools where race does not matter: The role and significance of race in the racial achievement gap. *In Motion.* Retrieved from http://www.inmotionmagazine.com/er/pn_creating08.html

Noguera, P., & Wing, J. Y. (Eds.). (2006). *Unfinished business: Closing the racial achievement gap in our schools.* San Francisco: Jossey-Bass.

Nussbaum, A. D., & Dweck, C. S. (2008). Defensiveness versus remediation: Self-theories and modes of self-esteem maintenance. *Personality and Social Psychology Bulletin, 34*(5), 599–612.

Oakhill, J., & Yuill, N. (1996). Higher order factors in comprehension disability: Processes and remediation. In C. Cornoldi & J. V. Oakhill (Eds.), *Reading comprehension difficulties: Processes and remediation*. Mahwah, NJ: Lawrence Erlbaum.

Obama, B. H. (2009, January 20). Inaugural address. Capitol Building, Washington, DC. Available: www.whitehouse.gov/blog/inaugural-address

Ogbu, J. (1987). Opportunity structure, cultural boundaries, and literacy. In J. Langer (Ed.), *Language, literacy and culture: Issues of society and schooling*. Norwood, NJ: Ablex.

Ogbu, J. (1988). Variability in minority school performance: A problem in search of an explanation. *Anthropology and Education Quarterly, 18*(4), 312–334.

Ogbu, J., & Davis, A. (2003). *Black American students in an affluent suburb: A study of academic disengagement*. New York: Lawrence Erlbaum.

Olsen, L. (2000). *Made in America*. New York: New Press.

Omi, M., & Winant, H. (1986). *Racial formation in the United States*. New York: Routledge.

Orfield, G., & Lee, C. (2006). *Racial transformation and the changing nature of segregation*. Cambridge, MA: The Civil Rights Project at Harvard University.

Paige, R., & Witty, E. (2010). *The black–white achievement gap*. New York: AMA.

Pajares, F. (2003). Self-efficacy beliefs, motivation, and achievement in writing: A review of the literature. *Reading and Writing Quarterly, 19*(2), 139–158.

Pajares, F., & Miller, M. D. (1994). Role of self-efficacy and self-concept beliefs in mathematical problem solving: A path analysis. *Journal of Educational Psychology, 86*(2), 193–203.

Paris, S., & Newman, R. (1990). Development aspects of self-regulated learning. *Educational Psychologist, 25*(1), 87–102.

Parker, M., & Hurry, J. (2007). Teachers' use of questioning and modelling comprehension skills in primary classrooms. *Educational Review, 59*(3), 299–314.

Patrick, H., Ryan, A. M., & Kaplan, A. (2007). Early adolescents' perceptions of the classroom social environment, motivational beliefs, and engagement. *Journal of Educational Psychology, 99*(1), 83–98.

Patterson, O. (2009, August 19). Crossroads: Race and diversity in the age of Obama. *New York Times*, p. 24.

Payne, R. K. (1996). *Framework for understanding poverty*. Highland, TX: Aha Process.

Perfetti, C. A., & Hogaboam, T. (1975). Relationship between single word decoding and reading comprehension skill. *Journal of Educational Psychology, 67*(4), 461–469.

Perry, T., Steele, C., & Hilliard III, A. (2003). *Young, gifted and black: Promoting high achievement among African-American students*. New York: Beacon Press.

Pew Center. (2011). *Recent trends in immigration*. Washington, DC: Author.

Pintrich, P. (2000) The role of goal orientation in self-regulated learning. In M. Boekaerts, P. Pintrich, & M. Zeidner (Eds.), *Handbook of self-regulated learning: Theory, research, & applicatons* (pp. 451–502). San Diego, CA: Academic Press.

Pressley, M., Wood, E., Woloshyn, V. E., Martin, V., King, A., & Menke, D. (1992). Encouraging mindful use of prior knowledge: Attempting to construct explanatory answers facilitates learning. *Educational Psychologist, 27*, 91–100.

Ramani, G. B., and Siegler, R. (2011). Reducing the gap in numerical knowledge between low- and middle-income preschoolers. *Journal of Applied Developmental Psychology, 32*(3), 146–159.

Ramirez-Smith, C. (1995). Stopping the cycle of failure: The Comer model. *Education Leadership, 52*(5), 14–19.

Ravitch, D. (2010). *The life and death of the great American school system*. New York: BasicBooks.

Reed, D. (2001). *On equal terms: The constitutional politics of educational opportunity*. Princeton, NJ: Princeton University Press.

Rickards, J. P., & Hatcher, C. W. (1977). Interspersed meaningful learning questions as semantic cues for poor comprehenders. *Reading Research Quarterly, 13*(4), 538–553.

Rohrbeck, C. A., Ginsburg-Block, M. D., Fantuzzo, J. W., & Miller, T. R. (2003). Peer-assisted learning interventions with elementary school students: A meta analytic review. *Journal of Educational Psychology, 95*(2), 240–257.

Rosenthal, R., & Jacobson, L. (1968). *Pygmalion in the classroom*. New York: Holt, Rinehart & Winston.

Roth, G., Assor, A., Kanat-Maymon, Y., & Kaplan, H. (2007). Autonomous motivation for teaching: How self-determined teaching may lead to self-determined learning. *Journal of Educational Psychology, 99*(4), 761–774.

Rothstein, R. (2004a). The achievement gap: Closing the achievement gap requires more than just improving schools. *Educational Leadership, 62*(3), 40–43.

Rothstein, R. (2004b). *Class and school*. Washington, DC: Economic Policy Institute.

Rubman, C. N., & Waters, H. S. (2000). A, B seeing: The role of constructive processes in children's comprehension monitoring. *Journal of Educational Psychology, 92*(3), 503–514.

Ryan, K. E., & Ryan, A. M. (2005). Psychological processes underlying stereotype threat and standardized math test performance. *Educational Psychologist, 40*(1), 53–63.

Ryan, R., & Deci, E. (2000). Self-determination theory and the facilitation of intrinsic motivation, social development, and well-being. *American Psychologist, 55*(1), 68–78.

Ryan, R. M., & Deci, E. L. (2006). Self-regulation and the problem of human autonomy: Does psychology need choice, self-determiniation, and will? *Journal of Personality, 74*(6), 1557–1586.

Saft, E. W., & Pianta, R. C. (2001). Teachers' perceptions of their relationships with students: Effects of child age, gender, and ethnicity of teachers and children. *School Psychology Quarterly, 16*(2), 125–141.

Schmidt, W. H., McKnight, C. C., Houang, R. T., Wang, H., Wiley, D., Cogan, L. S., & Wolfe, R. G. (2001). *Why schools matter: A cross-national comparison of curriculum and learning*. San Francisco: Jossey-Bass.

Schott Foundation. (2009). *The opportunity to learn*. Cambridge, MA: Author.

Schultz, G. F. (1993). Socioeconomic advantage and achievement motivation: Important mediators of academic performance in minority children in urban schools. *Urban Review, 25*(3), 221–232.

Schunk, D. H. (2003). Self-efficacy for reading and writing: Influence of modeling, goal setting, and self-evaluation. *Reading and Writing Quarterly, 19*(2), 159–172.

Schunk, D. H. (2005). Self-regulated learning: The educational legacy of Paul R. Pintrich. *Educational Psychologist, 40*(2), 85–94.

Schunk, D. H., & Rice, J. M. (1993). Strategy fading and progress feedback: Effects on self-efficacy and comprehension among students receiving remedial reading services. *Journal of Special Education, 27*(3), 257–276.

Schunk, D. H., & Zimmerman, B. J. (1997). Social origins of self-regulatory competence. *Educational Psychologist, 32*(4), 195–208.

Schunk, D. H., & Zimmerman, B. J. (1998). Conclusions and future directions for academic interventions. In D. H. Schunk & B. J. Zimmerman (Eds.), *Self-regulated learning: From teaching to self-reflective practice* (pp. 225–235). New York: Guilford Press.

Schunk, D. H., & Zimmerman, B. J. (2007). Influencing children's self-efficacy and self-regulation of reading and writing through modeling. *Reading & Writing Quarterly, 23*(1), 7–25.

Sealey-Ruiz, Y., Handville, N. L, & Noguera, P. A. (2008). In pursuit of the possible: Lessons learned from district efforts to reduce racial disparities in student achievement. *The Sophist's Bane, 6*(2), 44–63.

Seifert, T. L. (2004). Understanding student motivation. *Educational Research, 46*(2), 137–149.

Shell, D. F., & Husman, J. (2008). Control, motivation, affect, and strategic self-regulation in the college classroom: A multidimensional phenomenon. *Journal of Educational Psychology, 100*(2), 443–459.

Siegler, R. S., & Booth, J. L. (2004). Development of numerical estimation in young children. *Child Development, 75*(2), 428–444.

Siegler, R. S., & Ramani, G. B. (2008). Playing linear numerical board games promotes low-income children's numerical development. *Developmental Science, Special Issue on Mathematical Cognition, 11*(5), 655–661.

Silva, E. (2010, December 14). Measuring teacher effectiveness. *The quick and the ed*. Washington, DC: EdSector.

Sizer, T. (1984). *Horace's compromise: The dilemma of the American high school*. Boston: Houghton Mifflin.

Skinner, E. A., & Belmont, M. J. (1993). Motivation in the classroom: Reciprocal effects of teacher behavior and student engagement across the school year. *Journal of Educational Psychology, 85*(4), 571–581.

Slavin, R. E. (2002). Evidence-based educational policies: Transforming educational practice and research. *Educational Researcher, 31*(7), 15–21.

Slavin, R. E., & Fashola, O.S. (1998). *Show me the evidence: Proven and promising programs for America's schools*. Thousand Oaks, CA: Corwin.

Slavin, R., Lake, C., & Groff, C. (2009). Effective programs in middle and high school mathematics: A best-evidence synthesis. *Review of Educational Research, 79*(2), 839–911.

Sleeter, C. E. (2000). Creating an empowering multicultural curriculum. *Race, Gender & Class in Education, 7*(3), 178–196.

Smith, L. (2007). *Schools that change*. New York: Corwin.

Soric, I., & Palekcic, M. (2009). The roles of students' interests in self-regulated learning: The relationship between students' interests, learning strategies and casual attributions. *European Journal of Psychology of Education, 24*(4), 545–565.

Spring, J. (2009). *Deculturalization and the struggle for equality: A brief history of the education of dominated cultures in the United States*. New York: McGraw-Hill.

Steele, C. (2010). *Whistling Vivaldi: And other clues to how stereotypes affect us*. New York: Norton.

Steele, S. (1996). *The content of our character*. New York: St. Martin's Press.

Stevens, T., Olivarez, A., & Hamman, D. (2006). The role of cognition, motivation, and emotion in explaining the mathematics achievement gap between Hispanic and white students. *Hispanic Journal of Behavioral Sciences, 28*(2), 161.

Stevens, T., Olivarez, A., Lan, W., & Tallent-Runnels, M. K. (2004). Role of mathematics self-efficacy and motivation in mathematics performance across ethnicity. *Journal of Educational Research, 97*(4), 208–221.

Stewart, E. (2006). Family- and individual-level predictors of academic success for African American students: A longitudinal path analysis utilizing national data. *Journal of Black Studies 36*(4), 597–621.

Stewart, E. (2008). School structural characteristics, student effort, peer associations, and parental involvement: The influence of school- and individual-level factors on academic achievement. *Education and Urban Society, 40*(2), 179–204.

Stipek, D. (2002). Good instruction is motivating. In A. Wigfield & J. S. Eccles (Eds.), *Development of achievement motivation* (pp. 309–332). San Diego, CA: Academic Press.

Stipek, D., & Gralinski, J. H. (1996). Children's beliefs about intelligence and school performance. *Journal of Educational Psychology, 88*(3), 397–407.

Stipek, D., & Kowalski, P. S. (1989). Learned helplessness in task-orienting versus performance orienting testing conditions. *Journal of Educational Psychology, 81*(3), 384–391.

Stull, A. T., & Mayer, R. E. (2007). Learning by doing versus learning by viewing: Three experimental comparisons of learner-generated versus author-provided graphic organizers. *Journal of Educational Psychology, 99*(4), 808–820.

Sutherland, K. S., & Oswald, D. P. (2005). The relationship between teacher and student behavior in classrooms for students with emotional and behavioral disorders: Transactional processes. *Journal of Child and Family Studies, 14*(1), 1–14.

Takaki, R. (1989). *Strangers from a different shore*. New York: Penguin.

Taylor, B. M., Pearson, P. D., Peterson, D. S., & Rodriguez, M. C. (2003). Reading growth in high-poverty classrooms: The influence of teacher practices that encourage cognitive engagement in literacy learning. *Elementary School Journal, 104*(1), 3–28.

Tenenbaum, H. R., & Ruck, M. D. (2007). Are teachers' expectations different for racial minority than for European American students? A meta-analysis. *Journal of Educational Psychology, 99*(2), 253–273.

Thomas, E., & Weingart, P. (2010, March 6). Why we must fire bad teachers. *Newsweek*, pp. 16–27.

Tough, P. (2006, November 26). What it takes to make a student. *New York Times Magazine*, pp. 28–45.

Tough, P. (2008). *Whatever it takes*. Boston: Houghton Mifflin.

Tracy, B., Reid, R., & Graham, S. (2009). Teaching young students strategies for planning and drafting stories: The impact of self-regulated strategy development. *Journal of Educational Research, 102*(5), 323–331.

Trends in International Mathematics and Science Study (TIMSS). (2003). Washington, DC: Institute of Education Sciences.

Treisman, U. (1993). *Lessons Learned from a FIPSE Project*. Berkeley, CA: University of California Professional Development Program.

Tucker, C., Zayco, R., Herman, K., Reinke, W., Trujillo, M., Carraway, K., Wallack, C., & Ivery, P. (2002). Teacher and child variables as predictors of academic engagement among low-income African American children. *Psychology in the Schools, 39*(4), 477–488.

Turner, J. C., Meyer, D. K., Anderman, E. M., Midgley, C., Gheen, M., Yongjin K., & Patrick, H. (2002). The classroom environment and students' reports of avoidance strategies in mathematics: A multimethod study. *Journal of Educational Psychology, 94*(1), 88–106.

Tyack, D., & Tobin, W. (1994). The "grammar" of schooling: Why has it been so hard to change? *American Educational Research Journal, 31*(3), 453–479.

UNICEF. (2002, November). *Innocenti report card: A league table of educational disadvantage in rich nations*. Florence Italy: UNICEF Innocenti Research Centre. Available: http://www.unicef-irc.org/publications/pdf/repcard4e.pdf

Urbina, I. (2010, January 11). As school exit tests prove tough, states ease standards. *New York Times*. Available: http://www.nytimes.com/2010/01/12/education/12exit.html

Valiente, C., Lemery-Chalfant, K. S., Swanson, J., & Reiser, M. (2008). Prediction of children's academic competence from their effortful control, relationships, and classroom participation. *Journal of Educational Psychology, 100*(1), 67–77.

Vansteenkiste, M., Lens, W., & Deci, E. L. (2006). Intrinsic versus extrinsic goal contents in self-determination theory: Another look at the quality of academic motivation. *Educational Psychologist, 41*(1), 19–31.

Vansteenkiste, M., & Sheldon, K. M. (2006). There's nothing more practical than a good theory: Integrating motivational interviewing and self-determination theory. *British Journal of Clinical Psychology, 45*(1), 63–82.

Vansteenkiste, M., Simons, J., Lens, W., Sheldon, K., & Deci, E. L. (2004). Motivating learning, performance, and persistence: The synergistic effects of intrinsic goal contents and autonomy-supportive contexts. *Journal of Personality and Social Psychology, 87*(2), 246–260.

Vygotsky, L. S. (1962). *Thought and language* (E. Hanfmann & G. Vakar, Ed. and Trans.). Cambridge, MA: MIT Press.

Waldfogel, J., & Lahaie, C. (2007). The role of preschool and after-school policies in improving the school achievement of children of immigrants. In J. E. Lansford, K. Deater-Deckard, & M. H. Bornstein (Eds.), *Immigrant families in contemporary society* (pp. 177–193). New York: Guilford.

Walker, C., & Greene, B. A. (2009). The relations between student motivation beliefs and cognitive engagement in high school. *Journal of Educational Research, 102*(6), 463–472.

Ware, F. (2006). Warm demander pedagogy: Culturally responsive teaching that supports a culture of achievement for African American students. *Urban Education, 41*(4), 427–456.

Warikoo, N., & Carter, P. (2009). Cultural explanations for racial and ethnic stratification in academic achievement: A call for a new and improved theory. *Review of Educational Research, 79*(1), 366–394.

Weiner, B. (1986). *An attributional theory of motivation and emotion.* New York: Springer Verlag.

Weiner, B. (1994). Integrating social and personal theories of achievement strivings. *Review of Educational Research, 64*(4), 557–573.

Weiner, B. (2000). Intrapersonal and interpersonal theories of motivation from an attributional perspective. *Educational Psychology Review, 12*(1), 1–14.

Welsh, J. A., Nix, R. L., Blair, C., Bierman, K. L., & Nelson, K. E. (2010). The development of cognitive skills and gains in academic school readiness for children from low-income families. *Journal of Educational Psychology, 102*(1), 43–53.

Wenglinsky, H. (2004). The link between instructional practice and the racial gap in middle schools. *Research in Middle Level Education Online, 28*(1). Retrieved March 2, 2006, from http://www.nmsa.org/Publications/RMLEOnline/tabid/101/Default.aspx

Wheelock, A. (1992). *Crossing the tracks: How untracking can save America's schools.* New York: New Press.

White, R. W. (1959). Motivation reconsidered: The concept of competence. *Psychological Review, 66*(5), 297–333.

Wigfield, A., Guthrie, J. T., Perencevich, K. C., Taboada, A., Klauda, S. L., McRae, A., & Barbosa, P. (2008). The role of reading engagement in mediating effects of reading comprehension instruction on reading outcomes. *Psychology in the Schools, 45*(5), 432–445.

Williams, J. (2006). *Enough: Phony leaders, dead-end movements and the culture of failure that are undermining black America—and what we can do about it.* New York: Random House.

Williams, J., Hall, K., Lauer, K., Stafford, K. DeSisto, L., & deCani, J. (2005). Expository text comprehension in the primary grade classroom. *Journal of Educational Psychology, 97*(4), 538–550.

Williams, J. P., Brooke-Stafford, K., Lauer, K. D., Hall, K. M., & Pollini, S. (2009). Embedding reading comprehension training in content-area instruction. *Journal of Educational Psychology, 101*(1), 1–20.

Williams, J. P., Nubla-King, A. M., Pollini, S., Stafford, K. B., Garcia, A., & Snyder, A. E. (2007). Teaching cause–effect text structure through social studies content to at-risk second graders. *Journal of Learning Disabilities, 40*(2), 111–120.

Williams, T., & Williams, K. (2010). Self-efficacy and performance in mathematics: Reciprocal determinism in 33 nations. *Journal of Educational Psychology, 102*(2), 453–466.

Willms, J. D. (2006). Learning divides: Ten policy questions about the performance and equity of schools and schooling systems. Report prepared for UNESCO Institute for Statistics.

Winne, P. H., Graham, L., & Prock, L. (1993). A model of poor readers' text-based inferencing: Effects of explanatory feedback. *Reading Research Quarterly, 28*(1), 52–66.

Wolters, C. A. (2004). Advancing achievement goals theory: Using goal structures and goal orientations to predict students' motivation, cognition, and achievement. *Journal of Educational Psychology, 96*(2), 236–250.

Wood, D. (2007). Teachers learning communities: Catalyst for change or a new infrastructure for the status quo. *Teachers College Record, 109*(3), 699–739.

Woolley, M., Kol, K., & Bowen, G. L. (2009). The social context of school success for Latino middle school students: Direct and indirect influences of teachers, family, and friends. *Journal of Early Adolescence, 29*(1), 43–70.

Zeleny, J. (2010, March 1). Obama backs rewarding districts that police failing schools. *New York Times,* p. 6.

Zimmerman, B. J. (2002). Becoming a self-regulated learner: An overview. *Theory into Practice, 41*(2), 64–71.

Zito, J. R., Adkins, M., Gavins, M., Harris, K. R., & Graham, S. (2007). Self-regulated strategy development: Relationship to the social-cognitive perspective and the development of self-regulation. *Reading and Writing Quarterly, 23*(1), 77–96.

Index

The letter *f* following a page number denotes a figure.

About the Authors

A. Wade Boykin

A. Wade Boykin is a professor and director of the graduate program in the Department of Psychology at Howard University. He is also the executive director of the Capstone Institute at Howard University, formally known as the Center for Research on the Education of Students Placed At Risk (CRESPAR). Dr. Boykin has done extensive work in the area of research methodology; the interface of culture, context, motivation, and cognition; Black child development; and academic achievement in the American social context. He is coeditor of *Research Directions of Black Psychologists*, which was a finalist for the American Psychological Association's Book of the Year.

Boykin has served as a fellow at the Institute for Comparative Human Development; as an adjunct associate professor at the Laboratory of Comparative Human Cognition, Rockefeller University; as codirector of the Task Force on the Relevance of the Social Sciences to the Black Experience, Yale University; as a member of the American Psychological Association Task Force on Educational Disparities; as a Research Advisory Panel member for the National Minority Student Achievement Network; as a member of the Board of Directors for Project Grad USA, a national school reform organization; on the editorial board of the Sage Publications Book Series on Race, Ethnicity and Culture; and on the President's National Mathematics Advisory Panel, which advises the president of the United States and the secretary of education with respect to the conduct, evaluation, and effective use of the results of research relating to proven, evidence-based mathematics instruction in order to foster greater knowledge of, and improved performance in, mathematics among American students.

Pedro Noguera

Pedro Noguera is the Peter L. Agnew Professor of Education at New York University. He holds tenured faculty appointments in the departments of Teaching and Learning and Humanities and Social Sciences at the Steinhardt School of Culture, Education and Development and in the Department of Sociology at New York University. He is also the executive director of the Metropolitan Center for Urban Education and the codirector of the Institute for the Study of Globalization and Education in Metropolitan Settings (IGEMS).

Noguera is the author of *The Imperatives of Power: Political Change and the Social Basis of Regime Support in Grenada*, *City Schools and the American Dream*, *Unfinished Business: Closing the Achievement Gap in Our Nation's Schools*, and *City Kids, City Teachers* with Bill Ayers and Greg Michie. His most recent book is *The Trouble with Black Boys . . . and Other Reflections on Race, Equity and the Future of Public Education*. Noguera has also appeared as a regular commentator on educational issues on CNN, National Public Radio, and other national news outlets.

Related ASCD Resources

At the time of publication, the following ASCD resources were available (ASCD stock numbers appear in parentheses). For up-to-date information about ASCD resources, go to www.ascd.org. You can search the complete archives of *Educational Leadership* at http://www.ascd.org/el.

ASCD Edge Group

Exchange ideas and connect with other educators interested in urban education on the social networking site ASCD Edge™ at http://ascdedge.ascd.org/

Print Products

Educating Oppositional and Defiant Children by Philip S. Hall and Nancy D. Hall (#103053)

Meeting Students Where They Live: Motivation in Urban Schools by Richard L. Curwin (#109110)

The Motivated Student: Unlocking the Enthusiasm for Learning by Bob Sullo (#109028)

Motivating Black Males to Achieve in School & in Life by Baruti K. Kafele (#109013)

Raising Black Students' Achievement Through Culturally Responsive Teaching by Johnnie McKinley (#110004)

Teaching English Language Learners Across the Content Areas by Judie Haynes and Debbie Zacarian (#109032)

Teaching with Poverty in Mind: What Being Poor Does to Kids' Brains and What Schools Can Do About It by Eric Jensen (#109074)

What Works in Schools: Translating Research into Action by Robert J. Marzano (#102271)

Videos

Educating English Language Learners: Connecting Language, Literacy, and Culture (#610012)

How to Involve All Parents in Your Diverse Community (#607056)

How to Use Students' Diverse Cultural Backgrounds to Enhance Academic Achievement (#608031DL)

Teaching with Poverty in Mind: Elementary and Secondary (#610135)

THE WHOLE CHILD The Whole Child Initiative helps schools and communities create learning environments that allow students to be healthy, safe, engaged, supported, and challenged. To learn more about other books and resources that relate to the whole child, visit www.wholechildeducation.org.

For more information: send e-mail to member@ascd.org; call 1-800-933-2723 or 703-578-9600, press 2; send a fax to 703-575-5400; or write to Information Services, ASCD, 1703 N. Beauregard St., Alexandria, VA 22311-1714 USA.